Tropical Capitalism

Tropical Capitalism

The Industrialization of Belo Horizonte, Brazil

Marshall C. Eakin

palgrave

First published 2001 by PALGRAVE™
175 Fifth Avenue, New York, N.Y. 10010 and
Houndmills, Basingstoke, Hampshire, England RG21 6XS.
Companies and representatives throughout the world.

PALGRAVE is the new global publishing imprint of St. Martin's Press LLC
Scholarly and Reference Division and Palgrave Publishers Ltd. (formerly
Macmillan Press Ltd.).

ISBN 0-312-22306-4

Library of Congress Cataloging-in-Publication Data
Eakin, Marshall C. (Marshall Craig), 1952–
    Tropical capitalism : the industrialization of Belo Horizonte, Brazil /
Marshall C. Eakin.
       p. cm.
    Includes bibliographical references and index.
    ISBN 0-312-22306-4
    1. Industrialization—Brazil—Belo Horizonte—History. 2. Belo
Horizonte (Brazil)—Economic conditions. 3. Belo Horizonte (Brazil)—
Politics and government. 4. Industrialists—Brazil—Belo Horizonte—
History. I. Title.

HC189.B4 E25   2001
338.98'51—dc21

                                              2001021893

Design by Letra Libre, Inc.

First edition: January 2002
10 9 8 7 6 5 4 3 2 1

Printed in the United States of America.

for
Don and Ann Beatty

Contents

List of Maps

As is customary, the titles of works in Portuguese are spelled as they appear on the original title page. The spelling of names has usually been modernized in the text.

List of Tables

Acknowledgments

This book has taken so long to write that I have accumulated a substantial list of debts to a large number of people and institutions. I began this project in 1987 with a generous grant from the Tinker Foundation that allowed me to spend a sabbatical year in Brazil working out of the Fundação João Pinheiro in Belo Horizonte. When I put this project aside to complete another book in the mid-1990s, the Tinker Foundation ended up helping me with two books, rather than the one they initially funded. I took up the project again in 1997–98 with the help of Roberto Martins and funding from the Fundação João Pinheiro. Their support helped me spend another sabbatical in Brazil, and to finish the research for the project. Roberto's help and nudging played a major role in moving the book toward completion. For this assistance (and the nudging) I will always be grateful. *Muito obrigado,* Roberto.

As a quick look at the bibliography and endnotes will show, I could never have written this book without the help of many fine scholars in Minas Gerais. These mineiros offered me their writings, advice, and research notes. I would like to thank them profusely for their help over the last twenty years. Yonne Grossi and Douglas Libby, in particular, have gone out of their way over the past 20 years to facilitate my work in Belo Horizonte, and they are true friends. I cannot thank them enough for their support. Virgílio and Rejane Almeida took an interest in this project when Virgílio was a graduate student in computer science at Vanderbilt in the 1980s, and their support and encouragement once they returned home to Belo Horizonte has been much appreciated for more than a decade. They have helped me write the history of their own hometown.

My work in Minas Gerais has been made more difficult, but also more interesting and rewarding, by the absence of a central archive for the materials I needed to write this book. Although my work began in the Arquivo Público Mineiro—that mother church of mineiro archives—it quickly led to a widely dispersed series of archives and institutions. I am deeply indebted to the many archivists who provided me access and guided me in my search for documents. These dedicated archivists labor daily to rescue the history of Minas Gerais and to keep it alive. They are the true heroes of this story. In particular, Moema Gontijo at the Centro de Memória of the Federação das Indústrias do Estado de Minas Gerais has gone out of her way over the past 13 years to help me complete this project. I cannot thank her enough for her assistance and encouragement. Cristina Pereira Nunes of the Centro also deserves special mention for her support. Cleyde Grandinetti at the Associação Comercial de Minas opened the ACM's archives and library to me early in the project and, by doing so, significantly reshaped the nature of the project. *Obrigado pela sua gentileza,* Cleyde.

My old friend, Amilcar Martins, has intervened on my behalf at several key moments in my research to open doors to collections. Despite a very busy political career, he has always found time to share with me his knowledge of mineiro history and politics. I am especially thankful for his help in gaining access to the archives of the Prefeitura Muncipal de Belo Horizonte, the Câmara Municipal de Belo Horizonte, and in particular the Junta Comercial de Minas Gerais, one of the great untapped (virtually) business archives in Brazil. Access to this archive also fundamentally reshaped my project and I am grateful to Dr. Célio Cota Pacheco (then president of the JUCEMG) for allowing me to work in the Junta's records.

A number of companies and government agencies allowed me access to their collections. Special thanks to Ermelinda Ricoy at Fiat do Brasil's factory in Betim for her help with sources and for a fine tour of the assembly line. I am extremely grateful to José Eduardo Pereira de Lima, director of corporate affairs, at Fiat headquarters in Nova Lima for spending a long afternoon allowing me to interview him and probe his vast knowledge of business and industry in Minas Gerais. Officials at Centrais Energéticas de Minas Gerais (CEMIG), the Instituto de Desenvolvimento Industrial (INDI), the Secretaria de Planejamento (SEPLAN), the Assembléia Legislativa de Minas Gerais, the Prefeitura Municipal de Belo Horizonte, the Câmara Municipal de Belo Horizonte, and the Biblioteca Pública de Minas Gerais kindly allowed me access to their collections. I am especially grateful to Ivana Parrela of the Arquivo Público da Cidade de Belo Horizonte, an institution created after I began this project, and one that has become central to rescuing the history of the city.

For two decades I have benefited from the willingness of mineiro scholars to share their work with me and to guide me in the direction of sources and new ideas. Very early on in this project Mitiko Okazaki Khedy graciously provided me with the results of a survey she had carried out to catalog archives dealing with the economic history of Minas Gerais. Late in the project, Sérgio Birchal appeared on the scene to share his own work and to help arrange interviews. Paulo Sérgio Martins Alves, Eliana Dutra, Anne Hanley, Gail Triner, and Maysa Gomes also offered their help at various times. Two people, in particular, deserve special mention. In my yearlong sabbatical in 1987–88 I worked out of the Fundação João Pinheiro and Elândia Silva went out of her way to facilitate my work and make me at home in Belo Horizonte. At the Arquivo Público Mineiro, Hélio Gravatá spent hours orienting me to the history and historiography of Belo Horizonte. Until his recent death, "o Gravatá" was a legendary archival and bibliographical figure and he is greatly missed. He was a profound influence on my work and career.

A number of scholars in the United States have helped me nudge this book toward completion over the years. John Wirth, Steve Topik, Tom Skidmore, Betsy Kuznesof, Tom Holloway, Jeff Lesser, and the late Warren Dean all made their contributions to this book in very different ways. I have worked for the past 18 years in a wonderful setting in the Department of History and the Center for Latin American and Iberian Studies at Vanderbilt University. I owe an incalculable debt to my many supportive and stimulating colleagues at Vanderbilt who nurture a collegial environment that makes our work a pleasure. As always, the bibliographical expertise of Paula Covington is greatly appreciated. The Robert Penn Warren Center for the Humanities at Vanderbilt and its diretor, Mona Frederick, deserve special mention. Twice in the last ten years, I have been fortunate to have an office at the Center and to participate in yearlong faculty seminars that have helped me develop my ideas, and to write, write, write. For the second time I find myself polishing the final draft of a book manuscript in the outstanding facilities of the Center.

In addition to the Tinker Foundation and the Fundação João Pinheiro, the Vanderbilt University Research Council has generously funded several research trips to Brazil. I am fortunate to work at an institution that generously supports both teaching and research, support that was essential in developing and completing this book.

I would be remiss if I did not mention the support of Michael Flamini and Amanda Johnson, my editors at Palgrave. Several years ago, Michael saw the manuscript of my general introduction to Brazil, and he played a key role in turning it into *Brazil: The Once and Future Country* (1997). He had the confidence in me to take on this project, and my next book as well, and I am eternally grateful for his support for my work.

I owe my greatest debt to my partner, Michelle Beatty-Eakin, and our two daughters, Lee and Lacy. Over the past fourteen years I have constantly disappeared, at times for months, to work on this book. Michelle has made countless sacrifices to give me the time I needed to research and write. She has kept me going when I despaired of ever finishing. Without her, none of this would have been possible. Lee was barely one year old when I began this project, and Lacy did not appear until I was a year into the research. Both of them have grown up with this book, and they are both old enough now to ask me continually, "When ARE you going to finish that book, Dad?" I can finally give them an answer—and then disappoint them with the news that there will always be another book in progress. Thank you, Michelle, Lee, and Lacy for letting me steal away to work, and for keeping me going. Without you, I would never have finished.

Finally, this book is dedicated to my in-laws whose encouragement over the years has been exceptional. Thank you, Don and Ann, for your interest in Latin America and for your support for this Brazilianist.

Map 1 Brazil: States, Territories, and Neighboring Countries

Introduction ✠

Varieties of Capitalism

Capitalism has transformed the world over the last three centuries. Emerging out of the trading networks of medieval Europe, it propelled the Europeans out across the globe in search of markets, goods, and profit. Beginning in the late eighteenth century the rise of industrial capitalism in England, and then on the European continent, helped give birth to the modern world—one dominated at the beginning of the twentieth century by a handful of European nations and the United States. The "rise of the West" to global economic and political supremacy ultimately rested on its powerful economic system—industrial capitalism.[1] At the end of the twentieth century, the collapse of the Soviet Union and the end of the Cold War have produced something of a capitalist euphoria even leading some commentators to declare the final victory of capitalism and democracy over socialism, and even the "end of history."[2]

In Latin America over the last two decades, the end of the Cold War, the return of electoral politics, and a crisis of the Left across the region have been accompanied by a profound economic shift.[3] After centuries of state intervention, and a half-century of protectionism designed to build up domestic industry, across Latin America governments have moved toward a neo-liberal economic model. This approach accepts the triumph of capitalism, and attempts to integrate the region successfully into the world capitalist system through reduced state intervention, more open markets, privatization of state controlled enterprises, and a general acceptance of the "power of the market."[4]

Yet, in this rush to embrace capitalism and the free market, it is not even clear just what is being embraced. Should Latin American nations attempt to copy the successful economies of Europe, the United States, and Japan? If so, what does that mean given the profoundly different paths to economic success each has pursued? If Latin America is to embrace capitalism, what does that mean given that there is not even consensus on how to define capitalism? For at least 200 years, from Adam Smith to Karl Marx to Joseph Schumpeter and more recent economic gurus like Milton Friedman, the leading economic theorists in the West have tried to define the essence of capitalism. For Smith, living at the dawn of the Industrial Age, trade was the heart of the matter and the source of the "wealth of nations."[5] Nearly a century later, having witnessed the power of the Industrial Revolution in England, Karl Marx looked to the system of private property, free wage labor, and "relations of production" as the essence of capitalism.[6] Nearly a century after Marx, Joseph Schumpeter surveyed capitalism and socialism and emphasized the importance of the entrepreneur in the rise and power of capitalism.[7] In the second half of the twentieth century, Milton Friedman emphasized the importance of free markets and free people as the quintessential features of modern capitalism.[8]

In this study, capitalism is defined quite simply as a system with a market economy, some form of private property, and wage labor. It is also generally characterized by the availability of credit, legally binding contracts, a culture of entrepreneurship, and rapid technological innovation. This system emerged out of the European trading networks of the late Middle Ages, and flourished with European overseas expansion in the early modern era. By the end of the nineteenth century, its most advanced forms had developed in Western Europe and the United States out of two industrial revolutions.[9]

The great capitalist nations came to power in the modern world via industrialization, yet through a variety of paths. Is it possible at the dawn of the twenty-first century to industrialize in the same ways as nations that did so a century, or even more, ago? Furthermore, for at least four decades, analysts of the developed countries have been speaking of the emergence of "postindustrial" economies. What will Latin American industrialization look like in a postindustrial world? Equally important, how will the already long economic history of Latin America shape its economic future—especially if that future is industrial capitalism?

This book speaks to these questions by looking at industrialization and capitalism in Brazil in the twentieth century. It examines the rise of the second largest industrial center in the ninth largest economy in the world. Brazil has emerged at the end of the twentieth century at the forefront of the so-called "newly industrializing countries."[10] In the next few decades Brazil could move into the ranks of the five largest economies in the world.[11] Clearly, the Brazilian path to capitalist development—to industrial capitalism—merits careful attention, especially for what it might tell us about Latin American industrialization and the problems of and possibilities for the region. I argue that Brazil has industrialized through its own variety of capitalism—one characterized by strong state intervention, political patronage, clientelism, family networks, and a pronounced *absence* of technological innovation. Brazil has become capitalist and industrialized without an industrial revolution.[12]

The focus of this study is the city of Belo Horizonte, the planned capital of Brazil's second most populous state, Minas Gerais. Since the gold rush of the early eighteenth century, Minas Gerais has been one of the keys to the Brazilian economy, and one of the most powerful players in national politics. Along with the cities and states of Rio de Janeiro and São Paulo, Belo Horizonte and Minas Gerais form the economic and industrial heartland of Brazil in the twentieth century. While Rio emerged as Brazil's first major industrial center at the beginning of the century, São Paulo became the country's industrial giant by the 1930s, and remains the core of Brazil's industrial economy.[13] Politicians created Belo Horizonte as their new state capital in the 1890s, but it did not truly emerge as an industrial center until the 1950s. In the last two decades, it has surpassed Rio de Janeiro to become the nation's second largest industrial pole.[14]

This book examines how and why Belo Horizonte grew so fast, how it industrialized, and what this tells us about the nature of Brazilian industrialization. I argue that the form of industrial capitalism that emerges in Belo Horizonte and Minas Gerais exhibits characteristics that can be found in other parts of Brazil and Latin America. As a late industrializer (doubly so in Belo Horizonte since Brazil industrialized later than the North Atlantic world, and Belo Horizonte industrialized after Rio and São Paulo), Belo Horizonte is like Germany and Japan where the role of state intervention to promote economic development is pronounced. (Some, in fact, argue that Germany and Japan experienced a "revolution from above" that produced their late industrialization.)[15] Like Japan, patronage, clientelism, and family networks are also keys to Brazilian industrialization. Unlike Europe, the United States, and Japan, Belo Horizonte (and Brazil) industrializes without generating significant technological innovation, and this remains a pattern of Brazilian (and Latin American) industrialization. Belo Horizonte and Brazil experience a form of industrialization that has not been self-sustaining.[16]

Although the literature on Latin American economic development grew dramatically in the 1960s and 1970s, since the 1980s historians of Latin America have increasingly turned away from economic history to cultural and social history.[17] In earlier decades, economists and historians asked similar questions and read each other's work about Latin American economic development. In recent years, historians have become more interested in issues other than industrialization and economic development, and economists have become increasingly theoretical, uninterested in area studies (Latin American or elsewhere). Consequently, the history and historiography of Latin American industrialization have suffered.

Even in the heyday of social and economic history scholars of Latin America were more interested in the macroeconomic picture of national economies and regions rather than the microeconomic view of businesses and firms.[18] Only in recent years in Brazil have historians begun to pay serious attention to what would be recognized as business history in the United States, Europe, and Japan. In the last 20 years, an increasing number of Brazilians and Brazilianists have produced articles and books on topics that would fall within the field of business history.[19] There has certainly been nothing equivalent to the development of schools of business history, or even syntheses equivalent to Alfred Chandler's foundational works.[20] Even more underdeveloped in these years was the role of technology in the process of industrialization.[21] Furthermore, studies at the level of cities tended to focus on national capitals—Mexico City, Buenos Aires, Lima. The unusual case of São Paulo alleviates this problem in Brazil, but few studies ventured beyond Brazil's two major industrial centers. This book brings together my own interest in industrialization, business history, and the history of technology to study a "secondary" city.[22] As is the case in Mexico with Monterrey, or Medellín, Colombia, turning to a secondary industrial city "decenters" our view of industrialization.

My focus is on Belo Horizonte across the twentieth century. To carry out this study I have mined a variety of sources in Minas Gerais: the archives and libraries of government agencies, business associations, the state business registry, newspapers, and interviews, as well as state and municipal archives. My approach in this study has been quite consciously interdisciplinary and eclectic. I have tried to interweave five major strands throughout this book. The most important of these strands is the history of mineiro industrialization, especially in comparative perspective—within Brazil, Latin America, and the rest of the world. In particular, I emphasize the need to recognize the role of technological innovation—or more accurately, its absence—in the process of industrialization. The third major strand is the role of the State in Brazilian and mineiro industrialization.[23] In the case of Minas Gerais, it is both the central State and especially the state government that hold the key to industrialization. I also argue that three powerful interest groups play the major role in shaping the process of industrialization in Minas Gerais: politicians, technocrats, and entrepreneurs. Although I recognize the importance of other groups, especially the role of workers in the process, I firmly believe that these three elite groups play the most powerful roles in shaping mineiro industrialization. Consequently, the final strand I pursue is elite ideology. What was the mentality of these powerful elite figures? How did they envision industrialization, especially the role of the state and nonelite groups in the process? In my effort to pursue these diverse yet intimately linked strands, I borrow liberally from studies by sociologists, political scientists, and other historians while drawing on the literatures on state building, economic development, industrialization, the history of technology, business history, clientelism, and political patronage.

I should point out that the research for this book has been made more difficult (and in some ways, more rewarding) by the nearly complete absence of government documents in the state archive, the Arquivo Público Mineiro (APM). It seems that in the 1930s the archive stopped receiving government documents. After long and arduous searches, I discovered that not only did government agencies rarely send their materials to the APM, they also did not keep them or maintain their own archives. Much of the history of Minas Gerais has been lost over the last 60 years due to the absence of a systematic effort to collect and preserve government documents. As a result, the APM is largely a repository and vital source for materials on colonial, imperial, and early republican Minas Gerais. With the prominent exception of its excellent and very complete newspaper collection (recently moved to the state library several blocks away), the APM offers little to the historian of post-1930 Minas Gerais. Only in the last decade has the government moved fitfully toward the implementation of a policy of document collection.[24] Writing the history of post-1930 Belo Horizonte and Minas Gerais is no easy task.

The absence of documents in the state archives sent me off in search of alternative sources, a search that was both challenging and rewarding. The records of the Associação Comercial de Minas (ACM), the Federação das Indústrias do Estado de Minas Gerais (FIEMG), the Junta Comercial do Estado de Minas Gerais (JUCEMG), in particular, provided me with previously unexploited and important sources on the industrialization of Belo Horizonte. Newspapers, especially the official government daily, *Minas Gerais,* were an invaluable source, publishing the annual balance sheets of companies operating in the state. Finally, interviews with politicians, technocrats, and entrepreneurs gave me insights into the process of industrialization that proved invaluable. Although this story is largely the history of a process led and driven by elites, it is one that has been (re)constructed from a variety of nontraditional sources. This book is both a synthesis of an enormous literature on Minas Gerais (overwhelmingly written by Brazilians) while drawing on previously untapped primary sources. I would not have been able to write this synthetic survey of a century of industrialization without the excellent studies of various pieces of the story by scholars such as Clélio Campolina Diniz, Luiz Aureliano Gama de Andrade, Otavio Soares Dulci, Evantina Pereira Vieira, Ignacio Godinho Delgado, and Maria Auxiliadora de Faria, to name but a few of them.

To place this study of industrialization in perspective, chapter 1 provides a historical and theoretical discussion of industrialization, with particular emphasis on the role of technology. It then turns to the place of Brazil and Minas Gerais in this context. I then quickly sketch the economic and technological background in Brazil and Minas Gerais in the nineteenth century. Chapter 2 examines the construction of the city and the first networks of political, economic, and social power. During this period, politicians created and developed a new state capital while entrepreneurs began to lay the foundations of local industry. During the first half century of its existence, these entrepreneurs created the first industries, banks, and commercial establishments, largely through kinship networks. This chapter establishes the social and political basis of the city's industrialization.

In chapter 3 I present an aggregate overview of industrialization during this period, before concentrating on a detailed examination at the firm level of different industries and technologies. Textiles, electric power generation, and iron and steel manufacturing form the three key sectors analyzed. I emphasize the role of imported technology and its adaptation to local needs. It was not until the 1940s, and especially the 1950s, that industrialization finally surged in Belo Horizonte. Chapter 4 turns first to the kinds of industry and technology that formed the core of Belo Horizonte's industrial surge: textiles, iron and steel, electric power generation, mining and minerals processing, and construction. This period also marks the emergence of the state government as the key to industrialization, and of technocrats (especially engineers) as the principal players in the process. Although this is the golden era of politicians and technocrats, entrepreneurs (contrary to most of the literature and prevailing beliefs) did not disappear, nor were they weak. In fact, this period witnesses the entrance on a large scale of foreign investment, especially in alliance with local capital. This is the era in which a "quadruple alliance" begins to take shape. In this chapter I analyze the formation of this alliance, looking carefully at the networks of power, networks built in both the economic and political arenas on the foundations laid before World War II.

The most complex phase of industrialization in Belo Horizonte and Minas Gerais is the period from the mid-1960s to the mid-1990s. During these years the technocratic model of state intervention dominated, Minas Gerais became the second leading industrial state in Brazil, and Belo Horizonte emerged as the second largest industrial center in the country. Nevertheless, important continuities mark the process. In spite of impressive industrialization, the economy of Belo Horizonte and Minas Gerais continues to be dominated by a small set of industries, and a small group of firms continues to dominate each industry. Consequently, despite an enormous increase in the size of the business community, the "power elite" remains small. Despite an increasingly diverse entrepreneurial and political elites, kinship networks—many of them dating back to the nineteenth century—continue to frame and shape both industrialization and state politics. Perhaps most striking is the persistence of kinship networks in the economy of Belo Horizonte and Minas Gerais to the last years of the twentieth century. If there is anything close to Chandler's "managerial revolution" it is in the transformation of state enterprises by technocratic managers. In the last decade of the twentieth century the economy of Belo Horizonte and Minas Gerais have entered into a profound transition that will probably mark the end of the era of family-controlled businesses, the true globalization of the industrial base, and a new role for the state government in the process of industrialization in the twenty-first century.

In the conclusion, I return to the core issues—strong state intervention, political patronage, clientelism, family networks, and a pronounced absence of technological innovation. The industrialization of Belo Horizonte shows how a state government (sometimes with the help of the central State) intervenes to promote economic development with great success. This study also demonstrates the importance of disaggregating national studies of industrialization, especially in the debate over the role of the state, to examine regions and the success or failure of state efforts to promote economic development. Political patronage and clientelism clearly were central to both the development of state and national politics, as well as the process of industrialization. The system of patronage and clientelism are crucial to the interrelationships between politicians, technocrats, and entrepreneurs, and their efforts to promote industrialization. It is through patron-client ties that these groups operate and pursue their goals. This study should demonstrate clearly that previous discussions of Brazilian industrialization that treat these groups as mutually exclusive or separate simply do not work. Not only do these groups often overlap and intertwine through networks of patronage, key individuals frequently moved within all three groups at various times in their careers.

Unlike most previous studies of Brazilian (or Latin American) industrialization with their impersonal statistics and aggregate analysis, this book personalizes the process of industrialization with names and faces, showing who was behind the industrialization of Belo Horizonte. Most important, it shows that networks, or "webs of power," constructed through capital and kinship lay behind the creation of both the mineiro economy and mineiro politics, and that despite enormous economic and demographic growth, these ever evolving networks remained the keys to Brazilian capitalism throughout the twentieth century. In the final pages of this book, I return to the larger, comparative picture of industrialization within Brazil comparing Belo Horizonte with Rio de Janeiro and São Paulo, and then the Brazilian experience with the rest of Latin America and other regions of the world. I emphasize that although state intervention, patronage, clientelism, and family networks form the key social and political features of Brazilian industrialization, it is the continuing failure to move from the transfer of technology to technological innovation that so deeply mars economic development in Brazil, and so clearly defines tropical capitalism.

Chapter 1 ※

Industry, Technology, and Politics

The emergence of new industrial centers in the developing world is one of the most important transformations of the late twentieth century. In the decades since World War II, the economic dominance of the United States, Europe, and Japan has been increasingly challenged by the rise of industry in Asia and Latin America. Forty years ago the economies of South Korea, China, India, and Brazil, for example, primarily produced foodstuffs and raw materials, and their populations were overwhelming rural. The term "Third World," in fact, arose in the 1950s, in part, to highlight the underdevelopment in Asia, Africa, and Latin America characterized by a lack of industrial growth in largely agrarian societies.[1] With the emergence of significant industrial growth in a number of countries, the already suspect concept of a "Third World" has now become even more problematic. The industrialization of Brazil, South Korea, Taiwan, India, and Mexico (to cite a few examples) has been impressive and clearly sets them apart from much of the rest of the so-called Third World.[2] By the 1980s, this industrialization had begun to alter fundamentally the global dominance of the so-called First and Second Worlds that emerged out of World War II. Third World industrialization, however, has not simply recapitulated the industrialization of what used to be called the First and Second Worlds.

Stated simply, industrialization involves "the transformation of a traditional agrarian society into an urban society based on machine technology."[3] Beginning in the late eighteenth century, England became the first country to experience this transformation and has provided historians with the classic model of industrialization.[4] In the nineteenth century industrialization spread to the European continent, notably in Belgium, France, and then Germany and Russia.[5] Despite more than a century of research and writing on the causes and origins of British and continental European industrialization, the issue remains highly controversial and hotly debated.[6]

Less disputed are the general features of eighteenth- and nineteenth-century industrialization. Technological change formed the core of the process—new machines, new sources of power, and new processes of production.[7] Machines replaced human and animal power. Water, then fossil fuels, powered the new machines, and the steam engine and the railway were the most prominent examples of the new machine economy. The invention and use of new materials such as iron for wood, vegetable for animal matter, and mineral for vegetable matter, altered the nature of economic activity. This technological shift eventually forged industrial economies with unprecedented productivity, self-sustained growth, and "a large and sustained rise in real incomes per head."[8] The Industrial Revolution accelerated the technological supremacy of Europe over the areas of what would later become know as the Third World, a supremacy that begins to emerge at least as far back as the fifteenth century.[9]

The history of technology has long been a crucial part of the history of industrialization in developed nations. Despite sharp disagreement over the role of technology and the causes behind its development, technological innovation and diffusion form a central part of the history of industrialization for most economists and historians.[10] Although much less developed, scholarship on the history of Third World, and more specifically, Latin American, industrialization has grown considerably in the last 30 years. This literature has not, however, had much to say about the history of technology.[11] Generally, technology has been taken as a given, or "black box." This is unfortunate and misguided. We cannot understand the nature of Latin American industrialization without examining the technology underlying it, anymore than we can understand European or North American industrialization without analyzing its technological underpinnings.

In fact, this book argues that the single most characteristic feature of Latin American industrialization is the continuing absence of technological innovation and diffusion. Technology has long been transferred to Brazil and the rest of Latin America from the more developed economies.[12] For a variety of reasons that will be examined later in this study, Brazil (and, by extension, Latin America) has not been very successful at generating local technological innovation. The ability not only to copy the latest technological innovations, but also to generate their own versions and improvements on those technology transfers has been a key characteristic of modern industrial economies and modern capitalism.[13]

Industrialization, however, involved much more than technological change, for the new machines arose in a complex interaction with the surrounding social and political environment. The new machines and production processes required expanding markets and increasing demand to absorb the goods they produced. They required the existence of a labor force to run the machines, and historically this labor force originated in an exodus of workers from the countryside. The modernization of the agrarian economy supplied the emerging machine economy with its surplus laborers, the foodstuffs to feed an urban population, and capital for investment in new industry. How the landowners (who historically played the dominant role in the agrarian economy and national politics) accepted, promoted, or rejected agricultural modernization and the social and political changes it engendered also played a crucial role in the process of industrialization.[14] An activist group of entrepreneurs generally drove forward the process.[15] Their relationship to the landed class and their access to political power are essential in any analysis of industrialization.

In the late nineteenth and early twentieth century the State played a key role as the facilitator or driving force moving industrialization forward. In the early nineteenth century a noninterventionist state (England, for example) paved the way for industrialization by removing traditional obstacles facing capitalists. By the late nineteenth century, interventionist states (Germany or Russia, for example) often imposed industrialization on recalcitrant social and political groups. Indeed, the most prominent examples of late industrialization generally are characterized by interventionist and authoritarian regimes.[16]

In Latin America the State has played a prominent role in economic development since the Conquest. It has become quite fashionable in recent years to blame Latin America's underdevelopment on excessive State intervention.[17] In nineteenth- and twentieth-century Brazil, the State played a decisive role in the process of industrialization. Yet, this was not Bismarck's "revolution from above" or Stalin's "forced industrialization."[18] With the exception of two periods (1937–45 and 1964–85) Brazil has been ruled by some form of representative republic. Even during the two phases of dictatorship, the regimes allowed limited political representation and dissent.

The State has served a mediating role for the contending actors and institutions within Brazilian society. Although the planter class (especially coffee planters) dominated political and economic power in Brazil under the Empire and First Republic, no single class, certainly nothing that could plausibly be described as a bourgeoisie, has assumed power in Brazil since the collapse of the coffee economy in 1930. In many ways, Brazilian politics since the 1930s has been the search for a political formula to accommodate a wide variety of classes and groups vying for access to power. Industrialists and entrepreneurs have been two key groups, but their political power has come as a result of coalitions with other groups.[19]

In a political system characterized by weak or nonexistent parties, personalities and personal networks hold the key to political power and economic development.[20] Political clientelism and economic opportunity converge. The most important source of patronage in Brazilian society has long been the State, and personal networks has long been the key mechanism for distributing that patronage. One of the striking features of these networks, especially in the state of Minas Gerais, has been the longevity and durability of networks built on kinship. Much more so than in Europe and the United States, family capitalism and family political networks endured throughout the twentieth century.[21] Although Brazilian industrialization is not unique, its path diverges in important ways from the process in Europe, the United States, and Japan in the nineteenth and twentieth centuries.

Prior to the industrialization of Europe and the United States in the eighteenth and nineteenth centuries, cottage or handcraft industry had been dispersed in many areas of the globe. By the end of the nineteenth century, European and North American industrialization—accompanied by the deindustrialization of areas of the Third World—concentrated world manufacturing in the emerging First World. According to one authoritative estimate, in 1900 the United States and Europe accounted for 86.6 percent of world manufacturing, and the Third World just 11 percent. (The always difficult to categorize Japan accounted for the remaining 2.4 percent.) Industrial concentration continued in the early twentieth century with the share of the Third World falling to 7 percent by midcentury. The growth of manufacturing in the Third World in the past three decades represents a process of reindustrialization as these countries attempt to "catch up" with the developed industrial economies that left them behind between 1750 and 1950. By 1980 the Third World's share of world manufacturing had risen to 12 percent at the expense of the developed economies, although all had increased the absolute level of production.[22]

Brazilian Industrialization

Brazil offers scholars a fascinating case study of industrialization in the Third World. The extraordinary economic growth in Brazil, particularly since World War II, has made it the ninth largest economy in the world.[23] Several economists have estimated that the Brazilian gross domestic product has grown at an annual rate of 3 percent per capita since 1900, averaging over 4 percent per capita from World War II to 1980. These rates exceed those of the core industrial nations over the long term.[24] Although formerly part of the underdeveloped, colonial world, Brazilian economic growth during the past few decades places it on the verge of entering the ranks of the so-called Group of Seven (the major industrial, democratic nations—the United States, Japan, Germany, France, England, Italy, and Canada). Brazil, in effect, no longer fits within the Third World, yet it is not a First World nation either. Given past performance and potential, Brazil has for some time appeared poised to become the first Third World nation to experience a modern industrial revolution. The revolution, however, has not materialized, leading some analysts to conclude that Brazil has failed economically.

Unlike the countries of the North Atlantic world, nations of the so-called Third World have been very late starters in the drive to industrialize. From the mid-eighteenth century to the early twentieth century, much of Europe, the United States, and Japan built the world's first industrial economies, and, subsequently, became the most powerful nations on the planet. They exported their surplus manufactured goods and capital across the globe, while most of the rest of the world imported the goods and capital, exported minerals or agricultural commodities, and often fell under the colonial rule of the industrial nations.[25]

It has long been a truism of economic history that the later industrializers take different paths than their predecessors.[26] England industrialized when there were no other industrial nations. As the first industrial nation, England quickly achieved an enormous economic advantage over the rest of the world. As parts of Europe and the United States followed in the nineteenth century, they had to contend with England's formidable head start and the advantages of a commanding control of capital resources, technology, and production. Germany, Japan, and Russia, in particular, industrialized with much greater state support and direction than England. In all cases, protectionism supported by the State played a crucial role.[27]

Latin America offers an especially important opportunity to compare paths to industrialization. Achieving independence in the early nineteenth century, the nations of Latin America have a longer experience with nation-building and independence than any other area of the developing world. Today it is the most industrialized region of the developing world. Understanding the nature of Latin American industrialization, its successes and failures, its strengths and weaknesses, provides us with important perspectives on the routes to industrialization in the Third World, and a more critical perspective on the routes taken in the so-called developed world.[28] Clearly, the process of industrialization will benefit from the nineteenth- and early twentieth-century experience with textiles, iron and steel, and electricity, but it will involve profoundly different technologies in an already highly industrialized world economy.

In particular, Latin America offers us the opportunity to examine industrialization in a setting with strong state intervention but without a single class leading the process. Entrepreneurs and industrialists play key roles (as they do in Europe, the United States, and Japan) in the process of industrialization, but in political cultures that are profoundly corporatist and personalistic. In the case of Brazil, the State leads the process of industrialization but in an erratic fashion until late in the twentieth century. There is certainly no European-style bourgeoisie, and self-sustaining growth has not been achieved despite impressive economic development. Finally, the dynamic technological innovation that characterizes European, U.S., and Japanese industrialization has not taken hold in Latin America. Finally, it differs sharply from current East Asian industrialization (South Korea, Taiwan, and Singapore, for example).

Despite its flaws, and they are numerous, Brazil certainly stands out as an extraordinarily successful example of late industrialization. An agrarian, slaveholding society for centuries, Brazil has made the transition from rural to urban, and agrarian to industrial in the last century, but most dramatically in the past few decades. Like much of Latin America, Brazil was a classic, monocultural, export-oriented economy well into this century. At the turn of the century, coffee generated more than 90 percent of the value of all Brazilian exports. As late as 1960, 60 percent of the value of all exports still came from coffee. Today, manufactured goods generate more then 75 percent of exports, and coffee less than 10 percent.[29] The burdens of a colonial past have long hindered Brazilian industrialization.[30] The Portuguese first landed on the coast of South America in 1500.[31] After several decades of neglect while they concentrated on their lucrative trading empire in Asia and Africa, the Portuguese gradually implanted settlements on the coast, principally in the northeast. In the captaincies of Bahia and Pernambuco the Portuguese transplanted cane sugar from the Azores and Madeira. The rapid expansion of sugar production after 1570 made Brazil the world's first great sugar exporter and the first and largest slave plantation society in the Americas. Although the Brazilian sugar industry declined in the face of Caribbean competition in the late seventeenth century, colonists discovered gold in the Brazilian interior in the 1690s sparking the Western world's first great gold rush. For the first six decades of the eighteenth century Brazilian gold enriched the Portuguese monarchy and helped fuel the expansion of the European economy.[32]

The sugar and gold cycles followed the classic colonial pattern as the metropolis extracted enormous wealth from colonial Brazil while putting little back into the economy. Imperial restrictions hindered the development of local industry. In 1785, the Portuguese king issued a decree banning all manufacturing in his American colony.[33] Only the extraordinary transfer of the Portuguese monarchy to Rio de Janeiro during the Napoleonic Wars brought the lifting of these imperial restrictions. Brazil also suffered as the colony of a technologically and industrially backward metropolitan economy.

The transfer of the monarchy (1808) and independence (1822) opened the Brazilian economy to the outside world. Great Britain had traditionally been Portugal's oldest political and economic ally and quickly became the dominant foreign presence in newly independent Brazil. British investment funded the expansion of railways, port facilities, roads, and financial institutions, especially in the southeastern triangle of Rio de Janeiro-São Paulo-Minas Gerais.[34] While independence and British expansion clearly helped integrate Brazil into the emerging world economy in the nineteenth century, a long and heated debate has ensued over the extent of that integration and its impact on Brazilian development. A number of schools of thought stress dependency, the imperialism of free trade and the deleterious effects of the British role, while others argue that the impact is overstated and the integration relatively weak.[35]

The explosive expansion of coffee production and exports after 1830 provided Brazil with its most important linkage to the world economy. By the 1840s coffee accounted for 40 percent of export revenues, and in the coming decades would approach 80 percent at times. Expanding first in the region around Rio de Janeiro, coffee production also spread into the southern regions of bordering Minas Gerais. In the late nineteenth century production migrated westward into the state of São Paulo. Coffee made the city and state of São Paulo the economic heartland of the nation by the end of the century.[36] With the end of the Atlantic slave trade in 1850, and growing pressures for abolition after 1870, the coffee landowners turned to European immigration (especially from southern Italy) to satisfy their demand for labor.[37] The entry of more than two million Europeans (largely into the São Paulo region) between 1870 and 1914 eased a labor shortage and the demise of slavery (abolished by legislation in 1888).[38] Immigrants played a key role in the rise of industry in São Paulo, and revenues from coffee exports fueled industrial growth after 1890.

Political stability also facilitated economic modernization. In contrast to much of Latin America in the nineteenth century, Brazil achieved impressive political stability, allowing the country to embark on modernization decades before most of its neighbors. The rise of the coffee economy coincided with the end of significant internal revolts to central rule and the beginning of the long reign of Emperor Pedro II (1840–89). A relatively homogeneous political elite with an agrarian base controlled a parliamentary system styled after that of Victorian England.[39]

Although the rise of coffee cultivation after independence in the early nineteenth century continued the agroexport pattern of the colonial period, some primitive industry began to emerge principally in textiles, metallurgy, and food processing. Unlike previous export crops, coffee became an engine for growth for more diversified economic expansion in the southeast, first around the capital, Rio de Janeiro, and then later around the city of São Paulo.[40] A frontier town until the nineteenth century, São Paulo boomed as the commercial center for the rapidly expanding coffee fields, and the focal point for massive European (especially Italian) immigration after 1880. European demand for coffee and the export of its surplus peoples shaped the growth of São Paulo. During the last century, the city and its hinterland have become the most dynamic and largest industrial park in Latin America. By the 1930s the state of São Paulo had surpassed Minas Gerais as the most populous in the nation, and the city of São Paulo began to challenge Rio de Janeiro's traditional economic and cultural primacy. (Today the state of São Paulo has a population of 35 million, Minas Gerais has 17 million, and Rio de Janeiro, 14 million. The three states combined account for 40 percent of the nation's population.) Between 1880 and 1930, both cities experienced important industrial growth, but the main industrial surge in these two growth poles came after 1930 with government protection, especially via the policy later labeled import substitution industrialization.[41]

Successive Brazilian governments turned their attention to building a diversified domestic economy after the resounding shock of the Great Depression. In the decades after World War II Brazil also experienced major inflows of foreign investment as multinational corporations began to build manufacturing facilities in the Third World. Beginning in the 1950s, and accelerating in the late 1960s, multinationals poured billions of dollars of investment into manufacturing facilities in Brazil to supply protected domestic markets, and to export cheaply produced goods to other countries. Prior to 1970 the bulk of this investment went to the state of São Paulo, and secondarily to Rio de Janeiro. By the 1980s nearly 50 percent of Brazil's industrial production was concentrated in Greater São Paulo, and another ten percent in Greater Rio de Janeiro. This extraordinary industrial growth made Brazil the tenth largest economy in the world by the early 1980s.[42]

Brazil, like Mexico and Colombia, has also been characterized by a process of regional industrialization. Brazil has not suffered from the unbalanced "megacephalia" that has been so characteristic of countries like Argentina, Uruguay, Venezuela, and Peru. In Brazil, Rio de Janeiro emerged first (in the late nineteenth century) as the economic and industrial heartland, and in the early twentieth century, São Paulo not only challenged Rio's primacy, it left the nation's political capital far behind by the 1950s. Belo Horizonte, and, to a lesser extent, other state capitals, have also industrialized in the second half of this century (most notably, Porto Alegre and Curitiba). In this sense, Brazilian industrialization is similar to the pattern in Mexico (with the rise of Puebla and Monterrey) and Colombia (Bogotá and Medellín) but even more dispersed.[43]

Mineiro Industrialization

When measured against the explosive economic expansion of the São Paulo-Rio de Janeiro axis, the economy of Minas Gerais has fared poorly. Although the gold rush had made Minas the richest captaincy in Brazil in the eighteenth century, the exhaustion of gold by the 1770s left the region in decline and decadence.[44] Throughout the nineteenth century Minas grew slowly, largely on the basis of the production of beef, dairy products, and other foodstuffs for local and regional consumption. The economy turned inward after the frenetic export boom of the eighteenth century. Throughout the nineteenth century the provincial economy remained fragmented into highly diversified, relatively isolated and dispersed productive units, characterized by a high degree of self-sufficiency in a large number of small units of production producing largely for local consumption.[45]

As John Wirth has pointed out, Minas historically is a transitional region in the Brazilian heartland with complex connections to surrounding states. More so than any other political creation, Minas Gerais brings together a striking variety of landscapes. "That Minas is not one region," Wirth notes, "but rather a mosaic of seven different zones or subregions is fundamental."[46] The West and Triângulo are historically extensions of São Paulo characterized by cattle ranching and farming. The South and Mata, both extensions of the forested and mountainous regions, were historically an extension of the hinterland of the province of Rio de Janeiro, and were transformed by the expansion of coffee cultivation in the second half of the nineteenth century. The East and North, in contrast, are geographically an

Map 2 Regions and Cities of Minas Gerais

extension of the arid sertão that stretches into Bahia, Pernambuco, and Ceará. At the center of these diverse zone sits the old gold mining region that had entered into decline in the late eighteenth century. Once a densely forested region, much of the forest had been stripped for fuel and timber in the gold rush.[47]

The old mining zone (also known as the Zona Metalúrgica) remained in relative decline in the nineteenth century while the southern areas (South and Mata) of the province participated in the economic expansion generated by coffee production in the bordering provinces/states of São Paulo and Rio de Janeiro. (See map 2.) By the 1890s the state depended primarily on coffee taxes for its revenues, and the politicians of the South and Mata were among the most powerful in Minas Gerais.[48]

In the twentieth century, even as it industrialized, Minas grew in the shadow of São Paulo and Rio de Janeiro. In the language of dependency theorists, it developed on the "periphery of the periphery." This position, both geographic and political, has profoundly shaped the nature of mineiro industrialization. While scholars have long noted that Brazilian industrialization has been shaped by the intervention of the federal government, in Minas the hand of the state government has been decisive. If a "triple alliance" of the State, foreign investment, and national capital shaped Brazil's economic development, then the role of the state government has made mineiro industrialization a "quadruple alliance."[49]

The role of the state government in mineiro industrialization has been intertwined inextricably with the process of state-building (as opposed to the role of the State in nation-building). In the 1890s Minas Gerais was, arguably, a group of regions loosely tied together by a longstanding political demarcation that had yet to become reality. The construction of Belo Horizonte was originally designed to foster the political (as well as economic) unity of these diverse regions. The idea succeeded beyond the dreams of its creators. Belo Horizonte became a dynamic vortex pulling the political elites of the diverse regions inward toward power and unity while, at the same time, it gradually became an economic vortex as well, drawing economic activity and entrepreneurs into an increasingly powerful growth pole.[50]

The key to political and economic power in Minas Gerais has been a balance between unity and diversity through networks of kinship and capital. Powerful political clans, some with roots deep in the mineiro past, have built local and regional networks in the diverse zones of the state. Their success over the last century, however, has depended on the ability to claim a share in the power and resources of the state government. The state government and economy have been forged out of the clientelistic networks based in the regions of Minas Gerais. In economics and politics these clans' power originally arose out of their home regions, and eventually (in most cases) both politicians and economic activity migrated to the center—Belo Horizonte. This study traces the rise of Belo Horizonte as a major industrial center, but it is always against the backdrop of politics. The two are intimately intertwined in this story.[51]

This analysis divides the industrialization of Belo Horizonte and Minas Gerais into four main phases or periods. The origins of industrialization date from the late nineteenth century (the 1870s in Minas and the 1890s in Belo Horizonte) up to the 1940s. During these decades the first industries in the city and state took shape, principally in textile manufacturing, food processing, and metallurgy. In nearly all cases, the companies and industrial establishments were small, and generally their capital (rarely in large quantities) came from pooling the resources of family networks. Quite often this capital had been accumulated through agricultural or commercial pursuits. In these decades, a small but vibrant business community took shape in Belo Horizonte. By the end of World War II, the first phase of industry and industrialists came to a close.

From the mid-1940s (and especially in the 1950s) industry in Belo Horizonte and Minas surged forward. In these years, the role of the state government became the decisive factor in the process of industrialization. This activist state government aggressively pursued foreign investment, and the poorly capitalized local industrialists often found themselves the weak, third leg in ventures combining local, state, and foreign capital. It was also in these years that technocrats (primarily engineers and, later, economists) emerged as central players in the process of industrialization. Although they had played significant roles beginning in the 1930s, they became the third powerful player in the triad of politicians, technocrats, and entrepreneurs. With the national political crisis of the 1960s, the industrial surge of the 1950s entered into a period of stagnation and crisis.

The so-called economic "miracle" of the military regime after 1968 ushered in the third phase of industrialization. The 1970s, like the 1950s, were years of dramatic economic growth for Minas Gerais. During the 1970s Minas became a predominantly urban, industrial state, and the Center (more or less the old Zona Metalúrgica) grew dramatically in comparison to the rest of the state. While the Brazilian economy chalked up the highest growth rates in the world (10–11 percent per annum) in the late 1960s and early 1970s, Minas Gerais grew faster than its traditional rivals Rio de Janeiro and São Paulo, and the Zona Metalúrgica grew much faster than the rest of Minas Gerais. Foreign and state capital (both state and federal) transformed mineiro industrialization that had, until the 1960s, remained primarily small scale and family run, to large scale and dominated by foreign and state capital.[52] Two-thirds of all new industrial investments between 1970 and 1977 were state generated.

The debt crisis of the 1980s, however, followed the "miracle" of the 1970s. The government of Minas, like the federal government, had borrowed heavily to finance the industrial surge, and, with the oil shocks and rise in interest rates of the late seventies and early eighties, found itself cut off from new loans while unable to pay the old ones. Much like the 1960s, the 1980s were years of stagnation, high inflation, recession, and great pessimism. Belo Horizonte, however, reached its centennial well into a new phase of economic growth and industrialization. Like the 1970s and 1950s, the 1990s were another decade of growth. In the last half of the twentieth century the economy of Minas rode an economic roller coaster, roughly a decade of growth followed by a decade of stagnation, from the 1950s to the 1990s.

Politicians, technocrats, and entrepreneurs faced a series of obstacles in their efforts to industrialize Belo Horizonte and Minas Gerais. Geography, inadequate transportation networks, a scarcity of capital, and technological backwardness presented the greatest challenges to those promoting economic growth and modernization. Located four hundred kilometers inland, in a rugged, mountainous terrain, the inhabitants of the old Zona Metalúrgica had access to the ports of the Atlantic via unpaved mountain roads until the arrival of the first rail line with the construction of Belo Horizonte in the 1890s. Minas Gerais was also an anomaly in Brazilian settlement patterns. The gold rush made Minas the most heavily populated captaincy in Brazil in the eighteenth century, but the only major population center not along the Atlantic coast.

The merchants and industrialists of Rio de Janeiro and São Paulo had easy access to the rest of the world economy by the 1890s because of their locations on or near the coast. By the First World War, São Paulo also had an extensive rail network extending into the interior of the state as a result of the expansion of coffee production.[53] Throughout the twentieth century, the inadequate network of paved roads and rail service have held back the economic development of the state, and Belo Horizonte. The capital did not have a large-gauge rail connection to Rio de Janeiro until 1917, and was not connected with the state highway network until 1922.[54] The high costs of transportation—by road or rail—have been an obstacle to industrialization.[55] In the words of one astute mineiro, the state remained an "economic island" well into the mid-twentieth century.[56]

The inability of mineiros to mobilize capital has been an even more severe hindrance to industrialization throughout the past century. Although investors in Rio and São Paulo have also had difficulty mobilizing capital (a feature typical of underdeveloped or developing nations), mineiros have had even more trouble than their carioca and paulista counterparts. Prior to the 1920s, capital came almost exclusively from family networks. With the emergence of a rudimentary banking system by the 1920s, the opportunities for capital mobilization increased, but not nearly as much as in Rio and São Paulo, where much larger and more sophisticated banking and capital markets were emerging. This historical scarcity of capital is the major reason for the entry of the federal government into economic affairs in the 1930s, and of the state government into the economy of Minas Gerais in the 1950s.[57]

Finally, geography, poor transportation, and scarce capital contributed to the technological backwardness of the mineiro economy, a pattern going back to the colonial era when Brazil suffered from its dependence on the technologically backward Portugal. As this study shows, this historical pattern of technological dependence and the lack of local innovation continued throughout the twentieth century. Despite impressive economic growth and industrialization, mineiro politicians, technocrats, and entrepreneurs have not given a high priority to the promotion and diffusion of technological innovation. As a consequence, Minas Gerais (and Brazil as well) experiences a form of industrialization that depends heavily on technology transfer, and suffers from a continual inability to generate internal technological innovation. This lack of local innovation may be the most serious flaw of mineiro and Brazilian industrialization.

This study analyzes the industrialization of Belo Horizonte over the last century by focusing on three key (and sometimes overlapping) groups: politicians, technocrats, and entrepreneurs. These three groups confronted the obstacles to industrialization and made crucial choices that shaped the patterns of industrialization in Belo Horizonte. They strove to overcome the region's geographic isolation, its lack of adequate transportation, capital, and technology. Entrepreneurs struggled to make the city an economic (as well as bureaucratic) center, and technocrats—the last group to appear on the scene—played a decisive role in the postwar transformation of Belo Horizonte into Brazil's second largest industrial center.[58] It was politicians, however, who created and controlled the fate of the city, and politics has played the decisive role in the creation and growth of Belo Horizonte.

Brazilian Politics

During its first half-century, Belo Horizonte became a political (as well as an economic) vortex, pulling the state's political elites inward toward a physical center for their networks of power and influence. Although created as a distinct administrative entity (captaincy) in the early eighteenth century, and despite nearly seven decades experience as a powerful province in imperial Brazil, Minas Gerais was sharply divided politically and geographically at the end of the nineteenth century. Just as regionalism characterized national politics with provinces (and then states) vying for power and influence at the national level, regions within this region struggle to protect and advance their own interests.

By the late nineteenth century the state contained seven clearly distinct geographical and political zones (*zonas*). (See map 2.) The Zona Metalúrgica, sometimes referred to as the Center, had arisen as the first center of European occupation and economic activity with the gold rush at the beginning of the eighteenth century. It contained the first officially recognized *vilas,* one being the colonial and then imperial capital, Ouro Preto. With the sharp decline in gold production after 1770, and with the rise of coffee cultivation in the Zona Sul and Zona da Mata, the Center's economic power no longer matched its political importance. Landowners, especially coffee planters, in the Sul and Mata had emerged as a powerful force in state politics, often in conflict with the political elites of the less economically dynamic Center.[59]

The other four zones carried much less weight politically and economically than the Center, South, and Mata. The North and East, much less densely populated, and often geographically more a part of the Northeastern interior, had developed their own political elites. The West and the Triangle were also less densely populated, and contained a growing number of cattle ranchers on terrain that merged into the savanna of the Brazilian Center-West. It was the political elites of these zones who battled over the transfer of the state capital in the early 1890s, with the Center pulling together enough votes from the other zones to defeat the Sul and Mata's alternative to Belo Horizonte (Várzea do Maçal).[60]

As Belo Horizonte grew in the decades before World War II, the regional elites came to the capital to serve in the governor's palace, the state cabinet, the legislature, and the many other positions in the state bureaucracy. Many bought homes or created businesses in the area, sent their children to school in the capital, and effectively developed dual residences—in their hometowns (and political bases) in the interior as well as Belo Horizonte. The new state capital offered them political employment, sometimes economic opportunity, and served as a neutral ground for mediating the conflicts among regional elites.

Over the last two centuries, mineiro politics—like Brazilian politics—has been characterized by certain key features that have persisted tenaciously across time and regime changes. These features offer the keys to understanding how state politics operate, and why elite networks remain the key to both politics and the process of industrialization. Patrimonialism, elitism, clientelism, personalism, and regionalism have endured and evolved since colonial times. The growing power of the State (on a national scale) and the state government (that is, in Minas Gerais), has been an undeniable and fundamental element of the body politic (of both nation and state).

Historically, a growing and complex bureaucracy has long formed the skeleton of this body politic, a bureaucracy in which power flowed downward from the king (and then later the emperor or president) who headed the system. Powerful landowners, merchants, military officers, the clergy, and public functionaries kept the masses in check by dominating the State apparatus, and the patronage it dispensed. The State controlled and dispensed resources (patrimony) to allies and friends, denying patronage to enemies. The State bureaucracy took on a life of its own, certifying, verifying, and acting as the buffer between the powerful and the powerless (a "cartorial" state in the words of Hélio Jaguaribe). This patrimonial system with its corporatist ethos of hierarchy, stability, and concentration of power stood in stark contrast to the shifts taking place in western Europe, especially in England, by the sixteenth and seventeenth centuries.[61]

In Brazil, the influence of the Enlightenment and the struggle for independence did not produce a dramatic rupture with the corporatist, bureaucratic tradition. The transfer of the monarchy to Rio de Janeiro in 1808, and the unusual role of the Braganzas (both João and his son, Pedro) in providing a relatively bloodless transition to independence helped Brazil avoid the chaos and anarchy so characteristic of much of Spanish America. In many ways, independence signaled the transfer of power to a Brazilian elite who continued the process of extending the power of the patrimonial State over the vast regions of the Empire. In the nineteenth century, the Brazilian elite faced the task of forging a nation out of a colonial beginning, rather than creating a nation by breaking with a colonial past. Continuity rather than radical change characterized independence in 1822. In Brazil, a small landowning (and largely slaveholding) elite moved to impose centralized government and patrimonial politics, despite a rhetoric of classic liberalism.[62]

For most of the nineteenth century Brazil's experiment with monarchy made it unique among the nations of the hemisphere. The 67-year reigns of Pedro I and his Brazilian son, Pedro II, provided the country with a stability matched by very few nations in Latin America or by the United States. While civil wars tore apart most of Spanish America and the United States, Brazil's imperial system helped provide a gradual transition from colony to republic. The advantages of stability and gradual change, however, came at a very high price for the masses. Slavery remained intact until 1888, and the free masses had little voice in politics. The poor, rural, nonwhite masses occasionally expressed themselves through the regional revolts that challenged the central government (especially in the 1830s and 1840s). By and large, however, the elites remained firmly in control and the major crises in the imperial system generally came from intra-elite rivalries.[63]

These elites hold the key to understanding the workings of Brazilian (and mineiro) politics over the last two centuries. The ability of various elite groups to keep the masses at bay and maintain control of the reins of power—the patrimonial State and its bureaucratic machinery—has been impressive. Whether under an imperial monarchy, a republic, dictatorship, or mass politics, elite manipulation of the State machinery has continued—changing forms like a chameleon. In a sense, the State machinery has been the enduring constant in Brazilian political history, while the elites who have controlled the instruments of power have changed through the centuries. Sugar planters and merchants gave way to coffee planters, the military, and industrialists, who ultimately had to reach an accommodation with the urban middle classes.

Furthermore, until the rise of a small socialist and communist movement in the early twentieth century, no substantial ideological disputes divided the Brazilian elites. Virtually all of them accepted the rules of the system, and fought to control it, rather than to change it. The relatively small political elite came from a very homogenous background. Generally from landholding (and often slaveholding) families, they attended the same schools, graduated from one of Brazil's two law schools (Recife and São Paulo), and were generally inculcated with the same constellation of values. Most worked their way up through the political system following similar career patterns. Following a seemingly democratic set of rules, in reality the elites were engaged in a form of "shadow play" that hid the true mechanisms of power in Brazilian politics and society.[64]

Politics in modern Brazil has long been a sophisticated game of patronage. In the nineteenth century one rose through the system by becoming a client of the powerful, and building a clientele among the less powerful. The most important forms of patronage were the spoils of the State. Positions in government became a means to reward one's clients, and advance one's own interests. Brazilian politics became a giant spoils system, and politicians vied for control of the spoils. The State served as the apparatus for accumulating, controlling, and dispensing patronage.[65]

With severely restrictive requirements for voting, and careful scrutiny of the voting booth by local landowners, the electoral system became a means for legitimating the power of the elites. The only real question was which group within the elites would control more of the spoils. Rather than building political parties along the lines of ideology and issues, parties became networks of powerful clans whose political foundations were regionally based. Local bosses became clients of regional power brokers who then contended for power in state governments. The most powerful states (principally Minas Gerais, São Paulo, Rio de Janeiro, Bahia, and Rio Grande do Sul) then jockeyed for position on the national scene. Clans and state elites became the most important keys to understanding the networks of power in Brazilian politics.[66]

By the turn of the century, for example, the elites had developed a system known as *coronelismo* that beautifully illustrates the tradeoffs and creativity involved in maintaining elite power. At the time, the federal government did not have the resources to extend the central State's power into the vast interior. The regional elites wanted to keep central government intervention into state politics at a minimum. Large landowners (often with the honorary title of colonel in the local militia, much like the U.S. South) remained very powerful at the local level. The genius of coronelismo was in linking up the power of these rural landowners with the resources of the emerging State.[67]

The powerful landowners contended for supremacy in their locale with the support of the state government generally proving decisive in any power struggle. The state government could back the landowner with laws and legislation, resources, and, ultimately, with troops. In return, the colonel could guarantee his patrons in the state government the extension of the powers of the State into the countryside at a minimal cost. He also delivered the vote on election day. The ever increasing patronage power of the state and federal governments became even more important, and reinforced the hold on power of the elites. The real struggles for power in the First Republic were between elite groups for power at the state level. When these struggles threatened the stability of the Republic itself, the federal government would send in troops to restore order.[68]

This tradeoff, of state backing for large landowners in exchange for control of the vote, provided Brazil with stability in the short run, but at a very high price. The system gave new life to the old structures of power in the countryside. In effect, the modernizing, urban elites struck a deal with the traditional rural elites. The latter retained much of their power in the countryside in exchange for loyalty to the central government and the new "representative" republic. In the long run, the arrangement reinforced and perpetuated the worst features of the old power structure well into this century. Brazilian politicians constructed the facade of representative, democratic politics on the still very powerful structures of patronage, patrimonialism, hierarchy, and elitism.

Mineiro Politics

Minas Gerais has been one of the two or three most important administrative units in Brazil since its origins in the gold rush of the eighteenth century. By 1750, Minas had become the most heavily populated captaincy in Brazil, and remained the nation's most populated state until surpassed by São Paulo in the 1930s. (Minas is still second in population behind São

Paulo.) Clearly the colony's richest captaincy until the 1770s, the dramatic decline in gold production slowly diminished the captaincy's economic importance, as exports declined drastically and the mineiro economy diversified, fragmented, and turned inward.[69] Not until the rise of coffee production in the 1850s and 1860s in the Sul and Mata did Minas begin to recover an important role in the Brazilian economy.

Throughout Empire and Republic, despite Minas's relative economic decline (compared with Rio de Janeiro and the emerging São Paulo) its national political prominence continued and grew. Over the last two centuries, Minas Gerais has played a key—if not *the* key—role in nearly every major national political turning point. In the nineteenth century, mineiro politicians played leading roles in the imperial government, and the state played a decisive role in the stabilization of the Republic in the 1890s.[70] Although the state's republicans were in disarray in the first years of the Republic, they quickly regrouped to form a cohesive and unified political block, the largest congressional delegation in the national assembly.[71]

After 1898, along with the powerful paulista politicians, mineiros forged the so-called "politics of the governors" that dominated Brazilian politics to 1929. In effect, Minas and São Paulo (along with Rio Grande do Sul) dominated national politics, with Rio de Janeiro, Bahia, and Pernambuco playing secondary roles. In exchange for loyalty to the central government (and patronage from it), governors were left to run their states as they pleased. The states, in effect, became clients of the patrimonial national State. Governors essentially followed the same policy at home, allowing local power-brokers (the coronéis) to run their towns and villages in exchange for loyalty to the state government (and state patronage).[72]

Minas benefited enormously from the so-called "coffee and cream" alliance. Three mineiros served as president between 1904 and 1926 (Afonso Pena, Wenceslau Bras, Artur Bernardes), and the state enjoyed the role of kingmaker in national politics.[73] This political clout derived from the extraordinary cohesion and unity the state's politicians managed to maintain. Beginning with the administration of Governor Francisco Silviano de Bueno Brandão in 1898, the major political factions in the state came together to control state politics, and to exert national influence.[74] The Partido Republicano Mineiro (PRM) became the principal vehicle for achieving and maintaining this cohesion and influence. With one exception (the Partido Comunista do Brasil, formed in 1922), Brazil did not have national political parties until the late 1940s. Under the First Republic, state-level parties controlled politics and then negotiated with other parties at the national level. These parties (in many states the Partido Republicano) became the instrument of state political elites to dispense patronage, maintain traditional clientelistic ties, and manage personalism.[75]

Politics in Minas has been built on personalism, clientelism, and patronage since the eighteenth century. Despite the rise of mass politics, urbanization, and open elections, these traditional political forces continue to dominate in mineiro and Brazilian politics up to the present.[76] From the 1890s to the 1940s, the state government—via the PRM until 1930 and via Getúlio Vargas and his regimes until 1945—became the principal source of patronage, in the form of resources and jobs. Governors reinforced and rewarded their allies in municipios with patronage, and local leaders dispensed their rewards to their allies in the municipios. In Minas, competition was not between political "ins" and "outs," but among the regionally based clans and factions who sought their share of influence in state politics.[77]

The political elite in Minas has never been very large, and from the 1890s to the 1940s probably numbered in the hundreds (out of a state population of about 3 million in 1890 and nearly 7 million in 1940). The most thorough study of the political elite (defined as persons who were "members of the state and/or federal legislative congresses, or occupied major offices in the state and/or federal public administrations between 1891 and 1930") tallied 542 individuals.[78] This group was all white, all male, and nearly all had a college education, more than 60 percent with a law degree (and another 24 percent in medicine or engineering).[79]

All studies of the mineiro political elite agree that kinship ties were probably the most important characteristics of this group.[80] More than half of individuals in Martins' study had intra-elite family ties, and many came from entrenched family oligarchies with strong local or regional bases.[81] Martins, in fact, argues persuasively that "intra-elite family ties was the most important single factor for the upward mobility of members of the elite."[82] Wirth's analysis, part of a comparative study of Pernambuco and São Paulo, also stresses the insularity and homogeneity of the mineiro political elite. Very few members of his elite population were born outside of Minas (13 percent versus 19 percent for the paulista elite), and none were foreign-born.[83]

The principal means of recruiting and training elite politicians in Minas was known as the *sargentação* system. Young talented individuals (especially from the elite's own family networks) served in a sort of apprenticeship system, first in local politics as *vereador* or *prefeito,* then in the state assembly, before moving on to the federal congress. The more successful then moved on to a federal ministry, a state secretariat, and then—the select few—to governor or president of the republic. The PRM served as the vehicle for state-level leaders to recruit and reward local and regional aspirants to power. Its power was so great that in the first three decades of this century, the PRM executive committee drew up the lists of candidates for municipal, state, and national offices—and its candidates always won, often with near unanimity.[84]

This one-party rule (not unlike the PRI in modern Mexico) not only unified the state's political elite, it also eroded and suffocated regional, local, and private interests (both political and economic) increasing the centralization of power in Belo Horizonte. In 1903 the political elite modified the state's constitution (of 1892) stripping municipios of their political and fiscal autonomy, placing the appointment and transfer of municipal judges in the hands of the governor, and handing control of most electoral mechanisms (voter registration, vote counting) under the control of the state legislature and governor.[85] The executive committee of the PRM made every important political decision, from who would run for office, to the distribution of patronage.[86] In effect, the power brokers of the PRM in Belo Horizonte asserted a centralized, authoritarian, top-down control over the state's fiscal and political resources.[87]

The two most important resources the state controlled were tax revenues and jobs. The PRM doled out these resources from Belo Horizonte to local and regional political elites in exchange for their loyalty.[88] Employment, as it had been as far back as the colonial era, was the quintessential form of patronage. During the First Republic, on average, the government hired some two thousand new employees each year, most purely on the basis of political connections. This use of *empreguismo* (appointment to public office) has continued in states and the federal government up to the present.[89] For those who challenged the PRM or showed disloyalty, the denial of patronage and access to office could mean the end of a political career. Cooptation and coercion went hand in hand.

Mineiro politicians have achieved a certain fame and notoriety in Brazilian politics as astute power brokers. In the 1930 civil war, in the fall of Vargas in 1945, in the coup in 1964, and the transition to civilian rule in 1985, mineiro politicians have been among the decisive power brokers. As a result, Brazilians talk of *mineiridade* or *mineirice* referring to "political shrewdness, bargaining or compromise, frequently associated with a pragmatic, non-ideological and opportunistic trend to support the government, to be unstintingly pro-Establishment."[90]

As Martins has argued, the "secret of Minas" has been precisely the centralization and unification of the state's political elite that has allowed them to stabilize state governance and achieve power in national politics. This cohesion and unity, however, have been achieved at a price. The increasing centralization of power in the hands of a political elite in Belo Horizonte has weakened private interests, co-opting the upper and middle classes through patronage and compromise. Politics has sometimes become an economic end in itself as it offered a direct source of revenue. For a good number, politics became a lifelong career. Mineiro politicians became Max Weber's "professional politicians" who lived *off* politics and not *for* politics.[91]

As the following chapters will show, in a political system built on patrimonialism and patronage, virtually the only way for entrepreneurs to gain access to the resources they needed to survive and thrive has been through political influence. Put another way, economic development did not generate political success, but rather the opposite. Economic development depended on political success.[92] Political centralization became the engine (and the limiting factor) in the state's economic growth. Ironically, oligarchical politics provided impressive political stability and national influence, but it also limited the growth of open and truly competitive politics, while weakening the private sector and reinforcing entrepreneurs' dependence on the state.

Scholars have long debated the relationship between "economic" and "political" interests or elites in Brazilian and mineiro politics. Some have tried to demonstrate a correlation between specific elite groups (such as coffee planters) and various political outcomes (such as legislation to protect coffee interests). Others (Martins, for example) have turned this around to emphasize the disassociation between economic interests and politics, arguing that a bureaucratic elite in Minas dominated state politics in the early twentieth century creating a "white-collar republic."[93] For more recent decades, the debate has been over whether technocrats or politicians had the upper hand in state politics (Andrade and Hagopian, for example.) All of these studies have emphasized the power and importance of clientelism and patronage politics. They diverge in their analysis of who holds power—career politicians, technocrats, or businessmen.

While it is clear that no single economic interest group—coffee planters, industrialists, merchants—ever achieved political control of state politics, this seems to me to miss the point. In a relatively insulated society with a very small elite, the networks of power were very personalistic and interconnected. Sons of the same families went into a variety of careers, some as politicians, some as businessmen, and others as technocrats. Even when they did largely focus on one of these careers they continued to be tied by kinship and friendship to those in other careers. Furthermore, nearly all these studies assume a single career for every individual. As we will see in the following chapters, some of the most powerful and important figures in twentieth-century Minas have pursued multiple careers in politics, business, and the technocracy. In short, to categorize individuals, and then argue that they pursue only the interests of their career cohort is to lose sight of the connections among elite individuals they forged through clientelism and kinship—connections that integrated rather than divided politicians, technocrats, and entrepreneurs.

The mineiro political elite pulled together a diverse and relatively isolated group of regions (Centro/Metalúrgica, Norte, Oeste/Triángulo, Sul, and Mata) creating a unified elite and state. Belo Horizonte in the first half-century after its creation became a true bureaucratic and administrative capital and the locus of state political activity drawing the political elite inward. The city became the center for political negotiations and the locus of state patronage. The emergence of Belo Horizonte as the economic center of the state was a direct and logical result of this political centralization.

Chapter 2 ⬙

Building Belo Horizonte and a Business Elite, 1890s–1940s

On a warm December day in 1897, the political leadership of Minas Gerais converged on the small hamlet of Belo Horizonte to inaugurate a new capital for Brazil's most populous state. Foreshadowing the construction of Brasília six decades later, politicians and planners had transformed a rustic municipio of some 8,000 inhabitants into an enormous construction project. As with Brasília, those who promoted the move saw the new capital as a symbol and a catalyst. This planned city would symbolize the modernizing forces that were transforming Brazil and Minas Gerais as they entered the twentieth century. More important, the rationally designed political center would also serve as a catalyst in the economic growth and integration of the state. In short, a modern, planned city would provide Minas Gerais with the dynamic economic and political capital that it so badly needed.[1]

Belo Horizonte has grown beyond the wildest dreams of the fin de siècle politicians and technocrats who created it. A century later, rapidly approaching four million inhabitants, the city has become the second largest industrial center in the ninth largest economy in the world. Economic and political power have become so concentrated in Belo Horizonte that technocrats now grapple with ways to reverse the centralization of the past century. The growth pole has become too successful and has now taken on too dominant a role in the state economy.

In this chapter and the next I look at the creation and early industrialization of Belo Horizonte during the first half-century of its existence. Politicians and entrepreneurs established the foundations of industry that would make possible the large-scale industrialization of the postwar decades. They also put into place the networks of patronage, clientelism, and kinship that have dominated and characterized mineiro politics and industrialization throughout the twentieth century. This analysis of the early industrialization of Belo Horizonte concentrates on the networks of political, economic, and social power that form its most distinctive characteristics. This chapter examines in detail the elite networks that dominated political and economic power into the 1940s. Through personalistic and clientelistic networks, these elites dominated the politics of the city and the state, and laid the foundations for industrialization. Chapter 3 analyzes the process of industrialization, concentrating on technology and the growing role of technocrats.

Creating a New Capital

From the moment of its creation, the state government has played the central role in the growth of Belo Horizonte. The idea of moving the mineiro capital from the picturesque, but out-of-the-way, Ouro Preto to a more advantageous location dates back to the late eighteenth century.[2] Resurrected periodically throughout the nineteenth century, the issue came to the forefront with the new republican regime in the early 1890s. Augusto de Lima, president of the new state and a native of a municipio bordering Belo Horizonte (known today as Nova Lima), called for the constituent assembly to set in motion the process for selecting and building a new capital. According to Lima, the new capital would "be a center of financial, industrial, and intellectual activity."[3]

Unable to resolve the issue, the assembly gave the new legislature the authority to move the capital. A technical commission surveyed and suggested four possible sites. Politicians from the different zones fought bitterly over the location of the new capital with many favoring the status quo. Ironically, legislators from the Center, the North, and the East—areas in economic decadence—combined against those of the Sul and Mata—the two most dynamic economic zones in the state—and by a two-vote margin (30 to 28) selected Belo Horizonte as the site of the new capital in December 1893.[4]

Governor Afonso Pena—born in the mining zone near the future Belo Horizonte—moved quickly. The legislation authorizing the transfer of the capital stipulated that the inauguration had to take place within four years of the vote in favor of the move. Furthermore, Pena had less than a year left on his term, and he knew that his successor could easily drop the project if it were not well under way when power changed hands. Aarão Reis, a civil

Map 3 Original Plan of Belo Horizonte

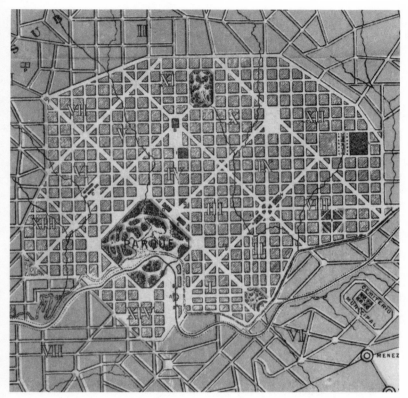

Source: Commissão Constructora da Nova Capital, *Revista geral dos trabalhos. I. Abril de 1895* and *II. Fevereiro de 1896* (Rio de Janeiro: H. Lombaerts, 1895 and 1986).

engineer from Maranhão with extensive construction experience in Rio de Janeiro, had headed the technical commission, and Pena now put him in charge of the construction of the new capital. Inspired by baroque city planning, and with Washington, DC and Paris as his models, Reis designed a geometric grid plan cut by diagonals. (See map 3.) While perhaps intellectually satisfying, the plan made few concessions to functional realities and topography, and most certainly did not anticipate the future demands of automotive transport. Reis envisioned an eventual population of up to 300,000 occupying the planned urban core, supported by watersheds and farming in the surrounding countryside.[5] Work on the site began in early 1894.

Construction of the new capital presented enormous technical and logistical problems. The railroad from Rio de Janeiro went only as far as Sabará (20 kilometers to the east), and a feeder line had to be constructed to bring in building materials, equipment, food, and workers. The government brought in thousands of workers, many Italian immigrants, to lay out the streets and avenues, and construct government buildings. On December 12, 1897, exactly four years to the day from the vote to move the capital, Governor Crispim Jacques Bias Fortes inaugurated the newly renamed Cidade de Minas.[6]

Reis designed streets 20 meters wide, and broad avenues 35 meters in width. The main avenue (later named Afonso Pena), an artery running north-south across the length of the city, measured 50 meters wide. The Avenida do Contorno circled the urban zone and served as the boundary with the suburban zone.[7] In the urban zone, the commission laid out nearly 4,000 lots. After setting aside nearly half of those for the government, for public officials, and for those local residents whose land had been expropriated for the new capital, the other half were put up for public sale.[8] The commission set about demolishing the old village and laying out the new streets and avenues. (The only pre-1897 structure to survive—an old farm house—today houses the Museu de Belo Horizonte.)

Much like Washington, DC, the new capital was administered as a virtual dependency of the state government. The *prefeito* was appointed by the governor until the mid-1940s. Rather than a *câmara municipal* with relative autonomy, Belo Horizonte had an elected *conselho deliberativo,* although the *conselho* did not even have a permanent home until 1914.[9] (The striking, cathedral-like structure is today the home of the Centro de Cultura Belo Horizonte in the heart of the central city.) The *conselho* did not become a *câmara municipal* until 1936 and quickly disappeared with the coup that created the Estado Novo dictatorship in 1937. The *câmara* was revived in 1947 and has operated ever since as an elected body, although under severe constraints under military rule (1964–85).

For the next four decades Belo Horizonte grew at a steady pace. By 1920, the municipio already ranked third in the state in the value of industrial production behind Juiz de Fora and Conselheiro Lafaiette (Queluz).[10] By World War II, the city had become Brazil's sixth largest urban center with a population over 200,000. (See table 2.1.) The city remained largely a bureaucratic and commercial center with some light industry.

By 1940, 25 percent of the labor force worked in industry, 18 percent in commerce, and 21.5 percent in public service jobs.[11] Textiles, food process-

Table 2.1 Population of Belo Horizonte, 1890–1991

Year	Municipio	Metropolitan area[10]
1890	8,009	—
1900	13,472	—
1920	55,563	—
1940	211,377	—
1950	352,724	507,993
1960	693,328	924,279
1970	1,255,415	1,669,392
1980	1,789,855	2,589,224
1991	2,048,851	3,461,905

Sources: Annuario estatístico, anno I-1921, volume IV, tomo I (Bello Horizonte: Imprensa Official, 1926) and national censuses, 1940–1991.

ing, woodworking, and clothing accounted for three-quarters of the value of industrial production in 1936, and, with very few exceptions, there was no heavy industry to speak of in the metropolitan region.[12]

The pages of the state government's official daily, *Minas Gerais,* are filled in the early decades of the century with the announcements of the opening of small, new industrial firms. These companies operated out of small buildings in neighborhoods around the city's periphery, especially along the Ribeirão das Arrudas that formed the edge of the central city. Shirts, socks, furniture, soap, carpentry, pasta, tobacco, beer, ice, bricks, and tiles were just some of the products produced in these small factories. Mechanical shops and small foundries also appeared. These small firms were largely individually owned or family enterprises employing at most 30 to 40 workers.[13] At times, the city government provided tax incentives or promises of electric power to encourage these businesses to set up shop in the new capital.[14]

Prior to the 1930s, successful industries were those that required relatively simple technology and could supply regional demand for simple consumer goods such as processed foods, textiles, and metal goods. By the early twentieth century, Minas had a long experience in these three industries. Throughout the nineteenth century these industries had developed quietly in Minas Gerais, and were more geographically dispersed than equivalent industries in Rio de Janeiro and São Paulo. The creation of Belo Horizonte would provide the industrial growth pole that Minas had lacked in the nineteenth century to accelerate the growth of these dispersed regional industries. A partial exception to this pattern was the iron and steel industry which began to take root in Minas because of its immense iron ore reserves. Yet, even in the case of iron and steel, the industry did not begin to grow substantially until after 1930.

In 1933, when the leading "industrial" entrepreneurs in the state formed the Federação das Indústrias do Estado de Minas Gerais (FIEMG), the group numbered some two dozen, and almost all of the member firms were small businesses.[15] Belo Horizonte had become the largest city in Minas Gerais, and its major industrial center by 1940, more a sign of the state's relative backwardness than the city's dynamism. Belo Horizonte remained smaller than Recife, Salvador, and Porto Alegre, as well as Rio de Janeiro and São Paulo.[16]

The Formation of a Business Elite

Belo Horizonte acted as a magnet attracting not only the state's political elite, but also its business elite, although the process took much longer and was not as complete as in politics. Business leaders could continue to operate successfully and profitably in their home regions and locales without moving the headquarters of their operations to Belo Horizonte. Although the capital had clearly become the home of most of the state's political elite (for at least part of the year) by the 1940s, the state's business elite continued to be fragmented regionally. Belo Horizonte, along with Juiz de Fora, were the two dominant business centers, but it would not be until the 1960s and 1970s that Belo Horizonte so clearly dominated the state's business community.[17]

In contrast to the fame and notoriety of mineiro politicians in national politics, scholars have nearly unanimously concurred on the relative weakness of mineiro entrepreneurs. In the late 1960s, for example, one of the principal assumptions of the landmark *Diagnóstico da economia mineira* was the historical weakness of mineiro entrepreneurs, especially when compared to the paulistas.[18] Nearly every important study by mineiro historians and social scientists points to this weakness as one of the prime factors behind the state government's role in the state economy. The state, so the argument goes, was compelled to step in with public capital because private capital simply could not provide the resources for industrialization and economic growth.[19] In effect, the argument reproduces at the state level the traditional argument for State intervention in the national economy that has been so central to developmental nationalism (of the Left and Right) in postwar Brazil (and the Third World, in general).[20]

Despite a considerable literature on Brazilian and mineiro economic history, very little has been written about businessmen and business communities. This book is, in fact, the first detailed historical analysis of the formation and evolution of the mineiro or *belorizontino* business community across the twentieth century.[21] Although smaller and less successful than their paulista contemporaries, it shows that mineiro businessmen (and occasionally businesswomen) most certainly were not lacking in entrepreneurial "spirit" or talent. Some of them, in fact, were (and are) among the most successful entrepreneurs in twentieth-century Brazil. The remainder of this chapter focuses on the origins, growth, size, and features of the business community in Belo Horizonte and Minas Gerais. The following chapter concentrates on the problems and choices they faced from the 1890s to the 1940s.

As a new city, Belo Horizonte had a very small business community in the first few decades after its creation, especially in comparison with Rio de Janeiro and São Paulo. In 1912, some 15 years after its official inauguration, the new capital had fewer than 40,000 inhabitants (versus more than a million in Rio and a half-million in the rapidly expanding São Paulo). Using a very expansive definition of commerce (that includes virtually anyone engaged in any kind of commercial, financial, or industrial activities), the business community numbered around 800. (See table 2.2.) (As a point of comparison, the same 1912 census counted nearly 600 civil servants [*funcionários públicos*].) Nearly half of these (345) are listed as *negociantes,* and another 187 are simply employees of commercial enterprises (*empregados no comercio*). The census tallied just 2(!) bankers, and some 38 industrialists. Given the structure of local industry, nearly all of these individuals ran small-scale operations.

By the early 1920s the size of the business community had doubled. Table 2.3 presents the breakdown (by category) for the municipal tax on professionals and industries in 1922.[22] The table breaks the list down into two parts: individuals paying the "professions" tax, and individuals and firms paying the "industry" tax. (For a complete listing of the subcategories, see appendix A.) Of the 500 individuals paying the professions tax, 32 percent (161) were artisans/craftspersons (from tailors to barbers and seamstresses), and another 33 percent (163) were professionals (attorneys, architects, dentists, engineers, and physicians). Managers/executives accounted for just over 4 percent (21) of those taxed. Office workers and the service sector accounted for 18 percent (91) and 13 percent (64) each.[23]

The breakdown of "industries" clearly indicates the commercial nature of the local economy in the early 1920s. More than 80 percent (701) of individuals/firms fall into this category. Factories and shops account for just 17 percent (145) of the total, and the financial sector makes up less than 1 percent (5) of the total. Nearly 80 percent (664) of all the "industries" taxed

Table 2.2 **Business Community of Belo Horizonte, 1912**

Profession	Total
Agents (Agenciadores)	19
Architects (Arquitetos)	12
Attorneys (Advogados)	68
Bankers (Banqueiros)	2
Bookkeepers (Guarda-livros)	22
Builders (Constructores)	25
Businessmen (Negociantes)	345
Capitalists (Capitalistas)	11
Contractors (Empreiteiros)	5
Employed in Commerce (Empregados no comercio)	187
Engineers (Engenheiros)	34
Hoteliers (Hoteleiros)	9
Industrialists (Industriais)	38
Merchants (Marchantes)	2
Money Changer (Cambista)	1
Pharmacists (Farmacêuticos)	36
Physicians (Médicos)	36
Total	812

Sources: Recenseamento de Bello Horizonte feito na administração do prefeito Dr. Olyntho Meirelles em 1912 (Bello Horizonte: Imprensa Official do Estado de Minaes Geraes, 1913), p. 51–53.

were owned by individuals, and the so-called "social" firms (to use the Brazilian tax terminology) were overwhelmingly partnerships or family businesses.

In the early 1920s, the business community in Belo Horizonte was quite clearly small, primarily composed of small businesses that were largely family-owned, and dominated by commerce rather than industry. Although the industrial sector was growing, it consisted largely of small factories to produce consumer goods, and artisanal shops. With a population approaching 60,000, the formal business community made up less than 3 percent of the population. Of that 3 percent (approximately 1,500 individuals exercising their profession or running industries), the business elite was drawn largely from the ranks of a few hundred professionals, industrialists, merchants, and bankers.

Census materials from the 1930s and 1940s also provide us with a glimpse of the size and structure of the business community, although the data are not precisely comparable.[24] Table 2.4 provides a rough breakdown

Table 2.3 Industries and Professions, Belo Horizonte, 1922

	Professions		
Profession			*Totals*
I. Professionals			163
II. Managers & executives			21
III. Office workers			91
IV. Services			64
V. Artisans/craftpersons			161
Total individuals			500

	Industries		
Industry	*Individuals*	*Firms*	*Totals*
I. Commercial	549	152	701
II. Financial	2	3	5
III. Factories	47	19	66
IV. Shops	66	13	79
Total for industries	664	187	851
Total for industries & professions			1351

Source: Minas Geraes, 28 December 1922, suplemento, 1–13.

of the nature of local business, with 71 percent (374) of all businesses classified as commercial, 23 percent (119) as industrial, and 6 percent (31) as other. Even more revealing is the value of the firms. Although commercial firms outnumber industrial ones by more than 3 to 1, the total value of industrial firms is nearly 90 percent of the value of all commercial firms combined. Quite clearly, the industrial firms are more highly capitalized and larger enterprises. The industrial sector continued to be dominated by firms that produced consumer goods for the local market (food processing, cloth, metals, wood). Retail cloth goods, retail goods, and restaurants/bars/cafes accounted for nearly 60 percent (220 of 374) of all commercial businesses.(See table 2.6.) The biggest businesses were cloth wholesalers. Just 4 firms accounted for nearly one-seventh of all commercial capital, and the firms had an average value of 275:000$, more than ten times the average for all commercial firms (just 20:000$).[25]

Table 2.5 breaks down the firms by type and capitalization. Of the 524 firms registered, 392 (or 75 percent) were owned by individuals, and the

Table 2.4 Mercantile Firms Registered by Junta Comercial, Belo Horizonte, 1936

Type of Firm	Number	Value of Firms (mil-reis)
Industrial	119	6.672:550$
Comercial	374	7.599:180$
Other	31	1.632:000$
Totals	524	15.903:730$

Source: Anuario estatístico de Belo Horizonte (1937), pp. 152–154.

Table 2.5 Composition of Mercantile Firms in Belo Horizonte, 1936

	Individual	Social	Totals
Number of firms	392	132	524
2 partners		86	
3 partners		23	
4+ partners		17	
cooperatives		3	
sociedade anónima		3	
Capital (mil-reis)	4.715:150$	11.188:584$	15.903:734$
Average capital	12:028$	84:762$	30:351$

Source: Anuario estatístico de Belo Horizonte (1937), pp. 124–151.

other 25 percent (132) were classified as "social firms." An analysis of these firms, however, shows that fully 65 percent (86 or 132) were partnerships of two individuals, and another 17 percent (23) were owned by three partners. Just 23 firms (just over 17 percent of all firms) had more than three partners. Of these, 3 were cooperatives. Of the remaining 20, just 3 were registered as *sociedades anónimas*. The 17 remaining firms were nearly all groups of 4–7 investors pooling their resources. The social firms were much better capitalized than the individually owned. Just 3 individually owned firms had capital of 100:000$ (a hotel, construction company, and a hardware business), 1 with 200:000$ (shoe company), and 2 with capital of 250:000$ (an automobile firm and a meat dealer). In contrast, 4 of the social firms had capital of 300 contos, 2 of 400 contos, 2 of 600 contos, 1 with 1,000 contos, and 1 with 1,500.

Although we do not have as detailed accounting of professions and businesses for the 1940s, the 1950 national census does give us a sense of the size

Table 2.6 Mercantile Firms Registered by Junta Comercial, Belo Horizonte, 1936
(by subcategories)

Type of Firm	Number	Value of Firms (mil-reis)
Industrial	112	6.672:550$
Food processing	28	2.862:000$
Construction	8	1.980:000$
Printing	8	328:000$
Footwear	9	168:000$
Woodworking	5	155:000$
Mining	4	110:000$
Furniture	3	110:000$
Pharmaceuticals	3	86:000$
Mechanical shops	8	58:750$
Others	46	814:000$
Commercial	374	7.599:180$
Wholesale cloth goods	4	1.100:000$
Clothing and shoes	15	911:000$
Butchers	7	733:000$
Retail cloth goods	38	682:000$
Restaurants, bars, and cafes	101	662:884$
Retail goods	81	577:500$
Farmacies	18	336:000$
Hotels and pensions	15	225:000$
Furniture stores	10	220:000$
Wholesale goods	3	160:000$
Electrical goods	3	80:000$
Others	79	1.911:000$
Other	31	1.632:000$
Real estate	2	684:000$
Procuratórios, commisões representações e conta própria	26	698:000$
Ginásios	2	120:000$
Rádio-difusão	1	130:000$
Totals	524	15.903:730$

Source: Anuario estatístico de Belo Horizonte (1937), 152–154.

Table 2.7 Population of Belo Horizonte, by Occupation, 1950

| | Number | | | Percentage |
Activity	Male	Female	Total	of Total
Agriculture, fishing, and forestry	3,131	99	3,230	2.5
Extractive industry	568	14	582	.5
Manufacturing	25,633	4,876	30,509	23.3
Commerce (goods)	13,970	2,093	16,063	12.3
Commerce (real estate, finance)	3,976	633	4,609	3.5
Services	12,829	24,852	37,681	28.9
Transport, communications, and warehousing	9,726	994	10,780	8.3
Liberal professions	1,742	397	2,139	1.6
Social activities	4,914	6,166	11,080	8.5
Civil servants	5,870	1,869	7,739	5.9
Military & police	6,019	68	6,087	4.7
Totals	88,434	42,061	130,495	100.0

Source: Recenseamento geral de 1950, Censo demográfico, 234.
Note: This table includes only the economically active population above ten years of age. It excludes those who are "inactive" (19,465), those with unclear occupations (707), and those engaged in "atividades domésticas não remuneradas e ativades escolares discentes" (116,532).

and structure of business activity in Belo Horizonte on the eve of its move toward heavy industrialization. Table 2.7 provides a breakdown of the economically active population in Belo Horizonte at the end of 1949. By midcentury the city clearly no longer served primarily as a bureaucratic-administrative center. Just under 6 percent of the individuals in the table worked as civil servants, and even if counting in military and police personnel, the civil service accounts for less than 11 percent of all workers. Belo Horizonte's emergence as an industrial center (albeit largely small industry) is also apparent with nearly a quarter of the workforce engaged in manufacturing. Commerce (counting both goods, real estate, and financial services) accounted for nearly 16 percent of the workforce, and when combined with the service sector and transportation, communications, and warehousing, commerce occupied nearly half the workforce.

These figures also give us a brief glimpse at the role of gender in economic activity. Women comprise just 20 percent of all those in the manufacturing sector, 14 percent in real estate and financial sector, and 13 percent in commerce involving goods. In contrast, they account for 66 percent of the service sector. Women played a very small role in the formal business sector, and almost no role at all in the business elite in Belo Horizonte. By the 1940s, that elite remained virtually entirely male, and still probably consisted of less than 300 individuals in a commercial, industrial, and service sector employing some 100,000 people in a city of about 350,000 inhabitants.

The business elite in Belo Horizonte was quite small at the beginning of the century. Virtually all of them were members of the Associação Comercial de Minas (ACM), which they had organized in 1901.[26] In fact, membership in the ACM was virtually synonymous with elite status. Nearly 100 businessmen attended the initial meetings of the ACM.[27] The state government also played a key role in the creation and support of this association, which was, after all, a classic example of a corporate interest group organized to defend its interests before the government.[28] The ACM held its first meetings in the Câmara dos Deputados, and did not have the means to construct a permanent headquarters of its own until the directors were able to secure a loan from the state government in 1921. For the next decade the ACM struggled to pay the loan back, eventually renegotiating for debt relief. The loan was finally paid off in 1929.[29]

Through the 1940s the membership of the ACM was never very large, and generally consisted of the most influential and important businessmen in the community. (Much like a country club, candidates for membership had to be nominated by a committee of current members, and then approved by a vote of the general assembly. Membership also required a substantial fee.) By the mid-1930s the Associação had about 100 voting members, and by the mid-1940s that number had risen to about 150.[30] A general assembly met once a month, but the real power in the ACM was the directory consisting of the president, first and second vice presidents, general secretary, first and second secretaries, first and second treasurers, and 15 or so directors, all elected by the general assembly in January each year.

Only the most powerful and influential businessmen were elected to the presidency. Typically, presidents were major businessmen who also often served in key political positions, elected and appointive. (See table 2.8.) The first president, Teófilo Ribeiro, was a partner in textile firms, served in many appointed political positions (including 14 years as the director of the state Secretaria de Finanças), and he had investments in a wide range of industries and companies.[31] José Pedro Drummond, who succeeded him in the presidency, was his son-in-law and the legislator who in 1893 had cast the decisive vote to move the capital to Belo Horizonte.[32] Christiano Teixeira Guimarães, who succeeded Drummond in the presidency, was the leading textile industrialist in the city, one of the founders of the Companhia Siderúrgica Belgo Mineira, and would eventually become an important banker as well.[33] (And the list goes on and on.) In short, in the half-century after its creation, probably fewer than 200 hundred businessmen dominated local commerce, finance, and industry, and the Associação served as their exclusive club and corporate haven.

By the 1930s a new elite group had emerged in Belo Horizonte, the Federação das Indústrias do Estado de Minas Gerais (FIEMG), a sign of the growing importance of the industrial sector in the state. Founded on February 12, 1933, the new organization elected its first directory in March. The new Ministério de Trabalho, Indústria e Comércio officially recognized the FIEMG in 1935 as the corporate representative of mineiro industrialists.[34] Like the ACM, the FIEMG gathered together the industrial elite of Minas Gerais, but unlike the ACM it would be a truly statewide organization. The Federation consisted of more than 150 members by the mid-1940s, nearly all representing small-scale enterprises.[35] Until the late 1940s, the only heavy industry in the region was the Belgo Mineira iron works in Sabará and Monlevade, and the Morro Velho gold mine in Nova Lima. Nearly all the founding members of the FIEMG were also members of the ACM.

A strongly corporatist ethos characterized the mentality of the business elite in Belo Horizonte, indeed, in all Brazil. In the formation of the ACM, the FIEMG, the Federação do Comércio, and other associations the business elite sought to use these corporate interest groups to lobby the state and national governments.[36] As they put it in the founding statutes of the ACM, they wanted "to be an entity addressing the public powers of the State and outside it made up of the classes that compose the association . . . presenting its complaints and defending its legitimate interests before any and all entities of public authority . . . to promote by all means within its reach the development and prosperity of the classes the entity represents."[37]

Very clearly the business elite saw themselves as a conservative force that would unify to provide stability and progress for the city, state, and nation. (They consciously and repeatedly referred to themselves as the *classes conservadoras.*) This sentiment was expressed repeatedly in the agricultural, commercial, and industrial congresses they organized in Minas in 1903, 1928, and 1935. In the words of one of the leading figures in the business community, Colonel Caetano de Vasconcelos, at the 1935 congress, "very soon we will form an indestructible block acting in the councils where the problems that affect the nation's potential are resolved. More than ever the *classes conservadoras* need to unite and impose through their prestige and authority the loyal fulfillment of their glorious objectives. . . ."[38]

Table 2.8 Presidents of the Associação Comercial de Minas, 1901–1945

Term	Name (Region) and Backgrund
1901	Teófilo Ribeiro (Center, non-mineiro) lawyer, textiles, banking, Secretary of Finance, Secretary of Agriculture
1911	José Pedro Drummond (Center) physician, lawyer, state senator, banker
1915	Christiano Teixeira Guimarães (Center) engineer, textiles, banking, insurance
1916	João Nepomuceno Licas de Lima (South) merchant, state tax collector
1918	Arthur Haas (Center, French) merchant, dry goods, automobiles
1919	Sebastião Augusto de Lima (North) merchant, textiles, banking, insurance
1924	Lauro Jacques (Center) merchant, state deputy, cinemas
1927	Eduardo Furetti (Center) director of Associação dos Empregados do Comércio
1928	Antônio Ribeiro de Abreu (West) industrialist, federal deputy
1930	Sebastião Augusto de Lima
1931	Lauro Jacques
1932	Artur Viana (Mata) merchant, industrialist, food processing, leather goods, agricultural implements, fertilizers
1933	Theódulo Leão (North) merchant, city council
1934	Cel. Caetano de Vasconcelos (Center) industrialist, banker
1937	Vitório Marçola (Mata) real estate
1938	José de Magalhães Pinto (West) merchant, banker, governor, various cabinet posts in state and federal governments
1939	Caetano de Vasconcelos
1941	Lauro Vidal
1943	Joaquim Vieira de Faria (South)
1944	Paulo Macedo Gontijo (West) engineer, textiles, construction
1945	José de Campos Continentino (West) engineer, furniture manufacturing

Sources: Luiz Sayão de Faria and Joaquim Ribeiro Filho, "Resumo histórico da Associação Comercial de Minas," *Revista Social Trabalhista* (December 1947), 360–7.

Periodically, the FIEMG and the ACM attempted to bring in new members and to help organize affiliate associations. In 1933, for example, the ACM proposed an "intense campaign" to create other commercial associations in municipalities that lacked them. The president remarked on "the necessity to undertake intense work to develop an associative spirit in the heart of the conservative classes of the State."[39] Jair Negrão de Lima, son of Benjamim Lima,

Table 2.9 First Directory of the FIEMG, 1933

Position	Name	Branch of Industry
President	José de Moraes Sarmento	textiles
1st Vice President	Alvimar Carneiro de Rezende	construction
2nd Vice President	José da Silva Brandão	iron & steel
1st Secretary	Augusto Gonçalves Filho	footwear
2nd Secretary	João Pinheiro Filho	iron
1st Treasurer	José Gonçalves de Souza	textiles
2nd Treasurer	Antônio Pereira da Rocha	textiles

Source: Vida Industrial 30:2 (February 1983): 13.

one of the most prominent business figures in the city and state, called for the ACM directors to support a proposal that would set aside spots for representatives of their "class" in the new constitution. He also wanted corporate representation in the federal assembly. The directors approved the proposal.[40]

The organizing commissions of each of these congresses were composed of a wide range of mineiro businessmen with interests in ranching, farming, industry, commerce, mining, and banking.[41] As with all the economic elites in this study, many of these men had multiple economic interests and circulated through careers in politics, business, and technocratic posts. Although one of the standard complaints coming out of these congresses, especially in 1928, was the lack of political representation for the "conservative classes" every study of the business community (Vieira, Delgado, Faria, Dulci, for example) shows that members of this elite were major political figures at the local and state levels throughout the first half of the century.[42] To use the terminology of Otavio Dulci, the mineiro elites were "polyvalent."[43]

As Dulci has persuasively argued, the mineiro economic elites in the first decades of the century had two visions of development that were not necessarily mutually exclusive. On the one hand, they promoted a vision of economic growth built on a variety of activities with a modernizing agricultural sector as the motor of industrial development. On the other hand, some of the elite promoted the idea of industrialization with an emphasis on intermediate goods. Both visions aimed to bring together the "disarticulated" geographic and economic zones of the state. There was near unanimity by all that the economic development of Minas Gerais could only come through state intervention, but by indirect means. In the words of João Pinheiro, perhaps the greatest political and business figure at the beginning of the century, the state could promote development in three ways: "substantial monetary prizes to stimulate private enterprise; indirect help of public powers to establish cooperatives, credit, and circulation; and, finally, protectionism for nationally produced goods."[44]

The 1928 congress emphasized the need to unite the conservative classes to achieve political representation that would work to address their main concerns: railway freight rates, the electrification of the Central do Brasil, the tax structure, agricultural credit, professional training, commercial legislation, defending coffee prices, social legislation, communication systems, and the exodus of rural workers to other states.[45] The proposals of the 1935 congress clearly demonstrate the statist orientation of the business elite. The proposals were directed to the state government and called for: more tariffs, credit, industrial assistance, nationalization of waterfalls, nationalization of mines, and greater state intervention to promote economic development.[46] Throughout the twentieth century the mineiro business elite has seen themselves as the men who would lead the process of industrialization and economic development, but they could not envision this happening without the assistance of the state and federal governments. They saw themselves as lobbyists cajoling the government to provide them with the means to promote economic growth. They also saw industrialists, merchants, bankers, and agriculturalists as a group with common interests.

The formation of the FIEMG represents the coalescence of a critical mass of industrialists, albeit mostly from small industries, hoping to promote the elite's vision of mineiro industrialization. Américo Giannetti, the greatest entrepreneur-politician-technocrat of his generation, expressed this vision in a speech praising the foundation of the FIEMG:

> We mineiro industrialists, who have always constituted a multitude of forces without objectives or direction, we are at this moment establishing for these forces the means of application from which will emerge results for all industries in our State. We are born of a preeminent need that is for us to come together and always be alert against any cause or eventual enemy who might come between us and our objectives . . . To come together and organize with the goal of achieving that which should be our reward . . . to shift the axis of national activities toward this part of Brazilian territory . . . [47]

Family, Entrepreneurs, and Politics

The business elite of Belo Horizonte in the half-century prior to 1945 engaged in three principal activities: commerce, industry, and banking. As with all the groups in this study, the three categories were not mutually exclusive and self-contained. Quite often, business leaders engaged in at least two of the three realms of business enterprise. Teófilo Ribeiro, for example, was on the boards of textile firms, banks, and served as a special legal and political advisor to the St. John d'el Rey Mining Company. Flávio Fernandes dos Santos practiced law, became one of the major partners in the Companhia Industrial de Belo Horizonte, and then served a term (1922–26) as *prefeito,* and then became a board member of a bank and several industrial firms.[48] In fact, very few of the business elite concentrated in a single sector of the economy, something that should not surprise us given the multiple activities of businessmen in more recent times.

The greatest entrepreneur of this era was Christiano Guimarães. Christiano Guimarães was born in Sete Lagoas in 1885. His father, Américo Teixeira Guimarães, was one of the founders of the Companhia Industrial de Belo Horizonte. Trained as an engineer, Christiano was the manager of the CIBH for 16 years. He was one of the four founders of the precursor of Belgo Mineira, and he founded the Banco Comércio e Indústria de Minas Gerais. He served on the Conselho Deliberativo de Belo Horizonte in the late 1920s and early 1930s. He also founded the Companhia de Seguros Minas-Brasil, and was a founder of the Faculdade de Ciências Econômicas of the Universidade Federal de Minas Gerais. He died in 1970 just short of his 85th birthday.[49] One could hardly imagine a more polyvalent figure.

The career of Christiano Guimarães also illustrates a crucial transition that took place during these decades in Belo Horizonte. The first great generation of entrepreneurs were generally the children of the generation that made the transition from landed and commercial wealth that they had begun to accumulate before the creation of Belo Horizonte. Men born in the years between 1860 and 1880 like Américo Guimarães, Benjamim Ferreira Guimarães, Benjamim Lima, João Pinheiro, and Augusto Gonçalves de Souza Moreira passed on to their sons and grandsons (Christiano Guimarães, Antônio Mourão Guimarães, Jair Negrão de Lima, Israel Pinheiro, and Miguel Augusto Gonçalves de Souza) the capital and industries that (beginning in the 1920s and 1930s) the second generation would parlay into the first phase of industrialization in Belo Horizonte and Minas Gerais.

Prior to World War II, most of this elite had its origins in other regions of the state.[50] Nearly all the presidents of the ACM were born outside the Center (and its subregion, the Zona Metalúrgica), not surprising for a still fairly new city. A handful of the prominent businessmen were foreigners, although their numbers were much smaller than those found in the business communities in Rio de Janeiro and São Paulo.[51] If textile industrialists are any indication, many of the elite had their origins in the countryside on the land. Of the 14 textile companies listed in appendix B, 12 were founded by directors who made their wealth through landowning, and two by men who generated their capital from commercial ventures.[52] Most had little prior knowledge of the cotton textile business, and nearly all hired managers (*gerentes*) with the experience they lacked. A number (most prominently the Mascarenhas family) built their initial factories on their rural properties, and some either produced or purchased their cotton from surrounding estates.[53]

Many of the factories were founded by families and their collective capital. The outstanding example, once again, are the Mascarenhas family enterprises started by three brothers in the 1860s with their father's blessing and landowning profits. By the 1920s the family controlled factories in several regions of the state, including two in the Center (Cia Cedro e Cachoeira and Cia Fabril Mascarenhas). The Cia Cedro e Cachoeira in Paraopeba was the first modern textile factory in Minas Gerais, and remains a very successful family-owned firm today.[54]

Another, more urban, example is the role of the Guimarães family. Once again, with capital generated initially from landowning, Américo Teixeira Guimarães either founded or gained control of four of the main cotton textile factories in central Minas (Cia Cachoeira de Macacos, Cia Industrial Belo Horizonte, Cia Industrial Paraense, and the Cia Renascença Industrial). In each case he pooled his own resources with those of his in-laws. In the case of the Cia Industrial Belo Horizonte he also had as one of his three partners Colonel Manoel Gonçalves de Souza Moreira, whose family founded the Cia de Tecidos Santannense, the Cia Industrial Itaunense, and the Cia de Tecidos Pitanguiense.[55]

These three families (Mascarenhas, Guimarães, Gonçalves de Souza) controlled nine of the thirteen firms in Belo Horizonte in the early 1920s. These firms accounted for three-quarters of the machinery (looms and spindles), workers, and production in central Minas Gerais in the 1920s. Clearly, a small group of family networks dominated the cotton textile industry in central Minas. Furthermore, they would continue to run the firms for decades. All three families retained control of these companies into the 1990s.

Another Guimarães family, that of Benjamim Ferreira Guimarães, illustrates the importance of family networks outside the textile industry. Born in 1861 in what is now Igaratinga, Pará de Minas (just to the west of Belo Horizonte), Benjamim Ferreira Guimarães began his life in fairly humble circumstances working as a peddler and merchant in Bom Successo. With the money he acquired in commerce he founded a textile factory in Valença,

Rio de Janeiro in 1906, and then others in Espirito Santo, Barbacena, and São João del Rei. He built a tanning plant in Curvelo, established shipping on the São Francisco River out of Pirapora, and in 1927 bought control of the Passagem gold mine (near Mariana). His son Antônio Mourão Guimarães would continue to diversify the family holdings, especially with the founding of the Banco de Minas Gerais in the 1930s and the establishment of Magnesita S. A. in the Cidade Industrial in the 1940s. Benjamim died in 1948 and his sons and grandsons continued to increase the family business empire. In the decades after the 1940s the family was best known for its banking interests.[56]

Family networks played a crucial role in the mobilization of capital for textiles, as well as other industries.[57] Entrepreneurs in Minas appear to have faced greater obstacles than their paulista or carioca counterparts in mobilizing capital in an underdeveloped banking system.[58] Until the 1940s, the banking elite remained very small. (Of the 21 banks with head-quarters in Minas Gerais in 1925, 14 had been founded in the previous five years.) By 1930 the mineiro banks had begun to acquire a national reputation and role, yet preliminary research seems to indicate that these banks exported capital to Rio de Janeiro and São Paulo.[59] In the absence of a strong banking community oriented toward local investment, family networks—and later, the state government—provided the capital for industry and commerce.[60]

The rise of banking through kinship networks and the use of this capital to finance the enterprises of kin are patterns found in early industrialization and the rise of modern capitalism in other areas of the world. In the early nineteenth-century in New England and in Porfirian Mexico, to take but two examples, early banking capital arose out of the pooling of resources in kinship networks. In the case of Mexico, bankers used this capital to finance the firms of their friends and kin. Naomi Lamoreaux's description of early banks in New England easily describe the setting a century later in early twentieth-century Minas Gerais: "Early banks in New England functioned not as commercial banks in the modern sense but as the financial arms of extended kinship networks. These groups used banks to raise capital for their diversified enterprises and give their operations a stable institutional base."[61] To some extent this lowered risk, as bankers could easily assess the pros and cons of lending to people they knew very well. Kinship ties allowed business leaders to "produce trust" in an era before institutionalized, impersonal banking. Banks, in effect, formed a crucial link in the webs of power within the business elite.[62] In the words of a famous local proverb, "Better to have friends in the marketplace than money in the till."[63]

Until the 1920s two banks dominated the small financial sector in Belo Horizonte and Minas Gerais: the Banco de Crédito Real and the Banco Hipotecário e Agrícola. The former was founded in 1889 in Juiz de Fora by businessmen who had primarily generated their capital from coffee production. Among the five founders was Bernardo Mascarenhas, the greatest mineiro entrepreneur of the nineteenth century, pioneer in the creation of the electric power industry and the textile industry in Minas Gerais. Another founder, João Ribeiro de Oliveira e Souza, would later become minister of finance (1919) and then found the Banco Mercantil do Rio de Janeiro. One of the founders was a viscount and another a baron. In 1913, the Banco Hipotecário e Agrícola bought controlling interest in the Banco de Crédito Real, eventually passing the stock over to the state government. When the state assumed controlling interest in the bank it became an instrument of the state to provide agricultural credit. The Banco Hipotecário e Agrícola was formed in 1911, primarily with French capital and expertise. The Périer group signed a contract with the state government guaranteeing that the new bank would provide credit for agriculture and loans to municipalities for public works projects. In exchange the bank was given tax exemptions and guaranteed interest rates. The bank's first president was Juscelino Barbosa, an ex-secretary of finance for the state government (1908–10).[64] It was the first bank headquartered in Belo Horizonte.[65]

By the end of the 1920s two other important banks had emerged in Belo Horizonte: the Banco do Comércio e Indústria de Minas Gerais and the Banco da Lavoura de Minas Gerais. The first was founded in 1923 by a group of the most prominent local planters, industrialists, and merchants—Américo Teixeira Guimarães and his son, Christiano; Sebastião Augusto de Lima; Vitorino Dias; José Antonio de Assunção, and Tomaz de Andrade. As we have seen, Américo and Christiano Guimarães had generated capital through their textile enterprises, most notably the Companhia Industrial de Belo Horizonte. Andrade was a prominent legal figure in Itaúna, while Dias and Assunção apparently were from landed families. Sebastião Augusto de Lima was a business associate of the Guimarães family. A native of Serro in the north of Minas, he had married a daughter of the famous Dayrell family in Diamantina. He moved to Belo Horizonte in 1913 (after serving as president of the muncipal council of Serro) and became a founder of the Companhia Industrial de Belo Horizonte, the Companhia Siderúrgica Mineira, the Banco de Comércio e Indústria, the Companhia Renascença Industrial, and the Compania de Seguros Minas-Brasil (all of these firms in conjunction with the Guimarães family). His son, Sebastião Dayrell de Lima later became president of the Banco. One of his daughters married Jair Negrão de Lima, son of another prominent businessman and later mayor of Belo Horizonte.[66]

The Banco da Lavoura, as its name indicates, originated as an institution to finance agriculture, and to a lesser extent, local businesses. Unlike most prominent business in Belo Horizonte at the time, it had substantial capital from immigrants, primarily the Italian community (the Savassi family, for instance) and some Syrian-Lebanese families (the Abras family, prominent local merchants). Its first president Hugo Furquim Werneck was a physician born in the city of Rio de Janeiro who had moved to Belo Horizonte in 1906. Throughout the early decades of the century he was repeatedly elected to the Conselho Deliberativo (the municipal council) and served as president from 1916 to 1930. Another founding member, Clemente de Faria, served as director-general of the bank. After World War II, his sons would take control of the bank and eventually transform it into one of the country's major financial institutions (after transferring its headquarters to São Paulo). In the late 1930s, Clemente de Faria brought in a promising young man from the interior to serve as the bank's manager—José de Magalhães Pinto.[67]

With the dominance of the Banco de Crédito Real and the Banco Hipotecário in the early decades of industrialization, banks had what has been described as an "intense relationship with the state" serving the financial function that was handled by the private sector in Rio de Janeiro and São Paulo. It facilitated the transfer of resources from the countryside to the city, from the agricultural sector to industry. In the words of Nogueira da Costa, "planters, merchants, industrialists and even foreigners applied their capital trying to implant a banking system in Minas, but it was the state, realizing the fragility of this embryonic development, that protected it, guided it, and commanded its growth."[68]

While some of these entrepreneurs did not run for political office or serve in elected positions, they were often allied with prominent political families through marriage, business partnerships, or both. In the case of the Cia Industrial Belo Horizonte, Flávio Fernandes dos Santos was one of the founding directors of the firm. In the 1920s he was the mayor of Belo Horizonte. One of the other key directors, Bernardino Vaz de Melo, was a major political figure in Sete Lagoas and his brother served as mayor in the early twentieth century. Manoel Thomaz de Carvalho Brito, who bought the Cia Industrial Sabarense (renaming it the Cia Fiação e Tecelagem Minas Gerais), was a major political figure in state politics throughout the first three decades of the century. Family business networks interlaced with the clientelistic family political networks.[69]

Over the past 15 years, mineiro historians and social scientists have repeatedly shown the intricate webs of family networks that wove together the business, political, and technocratic elites. Faria's work on the First Republic, Vieira's dissertation on the 1920s and 1930s, Delgado's on the 1940s and 1950s, and Dulci's as well on the postwar years, and Starling's book on the 1960s, all detail the overlapping and intricately interwoven elite networks.[70]

These families played a pioneering role channeling resources from agriculture and commerce into industrialization. The children of the pioneers would diversify industry, expanding banking, iron and steel making, and a wide variety of businesses. In the years prior to the development of an adequate banking system these families provided the meager capital resources to finance early industrialization, and they went on to found the banks they needed to provide larger capital resources for the next stage of industrialization. Their economic power would also eventually translate into political and technocratic power in state politics and the state government. Kinship and clientelism would converge by the 1940s to provide the driving force behind the next stage of mineiro economic growth.

Although a new and rapidly growing city, the patterns found in the formation of the business community in Belo Horizonte were probably not dramatically different than the process in Rio de Janeiro and São Paulo, the two major business centers in twentieth-century Brazil. The little information we have on the origins of the industrialists in São Paulo points to their own origins in landholding families.[71] This should, after all, hardly seem surprising in a society that was still overwhelmingly agrarian and rural at the beginning of the century.

In 1920, although Rio de Janeiro had more than a million population, and São Paulo more than half a million (the latter, ten times the size of Belo Horizonte), the occupational structures of the three cities do not show dramatic differences. In both Rio and Belo Horizonte, about 30 percent of the economically active population worked in industry (with a striking 48 percent in São Paulo). Rio clearly had a relatively larger commercial sector (18.3 percent) than São Paulo (14.7) and Belo Horizonte (10.5).[72]

By the end of the 1940s all three cities had grown dramatically, and Belo Horizonte's business community continued to be dwarfed by the other two cities. One indication of this is the structure of businesses in the commercial sector (see table 2.10) as seen in the 1950 census of business enterprises (albeit incomplete). Rio de Janeiro and São Paulo both had six to seven times as many businesses. Rio de Janeiro had more than 100 exporting firms, São Paulo some 28, and Belo Horizonte none, a clear sign of the more cosmopolitan and international nature of business in Brazil's two principal

Table 2.10   Retail Commercial Establishments, Rio de Janeiro, São Paulo, Belo
Horizonte, 1951

Type of Establishment	SP	RJ	BH
Housewares	83	79	9
Foodstuffs	380	306	51
Ceramics, hardware, and electrical goods	163	101	10
Machinery	58	103	15
Construction materials	120	117	21
Materials for industry	117	87	16
Chemical & pharmaceutical products	91	102	33
Textiles	342	298	46
Mixed activities	520	387	107
Export firms	28	106	0
Offices	191	211	7
Mixed establishments	0	53	8
Totals	2,093	1,950	323

Source: Anuário estatístico do Brasil (Rio de Janeiro: Instituto Brasileiro de Geografia e
Estatística, 1953), 331.

commercial centers. When one examines the total value of all business transactions in 1945, Rio's total is 13 times larger than that of Belo Horizonte,
and São Paulo's nearly 18 times.[73]

The state government also played a prominent role in the economic
growth of the city of São Paulo, most prominently in its powerful support
for immigration and the expansion of coffee cultivation in the late nineteenth century, and through protectionism in the twentieth.[74] As the Federal District and national capital, the city of Rio de Janeiro did not have a
state government, but had the direct support of the federal government in
promoting economic growth. Clearly, both cities were much larger, more
cosmopolitan, and had a greater participation of foreign-born entrepreneurs
than the smaller, more provincial Belo Horizonte.[75]

The patterns of family enterprise, political clientelism, and state protectionism are not foreign to the formation of business communities in Europe,
the United States, and Japan. What is striking in the Brazilian case is the persistence of family capitalism well into the late twentieth century, much
longer even than in England and Japan, two cases where family enterprises
also persist into this century.[76] Although state intervention takes place in Europe, Japan, and the United States, Brazil appears to be closer to the Japa-

nese case where the role of the state is much more pronounced in its efforts to nurture economic growth.

This mix of family enterprise, elite family networks, state intervention, political patronage, and elite domination of politics form the defining patterns in the formation of the business community in Belo Horizonte. The same features, albeit in differing degrees, probably define the formation of business communities in other major Brazilian economic centers in the first half of the twentieth century. Although the historiography is quite thin, further research will, no doubt, find many of these same features in other Latin American countries.[77]

The political and business elite of Belo Horizonte and Minas Gerais from the 1890s to the 1940s never numbered more than a few hundred individuals at any given moment. This elite was entirely male, overwhelmingly white, and generally had a university education. The creation of a state capital and the economic opportunity presented by the growth of a new urban metropolis around it drew nearly all this elite in from the surrounding regions. By the 1940s nearly all the political elite had dual residence, in their home region and in Belo Horizonte. All the business elite had moved to the city from elsewhere, even if just a short distance from the surrounding Zona Metalúrgica. It was not until the late 1930s and 1940s that a few young business leaders (usually the sons of the established elite) began to emerge, and who had grown up in the city.

It is clear that the political and economic elite was very small, heavily concentrated in Belo Horizonte in the decades before 1945, and they all knew each other and interacted frequently on a face-to-face basis. They were linked together (even when they are bitter political enemies or simply opponents on specific issues) through business ties, political activity, and— most importantly—through kinship. This was truly an "old boys" club. Whether they captured control of the state (as some would argue), or whether the state acted as a mediating force (as I believe it did) among them, a few hundred men dominated the political power and economic activity that shaped the lives of the tens of thousands who lived in Belo Horizonte, and the hundreds of thousands of mineiros outside the state capital.

Chapter 3 ▧

Technology and Industrialization, 1890s–1940s

Politicians, technocrats, and entrepreneurs pursued a very small number of technological paths to create key industries during the past century, paths that determined the nature of industrialization in Belo Horizonte and Minas Gerais. A good deal has been written about the aggregate features of this industrialization, and the politics and policies that shaped the process. Very little work has been done to disaggregate the characteristics of this industrialization within industries or to examine the process at the firm level.[1] This chapter turns from the earlier overview of Belo Horizonte's growth, a profile of the political and business elites, and the webs of power they created, to analyze the specific technological parameters that politicians, technocrats, and entrepreneurs faced in different industries and firms in the drive to industrialize Belo Horizonte and Minas Gerais.

Following a pattern that holds for Brazil, and for much of Latin America, mineiros imported foreign technology for their newly emerging industries. In textiles, iron and steel, and electric power generation, foreign technology (understandably) drove the initial industrial plants. This, in itself, is not unlike the story of early industrialization in many countries in the nineteenth and twentieth centuries—in Europe, the Americas, and Asia. As we shall see in chapters 4 and 5, this pattern of wholesale reliance on foreign technology, however, continues into the twenty-first century. In Minas, and indeed, in Brazil in general, industrialists do not follow the path of the United States, Japan, and many European nations. Rather than moving toward continual technological innovation—a true sign of self-sustaining and dynamic industrialization—the Brazilians continue to rely on others for technological advances and innovation.

This chapter examines not only the specific circumstances that entrepreneurs faced in Minas Gerais and Belo Horizonte, but also emphasizes the technological paths that they pursued in key industries. In particular, I concentrate on the most important industries in Belo Horizonte and Minas Gerais prior to 1950: textiles, iron and steel, and electric power generation.

Mineiro Industrialization to 1950

While mineiro industrialization at the firm level has not been very well studied, we do know a good deal about the aggregate features of the process. Mineiro scholars have produced a number of fine studies tracing the process of industrialization. These studies generally rely on national census data and, to a lesser extent, state census data. While the firm level data in this study do not drastically revise the standard view of the general process of mineiro industrialization, they do provide a very different view of how and why industrialization took place. In particular, it takes the traditional statistical, aggregate, skeletal overview of mineiro industrialization and adds to it the flesh and blood of individual actors and agency. This analysis shows who was behind the process of industrialization and the technological and entrepreneurial choices they faced.

Brazilian industrialization from the late nineteenth century to the late 1940s divides into two phases: before and after the economic and political crises of 1929–1930. Prior to the Great Depression, industry had been slowly and fitfully growing in a society that remained overwhelmingly agrarian and an economy that continued to be dominated by coffee production and exports. The twin stimuli of a world economic crisis and the rise of Getúlio Vargas to power moved Brazilian industrialization into a new phase. Despite the ad hoc and often haphazard efforts, the era of import substitution industrialization and greater state intervention to promote industry has its origins in the 1920s, and accelerates in the 1930s. It would not be until the late 1940s that the process became more consistent, conscious, and coordinated.

Prior to the rise of Belo Horizonte as a growth pole, mineiro industry was fragmented, dispersed, and largely oriented toward local and regional markets.[2] As John Wirth has pointed out, Minas was a "mosaic" of isolated and disarticulated parts.[3] Five of the state's seven regions had some significant industrial production (Mata, Metalúrgica, Sul, West, and East). These five regions accounted for three-quarters of the state's industrial production.[4] Only in the textile industry did significant concentration take place prior to the 1930s (and in comparison with Rio de Janeiro and São Paulo, even the mineiro textile industry is dispersed and fragmented). Most of the industry clustered in the Metalúrgica and Mata around Belo Horizonte and Juiz de Fora. In fact, until the 1930s, Juiz de Fora, a small town of some 40,000 inhabitants, was the closest thing to an industrial city in the state. As late as 1930, close to three-quarters of the state's production never left Minas. Textiles were the most export-oriented sector of the industrial or agricultural economy.[5]

Industry was widespread, but consisted largely of small shops to work cloth, leather, metals, foods, chemicals, and wood. In 1919, 80 percent of mineiro "factories" employed fewer than 10 workers, and over half had fewer than 5. A 1928 survey by the state government reveals that barely 7 percent of all mineiro factories employed more than 6 workers. Less than 3 percent employed 12 or more workers (and half of these factories produced textiles and clothing).[6]

In Minas, as in the Brazilian economy as a whole, textile manufacturing was the lead industry in the early twentieth century. In 1907, textile manufacturing accounted for 40 percent of total industrial capital investment and 34 percent of the industrial workforce.[7] Minas Gerais had been one of the principal centers of Brazilian textile production since the eighteenth century (along with Bahia, Rio de Janeiro, and São Paulo). Until the rise of Belo Horizonte in the early twentieth century, mineiro textile production was more widely dispersed and decentralized than the other three major producing states.[8]

Although the rise of industrial production has its origins as early as the 1830s, the beginning of modern industrial production really dates from the 1870s, in particular with the prominent role of the Mascarenhas family. More than two dozen factories were installed between 1872 and 1900, and by 1907 there were 36 factories operating in the state.[9] The patterns in the textile sector reflected those in the industrial sector in general in Minas. When compared with Rio de Janeiro and São Paulo, mineiro establishments were smaller, had fewer workers, and were less capitalized. While in the 1920s the number of spindles per factory in Rio and São Paulo averaged 7,000–8,000, in Minas the average was around 2,100. The number of workers per factory in Minas (300) also ran much lower than in Rio de Janeiro (544) or São Paulo (455).[10]

Although food processing accounted for nearly half (270 of 529) of all industrial establishments in 1907, it was highly dispersed in small establishments. The 36 textile factories accounted for 63 percent (16.884,3 contos) of the total industrial capital (26.820,3 contos), 40 percent of all industrial production, and 50 percent of all industrial workers (4,702 of 9,405). Food processing accounted for 35 percent of production and 20 percent of the industrial workforce. (See table 3.1.) No other industry remotely approached these two in the value of production, capital investment, or the size of the workforce.[11]

The Great Depression severely damaged the Brazilian textile industry in the 1930s and in Minas Gerais the industry lost ground relative to food processing and metallurgy. By 1939 textiles had fallen behind these two industries in the size of capital investment and the value of production, but continued to be the leading industrial employer. (See tables 3.2 and 3.3.) The three industries combined, however, dominated the manufacturing sector in the state.[12] Despite the decline (that would continue for decades), textiles were still the major industry in the zone around Belo Horizonte in 1940 with 32 establishments accounting for nearly 40 percent of capital investment (more than twice the second leading industry, food processing), and 23 percent of the industrial workforce.[13] Clearly, textile manufacturing played a central role in the industrialization of both Belo Horizonte and Minas Gerais prior to World War II.

By the 1940s, all the major sectors of industrial development in Minas Gerais and Belo Horizonte grew as a direct result of state intervention. Politicians and technocrats made a commitment to implanting critical infrastructural improvements through the creation of an electric power network and an integrated highway system. The government chose to stimulate the development of industry, especially in those sectors where the state had a natural resource base to provide key inputs (iron and steel, cement).

By World War II, mineiro politicians and technocrats were acutely aware of the backwardness of their state's economy relative to the states of Rio de Janeiro (including the Federal District), São Paulo, and even Rio Grande do Sul. Despite its crucial role in governing the nation during the previous half-century, the economy of Minas Gerais had lagged behind the economies of its powerful political partners. The opening section of the *Plano de recuperação econômica* (1947) offered a classic statement of the elite analysis:

> The geographic situation of Minas in relation to its brother states, its broken topography, the deficiency of its means of transport, as well as the growing and alarming decline in the fertility of its lands are the primary causes of the low level of our material progress. . . . The tendency to conservatism has brought Minas to the condition of a colonial economy. It sells and exports raw materials at low prices, and in exchange, buys and imports high quality manufactured articles.[14]

Table 3.1 Minas Gerais, Sectoral Structure of Manufacturing, 1907

Sector	Capital		Production		Workers	
	Contos	%	Contos	%	Number	%
Textiles	16.884,3	63.0	12.807,1	40.2	4.702	50.0
Food processing	5.307,4	19.8	11.078,7	34.7	1,899	20.2
Metallurgy & machinery	984,0	3.6	1.904,2	6.1	503	5.3
Subtotal	23.175,7	86.4	25.790,0	81.0	7,104	75.5
Total	26.820,3	100.0	31.879,4	100.0	9,405	100.0

Source: Clélio Campolina Diniz, Estado e capital estrangeiro na industrialização mineira (Belo Horizonte: Imprensa da UFMG, 1981), 29.

Table 3.2 Minas Gerais, Sectoral Structure of Manufacturing, 1919

Sector	Capital		Production		Workers	
	Contos	%	Contos	%	Number	%
Textiles	39.002	43.4	51.150	29.7	9,519	51.4
Food processing	31.782	35.4	88.613	51.6	3,936	21.3
Metallurgy & machinery	3.217	3.6	3.874	2.2	843	4.6
Subtotal	74.001	82.4	143.639	83.5	14,298	77.2
Total	89.768	100.0	172.055	100.0	17,522	100.0

Source: Clélio Campolina Diniz, *Estado e capital estrangeiro na industrialização mineira* (Belo Horizonte: Imprensa da UFMG, 1981), 29.

Table 3.3 Minas Gerais, Sectoral Structure of Manufacturing, 1939

Sector	Capital		Production		Workers	
	Cr$1.000	%	Cr$1.000	%	Number	%
Textiles	187.715	21.1	169.660	17.1	16,588	28.3
Food processing	240.166	26.9	415.466	41.8	11,384	19.4
Metallurgy & machinery	316.706	35.5	236.144	23.7	15,717	26.8
Subtotal	744.587	83.5	821.270	82.6	43,689	74.5
Total	891.973	100.0	994.047	100.0	58,624	100.0

Source: Clélio Campolina Diniz, *Estado e capital estrangeiro na industrialização mineira* (Belo Horizonte: Imprensa da UFMG, 1981), 29.

Table 3.4 Value of Industrial Production, 1907–1980 (percent by leading states)

	1907	1920	1940	1960	1980
São Paulo	16.6	33.0	38.6	55.1	51.9
Rio de Janeiro	39.9	28.5	27.9	16.0	10.9
Minas Gerais	5.0	5.8	7.8	6.0	8.7
Rio Grande do Sul	15.0	11.8	9.0	7.1	7.1
Totals	76.5	79.1	83.3	84.2	78.2

Note: Rio de Janeiro includes the Federal District and the surrounding state for 1907–1960.
Sources: Recenseamento de 1920, v. 5, pt. 1, p. viii; *Recenseamento de 1940*, v. III, p. 185;
Recenseamento de 1960, v. III, p. 76; *Recenseamento de 1980*, v. 3, t. 2, pt. 1, num. 1, p. 5.

In 1940, the states of São Paulo and Rio de Janeiro accounted for 66.5 percent of the value of Brazil's industrial production. (See table 3.4). Rio Grande do Sul and Minas Gerais ranked a weak third and fourth with the former accounting for 9.0 percent and the latter 7.8 percent of Brazil's industrial production. The four states combined generated 83.3 percent of Brazil's industrial production, a sign of the enormous concentration of industry in the south and southeast. One bright spot for Minas was that its industrial production had risen between 1907 and 1940, and its share of production had increased, while the relative shares of Rio de Janeiro and Rio Grande do Sul had dropped.

By 1940 the locus of economic and industrial power within Minas Gerais had also begun to shift. Coffee, the traditional base of economic and political power in the Sul and Mata, had suffered severe shocks for several decades culminating in the crisis of the 1930s. The once decadent economy of the Zona Metalúrgica had begun a resurgence by the twentieth century with the growth of Belo Horizonte, and the slow development of the iron and steel industry. Textiles and food processing remained the major industries in the state, but Belo Horizonte and its hinterland were becoming the most important producing region. Iron and steel, however, would provide the foundations for postwar industrialization in Belo Horizonte and Minas Gerais.[15]

The Textile Industry

Textile manufacturing in Minas Gerais has long been characterized by its dispersion, small-scale enterprises, and the dominant role of a relatively small group of entrepreneurs and enterprises. From the late nineteenth century into the 1920s the number of factories in Minas Gerais and São Paulo were roughly equal, but by the first decade of the twentieth century, the value of paulista and carioca production generally ran three times that of Minas—a clear sign of greater productivity per factory.[16] The number of factories rose from 43 in 1908, to 60 in 1920, to 85 by 1940. They were spread across 22 municipios in 1908, and some 38 by the 1940s. Most, however, were concentrated in the center and south of the state. In 1908, nearly half were in the Metalúrgica, and a quarter in the Mata. Nearly 90 percent of all factories were located in these two zones by the 1940s. The municipio of Juiz de Fora (Mata) dominated the industry with 7 of the 43 factories and 18 percent of all capital investment in 1908. By the early 1940s, 33 of 93 factories were in Juiz de Fora and they accounted for 15 percent of mineiro textile production.[17]

Although censuses list just four factories in the municipio of Belo Horizonte in 1908 and 1944, the city had become the center of the textile industry in central Minas by World War II. Many of the factories in the old Zona Metalúrgica were run and financed by entrepreneurs and families who either resided in the capital or turned to it as their principal commercial and business center. (See table 3.5.) Factories in Alvinópolis, Divinópolis, Itabira (2), Itabirito, Itaúna (2), Pará de Minas (2), Paraopeba, Pitangui, Santa Luzia, and Sete Lagoas, an additional 13 factories, had close ties to Belo Horizonte.[18] (See Maps 2 and 4.)

Along with the impressive (and larger) textile manufacturing center in Juiz de Fora, these firms formed the core of the most important industry in Minas Gerais, as well as Belo Horizonte and its surrounding region, in the first half of the century. This section examines these firms in detail looking at their owners and financing. It shows the importance of a relatively small group of families, most of whom originally obtained their wealth from exploiting the land, and their critical role in both the creation of local industry, but also a wide variety of economic activities at the heart of the economy of Belo Horizonte up to the 1940s.

Although it is not possible to identify all of the founders and major stockholders in the textile enterprises in Belo Horizonte (or Minas Gerais), we can reconstruct a fairly complete profile of the entrepreneurs who founded and ran textile businesses in the first half of the century. Appendix B contains a substantial listing of the founders and directors of the most important textile firms operating in Belo Horizonte and its surrounding region from the late nineteenth century to the 1940s. This list was compiled almost entirely from company balance sheets published in the official state newspaper, *Minas Gerais,* and with occasional help from secondary sources.

Map 4 Metropolitan Region of Belo Horizonte

As shown in chapter 2, most firms were founded by directors who made their wealth through landowning, and two by men who generated their capital from commercial ventures. Most had little prior knowledge of the cotton textile business, and nearly all hired managers (*gerentes*) with the experience they lacked. A number (most prominently the Mascarenhas family) built their initial factories on their rural properties, and some either produced or purchased their cotton from surrounding estates.[19]

The examples of the Mascarenhas, Guimarães, and Gonçalves de Souza families in chapter 2 demonstrate a clear set of patterns: family firms largely financed by family capital, a transfer of capital from landed wealth to industrial enterprises, and the importation of English and North American technology for their modest factories. Kinship networks played a crucial role in the mobilization of capital for textiles, as well as other industries. In the absence of a strong banking community oriented toward local investment, family networks—and later, the state government—provided the capital for industrialization.

Table 3.5 Key Textile Firms in Belo Horizonte and Surrounding Region, 1908–
1944 (by year of founding)

Firm	Municipio	Founded
Cia Cedro e Cachoeira	Paraopeba	1868
Cia União Itabirano	Itabira	1878
Cia Fiação e Tecelagem Minas Gerais (originally Cia Industrial Sabarense, 1880)	Belo Horizonte	1915
Cia Cachoeira de Macacos	Sete Lagoas	1886
Cia Fabril Mascarenhas	Alvinópolis	1888
Cia Fabril de Pedreira (originally Andrade, Guerra & Cia)	Itabira	1888
Cia de Tecidos Santannense	Itaúna	1891
Cia Industrial Itabira do Campo	Itabirito	1892
Cia de Tecidos Pitanguiense	Pitangui	1893
Cia Industrial Belo Horizonte	Belo Horizonte	1906
Cia Industrial Paraense	Pará de Minas	1906
Cia Minas Fabril (originally Cezar Braccer & Cia, 1907)	Belo Horizonte	1911
Cia Renascença Industrial	Belo Horizonte	1908
Cia Industrial Itaunense	Itaúna	1911
Cia Fiação e Tecidos São Gonçalvo	Pará de Minas	1922
Santa Luzia Industrial S/A	Santa Luzia	1925
Cia Fiação e Tecelagem Divinópolis	Divinópolis	1937

Sources: Domingos Giroletti, "A Modernização capitalista em Minas Gerais: a formação do operariado industrial e uma nova cosmovisão," Ph.D. Dissertation, Antropologia Social, Museu Nacional, Universidade Federal do Rio Janeiro, 1987, pp. 18, 79, 81, and 107; Alisson Mascarenhas Vaz, *Cia. Cedro e Cachoeira: história de uma empresa familiar, 1883–1987* (Belo Horizonte: Cia. de Fiação e Tecidos Cedro e Cachoeira S.A., 1990), p. 25; *Minas Geraes,* 12 September 1913, p. 3; Instituto Brasileiro de Geografia e Estatística, Departamento Estadual de Estatística, Minas Gerais–Brasil, *Indústria de fiação e tecelagem 1944* (Belo Horizonte: Oficinas Gráficas da Estatística, 1946).

Typically several family members pooled their resources to start a firm. The Mascarenhas and Guimarães families are good examples. Three Mascarenhas brothers founded the Companhia Cedro e Cachoeira in the 1860s with capital generated by their family, originally from landed estates around Curvelo, and partially from commercial, retail enterprises. The brothers, their in-laws, and their children eventually built or purchased other textile factories, as well as allied businesses.[20] Another key figure, Américo Teixeira Guimarães founded the Companhia Cachoeira de Macacos in Sete Lagoas

Table 3.6 Key Textile Firms in Belo Horizonte and Surrounding Region, 1925
(spindles, looms, workers, production)

Firm	Spindles	Looms	Workers	Production Contos
Cia Cedro e Cachoeira	15,000	420	750	5.200,0
Cia União Itabirano	1,300	60	90	858,8
Cia Fiação e Tecelagem Minas Gerais	3,764	306	475	3.895,6
Cia Cachoeira de Macacos	4,328	132	265	2.408,9
Cia Fabril Mascarenhas	4,200	138	250	1,355,8
Cia Fabril de Pedreira	1,440	60	90	562,0
Cia de Tecidos Santannense	3,916	150	180	1.564,0
Cia Industrial Itabira do Campo	3,716	140	200	1.800,0
Cia de Tecidos Pitanguiense	4,148	144	230	1.884,4
Cia Industrial Belo Horizonte	11,800	400	700	5.357,8
Cia Industrial Paraense	5,800	200	400	2.142,8
Cia Minas Fabril	4,000	55	120	395,2
Cia Industrial Itaunense	—	220	190	2.056,0
Total	63,412	2,425	3,940	29.481,3
Minas Gerais	167,660	5,843	9,894	89.891,9
as % of Minas Gerais	37.8	41.5	39.8	32.8

Source: Annuario estatistico de Minas Geraes. anno II (1922–25) (Belo Horizonte: Serviço de Estatistica Geral, 1929), 485–486.

along with the help of his father and a brother-in-law in the 1880s. By the 1920s the family network (led by Américo) controlled four firms in central Minas, and had bought factories in other areas of the state. Américo's son, Christiano Teixeira Guimarães, eventually became one of the most powerful businessmen in the state.[21]

The founders and directors of the firms in central Minas eventually were drawn to Belo Horizonte as it emerged in the early twentieth century. The city became not only the center of state political power, but also the commercial and financial hub of the state by the 1940s. Both the Mascarenhas and Guimarães families took up residence in Belo Horizonte and made the city the center for their business operations. In the first decades of the century they also founded businesses in the city. The Companhia Industrial de Belo Horizonte is a prime example. Led by Américo Teixeira Guimarães, members of the Mascarenhas and Gonçalves de Souza families (among others) founded what was (along with Cedro e Cachoeira) one of the two largest firms in central Minas. Christiano Guimarães became the manager of the factory and ran it for 16 years. In 1917 he joined with several other local businessmen to form the Companhia Siderúrgica Mineira, the precursor of the Companhia Siderúrgica Belgo Mineira. In the early 1920s he founded the Banco Comércio e Indústria de Minas Gerais, and in the 1930s, the Companhia Seguros Minas-Brasil. By the 1940s he was a central figure in an extended network of familial and business ventures at the core of the state's economy.[22]

The need to purchase textile technology for new factories, or to replace old machinery, was the principal factor driving the demand for capital investment. Textile manufacturers in Belo Horizonte, and in the rest of Brazil, have imported their machinery from abroad since the mid-nineteenth century. Up until the mid-twentieth century almost all textile technology in Brazil came from England, with a small percentage coming from manufacturers in the United States.[23] Beginning in the 1920s a small domestic machine industry emerged in the city of São Paulo, but it has never offered a significant challenge to foreign imports. Despite the enormous size of the Brazilian textile industry, it has never developed a significant domestic industry to produce textile machinery. Brazilian textile manufacturers continue to import their machinery from abroad or buy it from the local subsidiaries of these firms in Brazil.[24]

The industrial production of cotton textiles begins in Brazil in the mid-nineteenth century in the first decades after independence from Portugal (1822). During three centuries of colonial rule, the Portuguese Crown had viewed its American colony as a supplier of raw materials (such as cotton), and a market for its own exports.[25] In the late eighteenth century, the metropolitan government made efforts to develop Portuguese industry in response to its enormous dependence on English manufactures. In an effort to protect the nascent national textile industry, a 1785 decree prohibited textile manufacturing in the Brazilian colony with the exception of coarse cottons "fit for the use . . . of Negroes and for the wrapping and packaging of goods in general."[26]

The transfer of the monarchy to Rio de Janeiro (1808) and independence (1822) opened Brazilian ports to international trade, and the British (long the principal ally of Portugal) quickly established their commercial and economic supremacy. For the next century, England would be Brazil's principal trading partner and supplier of capital and technology.[27] Like many other sectors of the national economy in the nineteenth century, the fortunes of textile manufacturing were tightly bound to Britain's role in Brazil.

Like the rise of modern industry in Brazil, textile manufacturing advanced on two fronts facing two competitors: handcraft production and imports.[28] Tracing handcraft production in Brazil is problematic at best. No national census was taken before 1872, and censuses thereafter focus on modern factory production. Travel accounts, especially in the nineteenth century, consistently indicate widespread cottage production of textiles. In Minas Gerais, for example, the 1872 census documents textile workers in 54 of the province's 72 municipalities (*municipios*).[29] As late as 1903, imports of sewing thread and its consumption provide indirect evidence of widespread home production of cotton textiles.[30]

Imports are much easier to track than cottage production. In the first half of the nineteenth century, British imports dominated the Brazilian market, at least in urban areas. The rise of protectionist tariffs in the last half of the century contributed to the growth of domestic production, and by the turn of the century Brazil produced 85 percent of all cotton goods consumed in the country. Domestic production dominated in coarse goods, and most imports were of finer cloth goods.[31] By 1900, both handcraft production and imports had given way to the rise of a domestic cotton textile manufacturing industry.

Industrial cotton manufacturing begins in Brazil in the 1840s in Rio de Janeiro and Salvador. By the late 1860s, Brazil had 9 mills with some 14,000 spindles. A decade later, the number of mills had increased to 30, and by 1885 to 48 with some 66,466 spindles. Three-fourths of these mills were nearly evenly split between the provinces of Rio de Janeiro (11), Bahia (12), and Minas Gerais (13).[32] The 1870s mark the origins of industrial cotton textile production in Minas Gerais. In the three previous decades several entrepreneurs had made ill-fated efforts to establish textile factories in the interior of Minas. Lack of capital, the costs of transporting imported machinery into Minas (which had no railroad and virtually no paved roads), and problems of distribution plagued these early efforts.[33] Entrepreneurs set up at least six factories during the decade. The great pioneers in the origins of the industry were the Mascarenhas family, who established two of these factories.

The technological evolution of the Mascarenhas family's operations offer a view of the industry as a whole in Minas Gerais from the mid-nineteenth to the mid-twentieth century. (It should be kept in mind that their operations were also the most important and enduring in the state.) In the period prior to 1950, the Companhia Cedro e Cachoeira (which eventually came to include seven different factories) imported nearly all of its machinery from England, with some coming from the United States. Beginning in the 1950s, the company turned increasingly to imports from the European continent (especially Germany and Switzerland).

The experience of the Mascarenhas family illustrates many of the problems of early textile industrialists in Minas Gerais. Located nearly 500 kilometers inland, transportation posed major logistical problems. The rail line from Rio de Janeiro ended 300 kilometers south of the new Cedro factory. Like other early industrialists, one of the Mascarenhas brothers (Bernardo) toured other factories in Rio de Janeiro and São Paulo before designing and equipping their first factory in 1870. Based on his tour, Bernardo Mascarenhas ordered 50 tons of machinery from the U.S. firm of Arthur Danforth in Paterson, New Jersey (at a cost of US$20,358.28). Purchased in September 1870, the machinery arrived in the port of Rio de Janeiro a year later, and took another two months to make the trek to the factory site in a caravan of more than 20 oxcarts traveling on dirt roads. The machinist sent by the manufacturer to install the equipment was so exhausted by the trip that he had to be sent home, and his replacements turned out to be incompetent. The factory did not begin production until two full years after the original purchase of the machinery.[34]

When the family decided to construct a second factory they sent Bernardo to England and the United States to inspect both modern textile factories and producers of textile machinery. After comparing equipment and prices, he began a pattern that would continue for the next half century—purchasing nearly all the company's machinery in England, primarily from Platt Brothers and Company in Lancashire.[35] Bernardo Mascarenhas purchased 52 looms and nearly all the rest of the machinery for £4,000. Again, nearly two years passed between the purchase of the equipment (February 1875) and the initiation of operations (January 1877).[36]

In Minas Gerais, as well as the rest of Brazil, textile manufacturing began with the use of steam power and mostly made the transition to hydroelectric power by the 1920s. Given the abundance of streams and rivers in Minas Gerais, many of the early factories were located near waterfalls to generate power, and firms generally constructed their own power plants. It is no coincidence that Bernardo Mascarenhas is famous in Brazilian history as both a pioneer in the textile industry, and as the builder of the first commercial hydroelectric power plant in Brazil.[37]

Most of the mills outside of Minas Gerais prior to World War I were powered by steam engines. The engines were nearly all of English manufacture. In 1905, one survey of 110 factories in the country showed 89 using steam power. Buckley & Taylor from Oldham seems to have been the preferred choice.[38] By 1910, virtually every factory in Rio de Janeiro and São Paulo had converted to electric power. (In both cities, manufacturers had the option of purchasing power from the emerging electrical utility companies—nearly all foreign-owned.)[39] The major electric power utility in Minas Gerais developed later and slower than the (Canadian-owned) Brazilian

Traction, Light and Power Company in Rio and São Paulo. By 1915, three-quarters of all power generated in textile factories in São Paulo and Rio de Janeiro was electric, and only half in Minas Gerais.[40]

Although small in comparison to the United States, the textile industry in Brazil had become the twelfth largest in the world by the eve of World War I. With more than 200 active mills, and some 1.5 million spindles and 50,000 looms in operation (see table 3.7), the Brazilian textile industry was twice the size of Mexico's, the only other major textile producer in Latin America.[41] (As a comparison, the U.S. had nearly 1,500 mills, 35 million spindles, and 700,000 looms in operation in 1920.)[42]

The growth of the cotton textile industry in Brazil, however, depended heavily on machinery imports, and imports, in turn, hinged on factors such as the fluctuating exchange rate, tariff rates, and international trade patterns. Both World War I and World War II effectively halted textile machinery imports, and the Great Depression made purchases of machinery very difficult for man-

Table 3.7 Growth of Brazilian Cotton Mills, 1905–1921

Year and Area	Mills No.	Mills %	Spindles No.	Spindles %	Looms No.	Looms %
1905 Brasil	110	100	734,928	100	26,420	100
Rio de Janeiro	21		324,760		11,136	
São Paulo	18		110,996		3,907	
Minas Gerais	30		45,382		3,098	
Total (3 cities)	69	63	481,138	65	23,607	66
1915 Brasil	240	100	1,512,626	100	51,134	100
Rio de Janeiro	46		514,936		16,967	
São Paulo	51		378,138		12,743	
Minas Gerais	53		131,486		4,321	
Total (3 cities)	150	63	1,024,560	68	34,031	67
1921 Brasil	242		1,521,300		59,208	100
Rio de Janeiro	37		591,000		19,000	
São Paulo	55		415,900		14,700	
Minas Gerais	60		130,000		5,800	
Total (3 cities)	152	63	1,136,900	75	39,500	67

Notes: Rio de Janeiro includes the state and Federal District. Figures for São Paulo and Minas Gerais are state statistics.

Source: Adapted from Stanley Stein, *The Brazilian Cotton Manufacture: Textile Enterprise in an Underdeveloped Area, 1850–1950* (Cambridge, Mass.: Harvard University Press, 1957), 101.

ufacturers. According to one estimate, textile machinery imports from England declined at the turn of the century, rose dramatically between 1907–1913, dropped during the war years, rose again in the early 1920s, dropped again during the early 1930s, rising again dramatically in the late 1930s.[43]

The industry's dependence on imported machinery shaped its evolution. By World War II, most machinery in Brazilian factories predated World War I. Only in the late 1940s would a new wave of technological renovation take place. What this meant is that many factories in Minas Gerais and Belo Horizonte contained a mix of several generations of machinery, some of it obsolete. In 1936, of the 80,903 looms in operation in Brazil, only 6,657 were automatic looms.[44] Ironically, this technological backwardness stemmed, in large part, from the mill owners themselves.

The pattern in the textile industry well into this century has been for increases in machinery imports (i.e., technological renewal in the industry) at the end of periods of expanded production. Mill owners, in effect, had excess capacity that they utilized during periods of international crisis (World War I, the Great Depression, World War II). With profits generated by expanded production, they then turned to imports of new machinery (early twenties, late thirties, late forties).[45] During World War I the mill owners clearly recognized the excess capacity in their industry and used their political influence to ban imports of machinery in the early 1920s. With the onset of the Depression, they once again persuaded the government to ban textile machinery imports. They even went so far as to attempt to crush the incipient domestic production of looms, describing the locally produced looms as "crude imitations of French and English models."[46]

In effect, Brazilian mill owners attempted to control the market by restricting access to new machinery. They failed because domestic producers continued to utilize old equipment. Domestic loom manufacturers expanded production, and a thriving market in older machinery developed.[47] The prohibition, however, slowed down the technological evolution of the industry as a whole. Protectionism meant less competition from abroad, but less incentive internally to innovate in order to create a competitive advantage. As a result of the oligopolistic tendencies of mill owners, the domestic machine industry remained small, imports continued to dominate, and inability to import new machinery left the industry bloated and technologically backward.[48]

The Iron and Steel Industry

Like textiles, the iron and steel industry has roots as far back as the colonial era. Modern production of iron and steel begins to emerge in the mid-nineteenth century, and large-scale factory production in the 1920s. As the textile industry slowly relinquished its leading role, iron and steel would eventually become the primary industrial sector in the mineiro economy, a position it continues to hold at the end of the twentieth century. Although the iron and steel industry probably has been the focus of more studies than any other sector of the mineiro economy, few scholars have looked carefully at the role of entrepreneurs, and even fewer have emphasized the behavior of firms and their technological choices.[49]

Throughout the colonial period ironmongering had been a small-scale enterprise. Despite imperial restrictions on manufacturing in colonial Brazil, evidence of the use of small, Catalan forges is widespread. In 1811, the Crown decided to construct a weapons factory, and undertook the creation of two iron foundries using ore from Minas Gerais. Morro do Pilar (in Congonhas do Campo, Minas Gerais) and Ipanema (in Sorocaba, São Paulo) ran up deficits for the royal administrators. Morro do Pilar lasted about a decade, and Ipanema managed to survive until the 1890s despite huge losses. Small-scale forges spread throughout Minas during the empire. The Frenchman, João (Jean) Monlevade, a pioneer in the industry, counted some 84 forges in Minas in 1853, employing some 2,000 persons and producing over 2,000 tons of iron. In 1883, another survey found 75 forges in the province and estimated production at 1,500 to 1,600 tons.[50]

Foreign entrepreneurs played a role in the construction of some of the earliest foundries. King João VI brought the German engineer Ludwig von Eschwege to Brazil in 1810, and he stayed for more than a decade working on ways to improve mineral production and the nascent iron industry. Despite his efforts, with his departure in 1822, his projects were abandoned.[51] Monlevade, trained as an engineer in Paris, set up blast furnaces in Minas in the 1840s and struggled for decades to survive supplying a regional market. The most successful entrepreneurs were José Gerspacher (from Switzerland) and Carlos Wigg, the founders of the Usina Queiroz Júnior (Itabirito, 1889) and the Usina Wigg (Ouro Preto, 1893).

Although Minas has some of the largest iron ore deposits in the world, these early efforts to create an iron and steel industry were frustrated by the difficulties and costs of transport to domestic and foreign markets, inadequate capitalization, and an inability to compete with imported products. Early in this century, both foreigners and nationals began serious efforts to develop the industry in Minas Gerais. Yet once again, local investors were simply unable to mobilize the capital necessary for such large-scale industrial ventures. The structure of the national and international economy prior to World War II inhibited the formation of a mineiro iron and steel industry.

A small domestic market, high entry costs, and powerful competitors in the industrial nations stood in the way of the formation of a mineiro or Brazilian iron and steel industry prior to the mid-1940s.

Despite the lengthy experience with small-scale iron and steel production, the industry employed barely 500 workers at the beginning of the century and accounted for just 3.6 percent of investment in manufacturing.(See table 3.1.) At the end of World War I, the Usina Esperança in Itabira and the newly formed Companhia Siderúrgica Mineira (CSM) in Sabará were the only significant firms, and the latter was just beginning operations. Between 1918 and 1924, the state government offered tax exemptions and other fiscal incentives that directly led to the emergence of the mineiro iron and steel industry.[52]

Throughout the nineteenth and early twentieth centuries, mineiro elites had searched for ways to exploit their state's immense iron ore reserves. They lobbied the central government repeatedly, and business and political elites frequently called for the development of a modern iron and steel industry in Minas Gerais. In the absence of sufficient local private capital, the state and foreign investment held out the most promising means of developing iron and steel. In the celebrated case of Percival Farquhar, nationalism and the tenacious resistance of the state government blocked repeated efforts to develop the iron ore with North American capital during the 1920s and 1930s. Mineiro politicians desperately wanted an iron and steel industry, but feared foreign investors (such as Farquhar) would gain control of iron ore deposits, ship out the raw ore, and block development of local industrial development. In a conference of the leading figures in the industry at the governor's palace in November 1925, a 29-year-old Américo Giannetti roundly condemned "bad" foreign capital saying, "When I speak of foreign interests I refer only to that capital invested here in immense mineral deposits looking only to export our ore to supply foreign mills and to bring back to us manufactured products."[53] Leaders of both the ACM and the FIEMG regularly condemned Farquhar's efforts specifically, and "exploitive" foreign corporations in general.[54] In the famous phrase of Arthur Bernardes (governor of Minas from 1918–22 and president of Brazil from 1922–26), "Mining does not produce two harvests."[55]

Engineers and entrepreneurs based in Belo Horizonte founded the Companhia Siderúrgica Mineira in 1917. Christiano Teixeira Guimarães, his father, and Sebastião Augusto de Lima (their partner in the textile business), contributed half the start-up capital—175 contos (or roughly US$45,000). Amaro Lanari, his father (Cássio), and two brothers-in-law (Gil Guatimosim and Ovídio de Andrade), came up with another 175 contos. Christiano

Guimarães (who ran his family's textile factories) and Lanari had graduated in the same class (1909) from the Escola de Minas in Ouro Preto. (Although born in Argentina of Italian parents, Lanari was raised from early childhood in Minas.) All the initial technology was produced in Minas and São Paulo, and adapted by local firms in Sete Lagoas, Santa Luzia, Belo Horizonte, and Sabará.[56]

In stark contrast to the Farquhar affair, the CSM quickly found a foreign partner with capital to invest. After the visit of King Albert of Belgium to Minas in 1920, the Belgian consortium, Aciéres Réunies de Burbach-Eich-Dudelange (ARBED), took over the CSM and renamed the firm the Companhia Siderúrgica Belgo Mineira. ARBED invested 15,000 contos in their new firm (or nearly one-quarter the annual revenues of the state government). The original investors saw their 350 contos grow to 600 in the form of stock in Belgo Mineira. Christiano Guimarães became the first president of Belgo Mineira.[57]

In 1932, there were just eight iron and steel plants in the state, and by 1944, this number had risen to 11. (See table 3.8.) Nearly all were located in the region around Belo Horizonte, close to the enormous iron ore deposits, especially those near Itabira. The Usina Wigg in Ouro Preto and the Usina Queiroz Júnior in Itabirito were the true pioneers in the modernization of the industry beginning operations in the last years of the nineteenth century. Three more companies were founded in the 1920s, four in the 1930s, and a couple more in the 1940s. The enormous role of Belgo Mineira is obvious.[58] Accounting for three-quarters of all capital investment and 41 percent of all workers, Belgo Mineira's two plants (in Sabará and Monlevade) overshadowed all other operations. The third largest operation—the CBUM in Barão de Cocais—had barely one-tenth the capital of Belgo Mineira's two plants combined.

The experience of Américo Renê Giannetti provided a powerful lesson to politicians, technocrats, and entrepreneurs about the difficulties of promoting a metallurgical industry in Minas without the cooperation of foreign capital. Born in Rio Grande do Sul of Italian parents, Giannetti moved to the small town of Rio Acima (just to the southeast of Belo Horizonte) as a child. His father, Pedro, built a small foundry (Metalúrgica Santo Antônio S.A.) in Rio Acima and sent his son to school in Belo Horizonte. A graduate of the Escola de Minas in 1923, Giannetti was, at various times in his life, technocrat, entrepreneur, and politician. Between the 1920s and early 1950s, Giannetti founded and operated companies for road construction, and the production of paper, sulfuric acid, and pig iron. He was the greatest entrepreneurial figure of his generation, a man who circulated easily through political, business, and technocratic circles.[59]

Table 3.8 Iron and Steel Plants in Minas Gerais, 1944

Município and Company	Year Founded	Capital (CR$)	Employees
Cocais			
Companhia Brasileira de Usinas Metalúrgicas	1925	52,500,000	1,604
Belo Horizonte			
Companhia Industrial de Ferro	1937	5,293,606	242
Caeté			
Companhia Ferro Brasileiro	1931	79,240,935	3,194
Conselheiro Lafaiete			
Usina Queiroz Júnior	1921	2,178,005	177
Divinópolis			
Companhia Mineira de Siderúrgia	1944	5,000,000	148
Itabirito			
Usina Queiroz Júnior	1889	15,830,603	650
Nova Lima			
Companhia de Mineração N. L.	1941	6,000,000	663
Siderúrgica Gandarela	1931		
Ouro Preto			
Usina Wigg	1893	6,564,728	622
Rio Piracicaba			
Companhia Siderúrgica Belgo Mineira	1936	385,291,659	2,753
Sabará			
Companhia Siderúrgica Belgo Mineira	1921	130,972,971	1,266
Totals		688,872,507	9,745

Source: Instituto Brasileiro de Geografia e Estatística, *Usinas siderúrgicas em Minas Gerais— 1944* (Belo Horizonte: Oficinas Gráficas da Estatística, 1946).

Giannetti's most important project, undertaken after research trips to Europe (1938) and the United States (1941), was the construction of the first aluminum foundry in Latin America. The technology was entirely imported from the United States. Despite constructing his own hydroelectric power plants and having access to nearby bauxite deposits, Giannetti's project failed in the late 1940s. Unable to gain access to large amounts of capital investment at a crucial moment, the enterprise failed just as he was starting up operations. (Many accounts blame Giannetti's financial problems on an aluminum cartel—led by Alcoa—which supposedly blocked his access to credit from the Banco do Brasil.)[60]

Despite Giannetti's failure, the success of Belgo Mineira, and some smaller companies, made Minas Gerais the nation's major iron and steel producer by World War II and helped Brazil significantly reduce its dependence on imported iron and steel. In the early 1940s, imports of iron and steel were at the same levels as in the 1920s (despite increasing consumption), and Minas Gerais produced two and one-half times as much as it imported. The state accounted for nearly three-quarters of Brazilian iron and steel production.[61] On the eve of World War II, the metallurgical industry was the most heavily capitalized in the state with 35.5 percent of all manufacturing capital. The industry employed nearly as many workers as textile manufacturing. (See table 3.3.)

The growth of iron and steel production also played a major role in shifting the locus of industry in Minas from Juiz de Fora to Belo Horizonte. In 1920, the Mata (the zone around Juiz de Fora) accounted for 35.6 percent of the state's industrial production. By 1947, this figure had dropped to 20 percent (and that, to a large extent, due to the growth of the food processing industry—dairy products and sugar). At the same time, the Zona Metalúrgica's share of the state's industrial production had risen from 32 to 44.7 percent.[62] In 1939, the value of Belo Horizonte's industrial production was one-third larger than that of Juiz de Fora. Its food processing industry was nearly twice that of Juiz de Fora's, and its electrical industry nearly five times larger.[63]

Despite this success, mineiro politicians, technocrats, and entrepreneurs lost out in the competition for the construction of Brazil's first integrated iron and steel complex. With North American and federal monies, the Vargas regime constructed the Companhia Siderúrgica Nacional (CSN) at Volta Redonda, Rio de Janeiro in the 1940s.[64] The shock of the loss and the experience of Giannetti, combined with the continuing relative backwardness of the state's economy, were crucial in the forging of a consensus among an emerging technocracy that the time had come for the state government to plan and promote industrialization.[65]

This technocracy (discussed in greater detail in chapter 4) consisted largely of engineers, most of them graduates of the Escola de Minas, and the most important nucleus was concentrated in the Secretaria da Agricultura, Indústria, Comércio e Trabalho beginning in the 1930s. The Escola played a major role in the formation of the mineiro technocracy. Nearly three-quarters of its graduates in the early twentieth century went into public sector jobs. As José Murilo de Carvalho and Clélio Campolina Diniz have pointed out, these engineers played a crucial role in the formation of a natural resources policy, and the most important resource of the state was iron ore.

From 1933 to 1942 the Secretário de Agricultura was Israel Pinheiro da Silva, an Escola graduate, and the son of former governor João Pinheiro.[66]

The decisive shift toward state intervention in the leading sector of the mineiro economy came during World War II. The Vargas regime, playing off British and U.S. fears of German influence in Brazil, convinced both governments to loan the Brazilian government the necessary funds to create a state-controlled iron mining company, the Companhia Vale do Rio Doce (CVRD) in 1942 (as a part of the deal to built the CSN). The U.S. loaned Brazil $14 million to begin the project, and reserved the right to name two of the five members of the board of directors. Israel Pinheiro became president of the CVRD. The Brazilian government bought up Farquhar's iron ore lands around Itabira, and expropriated the Vitória to Minas railway to carry the ore to the coast. Economic nationalism and the inability to mobilize private domestic capital brought the state and federal governments into the core of the mineiro economy.[67]

At the end of the war, the United States and Great Britain backed out of the project, and it survived only with massive investment from the Brazilian government. In 1944, Farquhar had formed his own steel corporation— Aços Especiais Itabira S.A. or Acesita—along with two mineiro engineers, Athos de Lemos Rache and Aminthas Jacques de Morais. High start-up costs plagued the project, and the Banco do Brasil stepped in with more funds. The experience of both the CVRD and Acesita, both barely surviving their creation, impressed on mineiros the need for the state and federal governments to provide public capital investment in the absence of private capital (both foreign and national).[68]

Two fundamental challenges drove the demand of large-scale capital investment: technology and coal. Despite its abundant iron ore reserves, Brazil has very small and low-quality coal reserves (and Minas has none).[69] This presented the iron and steel industry with two clear choices: import costly coal from overseas or turn to the use of charcoal for fuel. Importing coal would be an expensive proposition, especially due to the need to invest heavily in transportation infrastructure—mainly railway improvements. The use of charcoal meant turning to a different kind of technology, and the need to constantly replenish woodlands, the source of fuel.

The paths of the two major steel producers—the CSN and Belgo Mineira—offer two different paths shaped by two very different technological choices. Belgo Mineira, first in Sabará in the 1920s and then at João Monlevade in the 1930s, constructed the world's largest charcoal-fuel steel plants. Rather than import expensive coal, Belgo pursued a program of reforestation (with fast growing eucalyptus trees) in the central region of

Minas Gerais to provide its plants with charcoal for the process of transforming iron ore into iron and steel. The European capital of ARBED financed a development program that made Belgo the largest steel producer in Brazil by the 1940s.[70] The CSM had turned to the experienced José Gerspacher to build their initial blast furnace. Belgo brought in Belgian technicians who imported a series of Siemens-Martin furnaces in the 1920s and 1930s, adapting them to local conditions and materials.[71] One of these technicians, the 32-year-old Louis Ensch, arrived in 1927 and became the dominant figure in the development of the company for the next quarter-century.[72]

The CVRD was created to exploit the vast ore deposits in Minas near Belo Horizonte. It was created as a mining company to supply the Companhia Siderúrgica Nacional (CSN), which was constructed at Volta Redonda between Rio de Janeiro and São Paulo. Volta Redonda was built almost entirely with U.S. technology and expertise. The CSN's executive committee selected Arthur G. McKee and Company of Cleveland, Ohio to serve as the chief engineering consultant on the project. McKee and Company had built iron and steel plants in Russia, England, and the United States. Most of the machinery and materials came from companies in Pittsburgh, and the orders went through shortly before the Japanese attack on Pearl Harbor in late 1941.[73] The CSN chose to export most of the ore mined by the CVRD and to bring back coal for its operations in the ships that transported the ore to Europe and the United States.[74] In a sense, from the perspective of mineiros, both companies were foreign-controlled: Belgo Mineira through ARBED in Luxembourg, and the CVRD through the federal government in Rio de Janeiro. Although nearly all of its operations took place in Minas until the 1960s, the federal government chose to headquarter the firm in the national capital and not in Belo Horizonte.

Iron and steel production offers a very different story from that of textiles. Unlike textiles, the barriers to entry are very high, in particular, the need for massive amounts of capital to finance infrastructure and sophisticated technology. In the textile industry, technological lag became a constant problem as entrepreneurs were unwilling or unable to finance not only the transfer of new technology, but also failed to develop their own domestic textile machinery industry. In the iron and steel industry, the state and foreigners became the leading entrepreneurs, and both mineiro businessmen and technocrats their principal associates. They did import sophisticated technology and adapt it to local circumstances, but (perhaps due to economies of scale) all major technological innovation came from the iron and steel producers in the developed economies of Europe, the United States, and Japan.

The Electric Power Industry

Although the electric power industry was not large in terms of capital investment, workers employed, or output, it was a crucial piece of the process of mineiro industrialization in the years prior to World War II, and it would become even more important after the war. Blessed with abundant streams and rivers, in the eighteenth and nineteenth centuries mineiros began using waterwheels to supply the force for machinery.[75] Although steam engines appeared in Brazil in the nineteenth century, they never played a very significant role in Minas Gerais. With the rise of the factory system at the end of the nineteenth century in the textile industry, entrepreneurs initially turned to waterwheels to power their mills. Hydroelectric power came soon after.

In Minas Gerais, as well as the rest of Brazil, manufacturing began with the use of steam power and mostly made the transition to hydroelectric power by the 1920s. Given the abundance of streams and rivers in Minas Gerais, many of the early factories were located near waterfalls to generate power, and firms generally constructed their own power plants. The pioneering role of Bernardo Mascarenhas in Juiz de Fora was followed by other firms across the state in the early decades of the century.[76]

The structure of the electric power industry, once again, reflects the greater degree of dispersion and fragmentation in mineiro industry when compared with São Paulo and Rio de Janeiro. In 1939, the three states accounted for more than 80 percent of all Brazil's electric power capacity. São Paulo alone generated nearly half (48 percent of Brazil's 1,044,738 kilowatts), Rio de Janeiro produced 28 percent, and Minas just 11 percent. Minas, however, had 314 generating plants, or 61 percent of the plants found in all three states. In other words, it had more, but smaller, plants. The average size of a power plant in São Paulo and Rio de Janeiro was 3,600 to 3,700 kilowatts, while in Minas it was a meager 356 kilowatts.[77]

In Minas Gerais, lots of small companies generated power in small quantities. At the end of World War II, in the region around Belo Horizonte, 25 different firms supplied about one million people with 370 million kilowatt-hours (kWh) of power. In São Paulo, a single company—The Light—supplied two and one-half million people with nearly ten times as much power (3,173 million kWh). In Rio de Janeiro, The Light generated nearly four times as much power as the firms in Belo Horizonte.[78]

The first hydroelectric plants in the region surrounding Belo Horizonte were built by the St. John d'el Rey Mining Company, Ltd. in the 1890s to supply power for its enormous gold mining operations. This British-owned company, in fact, was the major generator of hydroelectric power in the state until the end of World War II. The St. John imported all of its electrical equipment from General Electric (England) until World War II when it was forced to turn to U.S. suppliers.[79] The construction of the first hydroelectric plants in Belo Horizonte formed part of the original design for the city. These plants, however, were generally not very large, and were primarily designed to supply electric power for residential use.

Until the rise of CEMIG in the 1950s and the use of expropriation in the 1960s, Belo Horizonte would suffer continual shortages of electric power, for industry, for lighting (both public and private), and public transport (*bondes*).[80] The city built a small power plant (*usina*) on the Ribeirão das Arrudas in the first decade of the century, but its most important source of electric power was the hydroelectric plant the city constructed in Itabira on the Rio das Pedras in 1906–7.[81] By 1912, the city leaders had decided to hand over all electric power, bonde, and telephone service to a private company via concession. After a public auction, the prefeitura signed a contract with Sampaio Corrêa & Cia (from Rio de Janeiro).[82]

The concession was exercised by the most important source of electric power in the city prior to the 1930s, the Companhia de Electricidade e Viação Urbana de Belo Horizonte. Formed in 1911, this firm had a monopoly on power generated for the municipality, primarily for electric lighting and public trolleys. Its owner and president, Manuel Tomás de Carvalho Brito, successfully blended the careers of politician, technocrat, and entrepreneur. The son of a rural colonel, Carvalho Brito was born in Antônio Dias in 1872 in what today is the municipio of Itabira. After completing a law degree at the Faculdade de Direito de São Paulo, Carvalho Brito served as state deputy, federal deputy, state senator, and state secretary of finance. While secretary of Interior and Justice he carried out an important reform of the state educational system. One of the most powerful politicians in Minas during the First Republic, he had the misfortune of siding with President Washington Luís against Minas' governor, Antônio Carlos, in the bitter political dispute that led to the Revolution of 1930. The defeat of Washington Luís sent Carvalho Brito off into exile and effectively ended his political career. He owned and directed one of the biggest textile mills in Belo Horizonte, the Companhia Fiação e Tecelagem Minas Gerais (founded in 1880 as the Companhia Industrial Sabarense, see table 3.5).[83]

In October 1929, the state government sold the exclusive electric power monopoly in the municipality of Belo Horizonte to the North American utility, Electric Bond and Share, a subsidiary of American and Foreign Power Company (AMFORP).[84] When Bond and Share purchased what became the Companhia de Força e Luz de Minas Gerais, the company had just two hydroelectric power stations producing 12,000 kW, and nearly all of it from just one power plant, Rio de Pedras in the municipio of Itabirito. In the early 1960s, the CFLMG had not even doubled the generating capacity of that which existed in 1929.[85]

In the early decades of the century, the prefeitura offered to supply electric power to companies as an incentive to attract industry to Belo Horizonte. By 1919 just over one hundred industrial establishments were receiving electric power from the city, and 22 of those were on concessions subsidized by the prefeitura. The most important subsidy went to the Companhia Industrial Belo Horizonte located near the train station.[86] By the 1920s, the chronic shortages of electric power had become a regular headache for the prefeitura. The prefeitura asked Carvalho Brito's Companhia de Eletricidade e Viação Urbana to provide more electric power, more bonde service, and a new phone system. The company agreed only after getting a rate increase.[87] When the prefeitura took the concession back from Carvalho Brito's firm in 1926, local elites expected a dramatic increase in the quality of service and the availability of electric power, especially for the bondes. The prefeitura's newly created Departamento de Eletricidade, however, did not achieve any noticeable improvement in service, prompting severe criticism and the eventual contract with Bond and Share.[88] Despite the privatization of the electric concession, after 1929 the complaints about the service provided by the Companhia Força e Luz became frequent and more strident with each succeeding decade.[89]

Nearly all the technology for the electric industry was imported, primarily from the United States. Part of the logic of expansion that attracted foreign capital into public utilities in Latin America was the desire to expand markets for the machinery produced in North America. General Electric created AMFORP in 1923 as part of its strategy to secure overseas markets for its technology and to defend its patent rights. By the end of the 1920s, General Electric had invested more than $500 million in electric companies in 11 Latin American countries.[90]

Politicians, technocrats, and entrepreneurs constantly expressed dissatisfaction with the operations of the electric company in Belo Horizonte from its creation in the 1890s until the expansion of CEMIG in the 1950s. Whether under municipal control or after auctioning off the monopoly through a public bidding process in 1911, complaints of poor service, inadequate power, and an unwillingness to expand the capacity and number of generating plants plagued the electric utility in Belo Horizonte. The state government expropriated the company in 1926, apparently due to the long-standing complaints that, ironically, continued after the sale of the utility to Bond and Share in 1929.[91] In the mid-1940s, technocrats and politicians would locate the new Cidade Industrial in neighboring Contagem in order to build and control an adequate power supply for industry outside the Bond and Share monopoly in Belo Horizonte. A hydroelectric plant (Gafanhoto) located some 90 kilometers from Belo Horizonte on the Rio Pará, would eventually supply 10,000 horsepower to the Cidade Industrial (or nearly 50 percent of the amount of power generated by Bond and Share's five plants).[92] As with iron and steel, the scale of investment required for electric power generation drew state and foreign capital into another important industrial sector. This process would accelerate dramatically in the 1950s.

Conclusion

By the mid-1940s Belo Horizonte had emerged as a sizable city with nearly a quarter of a million inhabitants. By the 1950s the demographic and economic reach of the city had drawn at least a dozen surrounding municipios into the orbit of an emerging metropolitan region that would continue to expand over succeeding decades. Belo Horizonte had firmly established itself as the political center of the state, and as a magnet for business enterprise. Home to a substantial business community, and more importantly, a growing business elite, Belo Horizonte was also becoming the economic center of Minas Gerais. The core industries that would dominate the state's economy in the twentieth century—textiles, iron and steel, and electric power were in place and beginning to gravitate toward the region around Belo Horizonte. These key sectors of the economy, along with banking, had emerged out of the kinship and clientelistic networks of the First Republic, with the assistance of state support or foreign capital.

By the 1940s the Associação Commercial de Minas and the Federação das Indústrias do Estado de Minas Gerais had emerged as the leading interest groups for the business community, and the principal corporate entities for the business elite of Belo Horizonte and central Minas Gerais. Throughout the first half-century of the city's history, these groups continually analyzed the region's economic and industrial problems and lobbied government officials for solutions. In some cases, those officials were members of the ACM or the FIEMG. The litany of complaints remained relatively constant throughout these decades: a scarcity of capital investment and currency for transactions, the need for more banks and other financial institutions, better roads and rail service, lower freight rates and taxes, access to more and cheaper electric power.[93]

The leaders of the ACM were staunch supporters of the industrial development of Belo Horizonte, appealing to the prefeitura in the mid-1930s to create a plan that would attract new industry to the city. They heaped praise on Prefeito Otacílio Negrão de Lima (a member and a son of former ACM president Benjamim Lima) after he created an "industrial park" along the banks of the Arrudas in 1936.[94] Following the lead of the ACM and the FIEMG, the leaders of different industries began to organize corporate entities to defend the interests of specific industrial sectors. In 1932, for example, textile industrialists founded the Centro de Fiação e Tecelagem de Minas Gerais. The center was given office space in the ACM's building on the Avenida Afonso Pena, and all of its members agreed to join the Associação Comercial.[95]

By the mid-1940s, three of the key industries that would dominate Belo Horizonte were firmly in place, each with its own characteristics and trajectory. Textiles was the classic case of early industrialization, financed by kinship networks, and built with imported technology. Controlled by a small group of families, the textile industry in central Minas Gerais was the epitome of the convergence of kinship and capital that so characterized the first half-century of the industrialization of Belo Horizonte. Undercapitalized, largely serving protected regional markets, and showing little technological dynamism, the textile industry did help diversify the economy as these families also channeled some of their profits into banking, insurance, and other enterprises.

Iron and steel also suffered from lack of capital and technological backwardness, as well as locational disadvantages. With the influx of European capital (Belgo Mineira) and state capital (CVRD), the industry began to expand by the 1930s and 1940s. In both these cases, however, mineiro clientelism and kinship networks were critical, as foreign capital allied with the family networks emerging out of the textile industry (Christiano Guimarães being the prime example) and technocrats from these same networks organized and developed the CVRD (Israel Pinheiro being the key example).

The electric power industry, so crucial for the advancement of industry, stumbled under poorly capitalized local entrepreneurs (Carvalho Brito, for example), and then under the control of foreign capital that was also insufficient. Not until the state stepped in with its own resources in the 1950s and 1960s would the electric power industry have sufficient capital for expansion and, once again, it would be with the technocratic expertise emerging out of the kinship and clientelistic networks so important to traditional mineiro politics. In the 1950s and 1960s it would be a larger and much more influential generation of technocrats and entrepreneurs who would build on the work of the politicians, technocrats, and entrepreneurs who built Belo Horizonte and laid the foundations of its industrialization in the half-century after its founding.

Chapter 4 🗹

Technocrats, Politicians, and Industrialists, 1940s–1960s

By the mid-1940s, Belo Horizonte and Minas Gerais had begun to enter a new phase of industrialization. In the decade of the 1950s, the city and state experienced the first of three major industrial surges during the last half of the twentieth century (the 1950s, 1970s, and 1990s). This first major wave of industrialization built on the foundations laid in the previous decades—especially in the transformation of mineiro raw materials, most notably iron ore and water. Entrepreneurs had put in place a basic infrastructure of banks, transportation, electric power, and commercial networks. Technocrats and politicians would transform this fragile foundation through planning and the mobilization of massive new capital investment—both public and private. Entrepreneurs found themselves in a very different business environment from the prewar decades.

Politicians, technocrats, and entrepreneurs had learned a fundamental lesson from the experience of the previous decades: The industrialization of the state would not be possible without large infusions of capital, and the mineiro private sector quite simply could not mobilize that capital. The decade of the fifties marks the entrance of state and federal funds into mineiro industrialization in a big way, and by the entrance of foreign capital from multinational corporations. In analyzing Brazilian development during the 1960s and 1970s, Peter Evans described the convergence of capital from the federal government, the Brazilian private sector, and multinational corporations as a *tripé* or "triple alliance."[1] In Minas Gerais, this three-legged stool became a four-legged chair. The crucial role of public funds and support from the state government made this convergence of investors into a "quadruple alliance."

This chapter examines the industrialization of Belo Horizonte and Minas Gerais from the mid-1940s to the mid-1960s. The first section traces the outline of the industrial surge of the 1950s concentrating on the key industries: textiles, iron and steel, electric power generation, minerals processing, and (very briefly) construction. The next section returns to the people behind the process of industrialization, in particular, the crucial role of an emerging group of technocrats in the state government and state enterprises. I then turn to the role of politicians, the leaders who were eventually persuaded by the arguments of the technocrats that Minas could move forward only if it made major efforts to industrialize, and only if the state government stepped in to move that process forward. Finally, at the end of the chapter I come back to the role of entrepreneurs. The emergence of politicians and technocrats at the forefront of industrialization did not completely push entrepreneurs out of the picture. It did, however, fundamentally alter their role in the process of industrialization. They were the weakest partner in the alliance.

Outlines of the Industrial Surge

The industrial surge in Minas Gerais in the 1950s formed an important part of the industrial transformation of the Brazilian economy during the same decade. As Werner Baer has pointed out, "By the 1950s, industrialization was no longer a defensive reaction to external events. It had become the principal method for the government to modernize and raise the rate of growth of the economy."[2] The ideology of developmentalism (*desenvolvimentismo*) dominated among politicians, technocrats, and entrepreneurs, not only in Minas but in Brazil as a whole in the postwar decades. As Kathryn Sikkink has so clearly shown, developmentalism in Brazil was based on the belief that industrialization was necessary for development, in particular "heavy industry and the basic infrastructure that would facilitate the emergence of an integrated industrial structure."[3] Although private capital would play a key role in this process, it could not produce industrialization without help from the State.

Juscelino Kubitschek played a central role in the industrialization of Minas Gerais and Brazil in the 1950s, first as governor of the state and then president of the nation. As governor, Juscelino forged a coalition of politicians, technocrats, and entrepreneurs around his plans to develop Minas concentrating on energy and transport. As president, he brought his immense political skills to national politics, promising "fifty years' progress in five." In a sense, Juscelino's mineiro model of development became the

Brazilian model in the late fifties, and Brazil did experience impressive economic growth built on industrialization.

> Between 1955 and 1961 industrial production grew 80 percent (in constant prices), with even higher percentages recorded by the steel industry (100 percent), mechanical industries (125 percent), electrical and communications industries (380 percent), and the transportation equipment industries (600 percent). From 1957 to 1961 the real rate of growth was seven percent per year, and nearly 4 percent per capita. For the decade of the 1950's, Brazil's per capita real growth was approximately three times that of the rest of Latin America.[4]

In Minas, the industrial surge of the 1950s arose on the foundations laid in the interwar years. The textile industry continued to play an important, although diminishing, role in the mineiro industrial economy. Iron and steel, electric power generation, minerals processing, food processing, and construction emerged as the principal pillars of the growing industrial sector. Nevertheless, the state continued to lag behind Rio de Janeiro and São Paulo (especially the latter), and the major industries were those that transformed the natural resources of the state: water, iron, and other minerals. Furthermore, despite the growth of the iron and steel industry, it served primarily as a supplier for paulista and carioca industry. Despite impressive industrial growth after World War II, by the mid-1960s Minas remained primarily a supplier of inputs to the more sophisticated industrial parks in Rio de Janeiro and São Paulo.

Textiles, metallurgy, and food processing remained the three major pillars of the industrial economy of Belo Horizonte and Minas Gerais into the 1960s. (See table 4.1.) In 1919 the three accounted for 83.5 percent of all industrial production in the state. This figure went down to 68.5 percent by 1940, rose to 71.6 percent in 1950, and reached 77 percent of all industrial production by 1970. The relative position of the three industries, however, shifted quite dramatically in the three decades after 1940. The relative share of food processing remained strong into the early sixties at nearly half of all industrial production, but declined to less than a quarter of all production by 1970. Textiles also decline by nearly half (from 29.7 to 15.5 percent) from 1919 to 1940, and then by half again by 1970 (to 7.2 percent). Metallurgy, however, surged in the 1960s, nearly tripling its share of industrial production from 1950 to 1970 (from 11.7 to 34.4 percent). Furthermore, those industries that essentially mined and processed the state's minerals (mining, the transformation of nonmetallic

Table 4.1 Industrial Structure of Minas Gerais, 1919–1980 (percent of value of production by industry)

Industry	1919	1940	1950	1960	1970	1980
Food processing	51.5	34.1	45.5	48.9	24.2	20.9
Textiles	29.7	14.4	14.4	15.5	7.2	6.5
Metallurgy	2.3	20.0	11.7	12.6	34.4	31.8
Leather, wood, clothing	9.9	7.9	6.5	7.0	2.7	2.5
Chemicals	1.3	1.9	1.5	1.1	5.9	8.9
Nonmetallic minerals	—	3.3	4.1	4.4	6.5	7.2
Mining	—	4.0	2.8	2.8	6.0	7.4
Other	5.3	14.4	13.6	7.7	13.1	14.8
Totals	100.0	100.0	100.0	100.0	100.0	100.0

Sources: Recenseamento de 1920, v. 5, pt. 1, 394–5; *Censo industrial [de 1940]*, pt. XIII, t. 3, 475; *Censo industrial de Minas Gerais [1950]*, 1; *Censo industrial [de 1960]*, V. III, t. IV, 69; *Censo industrial de Minas Gerais [1970]*, 2–3; *Censo industrial [de 1980]*, v. 16, 2.

minerals, and chemicals) accounted for another 18.4 percent of industrial production by the end of the sixties. The metallurgical-minerals industries, then, accounted for more than half of mineiro industrial production (52.8 percent) with food processing and textiles combining for nearly another third (31.4 percent).

The tremendous expansion of the main industries can also be seen in the figures in tables 4.2 and 4.3. The number of industrial establishments tripled between 1940 and 1970. The number of firms in textiles and food processing doubled while in nonmetallic minerals the number quadrupled and in metallurgy there were eight times as many firms in 1970 as in 1940. When gauging growth with the size of the industrial workforce, the number of workers in all industries tripled between 1940 and 1970. In nonmetallic minerals the number grew by a factor of five. In short, all the major industries surged forward, but especially those associated with the mining-minerals processing-metallurgical sectors.

Textiles

By the 1940s the textile industry in Minas Gerais was more than half a century old. With the war in Europe in the early 1940s, production and productivity in the Brazilian textile industry rose, not so much to meet the demand normally supplied by imports (which was small) but rather to sup-

Table 4.2 **Major Industries in Minas Gerais, 1940–1970, Number of Establishments**

Industry	1940	1950	1970	1980
Nonmetallic minerals	677	1,623	2,030	2,854
Metallurgy	122	186	406	972
Textiles	123	138	182	294
Food processing	2,645	5,672	5,075	5,900
All industries	5,027	10,394	12,028	16,673

Sources: Censo industrial de Minas Gerais [1950], 1; Censo industrial de Minas Gerais [1970], 2–3.

Table 4.3 **Major Industries in Minas Gerais, 1940–1970, Number of Workers**

Industry	1940	1950	1970	1980
Nonmetallic minerals	4,489	7,696	13,325	21,602
Metallurgy	15,717	14,823	27,879	33,984
Textiles	16,588	28,188	32,020	32,440
Food processing	10,741	15,185	23,311	32,759
All industries	58,783	87,661	130,830	186,355

Sources: Censo industrial de Minas Gerais [1950], 1; Censo industrial de Minas Gerais [1970], 2–3.

ply external markets cut off from traditional centers of production (England, Japan, Germany). As Versiani has pointed out, however, this increase came largely through the utilization of idle plant capacity and outmoded machinery.[5] In the decade after the war, textile producers imported large amounts of equipment, but production in the 1950s remained relatively level. By the early 1960s, the textile industry in Minas was in full-scale crisis with low productivity, declining production, and obsolete machinery.[6]

Belo Horizonte's role in the textile industry became even more pronounced in the postwar years. A survey in 1970–71 tallied 83 textile mills in Minas (controlled by 73 firms). Thirty-two (38.5 percent) were located in the Zona Metalúrgica around Belo Horizonte. Another 21 (25.3 percent) were clustered in the Zona da Mata around Juiz de Fora.[7] These two cities that had dominated the decentralized industry of the early twentieth century had become the dominant centers of an increasingly concentrated industry by the 1960s. The pattern of ownership had also not changed in the industry since the 1940s. The same set of family-owned firms continued to dominate the industry (as was also the case in Juiz de Fora). In the case of Belo Horizonte, only a handful of firms had their plants located in the municipio. Most factories were in the metropolitan area (which was constantly growing and expanding) and adjacent areas. All the major firms, however, had their headquarters or an office in the capital.

Iron and Steel

Unlike the textile industry, which remained largely in the hands of local capital and fragmented into dozens of firms, the iron and steel industry in the postwar decades was dominated by a handful of companies and by a combination of public and multinational capital. Requiring highly sophisticated and extremely expensive imported technology, and with very high capital investment requirements, the iron and steel industry became the domain of politicians, technocrats, and foreign capital. It also became the keystone industry in mineiro industrialization, and the centerpiece of the industrialization of Belo Horizonte.

Four firms dominated the iron and steel industry in central Minas in the two decades after World War II: Belgo Mineira, Mannesmann, Acesita, and Usiminas. Belgo Mineira, the pioneering giant that had begun operations before the war, continued to expand its operations in Sabará and Monlevade producing pig iron and rolled steel products. Acesita (Aços Especiais Itabira) was originally founded by Percival Farquhar, but as with his other iron and steel plans, he found himself short on capital and was eventually forced to hand over control of the company to the Banco do Brasil. The German firm, Mannesmann, built its first plant in Belo Horizonte in the mid-1950s. Usiminas, which combined state and Japanese capital, began construction in Ipatinga (east of Belo Horizonte) in the late 1950s and entered into full production in 1962. The story of each of these huge firms illustrates the different roles of politicians, technocrats, and entrepreneurs in the postwar decades.

Until the emergence of the CSN at Volta Redonda in the mid-1950s, Belgo Mineira was the largest integrated iron and steel producer in South America. It was (and remains) the largest charcoal-based integrated iron and steel works in the world. Although the company had begun under the leadership of mineiro entrepreneurs, and despite the fact mineiros remained prominent executives in company operations, Belgo Mineira was (and is) the subsidiary of a very powerful multinational corporation. The role of local entrepreneurs was visible but ultimately a minor voice in controlling company operations. The company carefully cultivated politicians and has long been very successful at operating a foreign firm in a very nationalistic environment. Like local entrepreneurs, technocrats had little role in Belgo Mineira, although some did gain valuable experience working with the company.

ARBED chose to send out its principal technicians and directors from Luxembourg rather than drawing on local expertise and entrepreneurs. In some ways, this foreshadowed the policies of Fiat beginning in the 1970s. The influential Louis Ensch followed by Albert Scharlé in 1953, and then Joseph Hein in the 1950s and 1960s, were all European engineers sent out to run the company's operations in Minas Gerais.[8] All three spent decades in Brazil, married into prominent local families, and became part of the powerful local webs of power and influence.

Map 5 Iron and Steel Works, Zona Metalúrgica, 1964

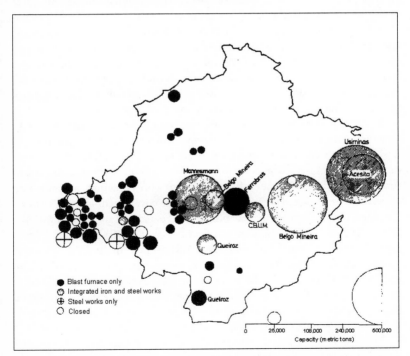

Derived from: John Philip Dickenson, "Zona Metalúrgica: A Study of the Geography of Industrial Development in Minas Gerais, Brazil," Ph.D. diss., University of Liverpool, 1970, 177.

Likewise, Mannesmann is the subsidiary of a powerful multinational corporation. When a German mission arrived in the early fifties looking to build a plant in Brazil, they ultimately decided on Belo Horizonte. (According to Lucas Lopes, Getúlio Vargas directed Mannesmann to the mineiros as a way of soothing their irritation over the earlier selection of Volta Redonda for Brazil's first iron and steel mill.)[9] Located in the Barreiro district alongside the Cidade Industrial in the southwestern portion of the municipio, the Belo Horizonte plant was close to mineiro iron ore deposits, rail lines and highways, and the soon to be abundant electricity supplied by the recently formed CEMIG. The plant went into operation in 1956 producing seamless steel tubes primarily with electric furnaces. By 1964 the plant was producing 200,000 tons of ingot steel and 160,000 tons of rolled products a year.[10] It was the fifth largest steel mill in the country (as measured by nominal capital invested).[11]

Acesita was an offshoot of the expropriation of the Itabira iron lands from Percival Farquhar for the creation of the CVRD. Farquhar invested his funds in the creation of a mill to create specialized steel products for tools and machinery. Located at Coronel Fabriciano on the Vitória-Minas railway, the company used blast furnace and charcoal technology and ore from the Rio Doce Valley.[12] Like Belgo Mineira and Mannesman, Acesita began with foreign capital. Unlike these two companies, Farquhar could not sustain the capital flow he needed, and the Banco do Brasil eventually took over control of the firm making it, in effect, a state-controlled enterprise.

In the eyes of many mineiros, the creation of Usiminas in the late 1950s represented the culmination of the long dream of a locally-controlled iron and steel industry.[13] Although initially the dream of local entrepreneurs, Usiminas came about because of the desire of Japanese investors to expand into Latin American markets in the late fifties. After intense negotiations, a consortium of Japanese firms signed an accord with the state government in 1957 to build the plant. Originally, the Japanese provided 40 percent of the capital, with the Banco Nacional de Desenvolvimento Econômico (BNDE) providing 25 percent, the state another 24 percent, the CVRD 9 percent, and the CSN and private Brazilian investors accounting for about 2 percent. Eventually, high costs forced the BNDE to raise its stake and the Japanese portion declined to about 20 percent. Built at Ipatinga in the Vale do Rio Doce, Usiminas turned the abundant ore reserves of the surrounding region into flat steel products. By 1966, the company was producing more than a million tons of rolled steel.[14]

These four firms played a very large role in the national industry, and they dominated the industry in Minas. They accounted for more than 90 percent of nominal capital invested and more than 80 percent of the workforce in the mineiro iron and steel industry. Along with the CSN these four companies accounted for nearly 80 percent of the nominal capital in the Brazilian iron and steel industry and close to 60 percent of the workforce in the industry. In 1964, Minas had 40 percent of the total capacity for producing rolled steel while Rio de Janeiro (36 percent) and São Paulo (23 percent) accounted for the rest of the nation's capacity.[15]

The 1950s were also the heyday of the smaller iron producers in Minas. As the integrated plants took shape they often lagged in their ability to produce enough pig iron for their steel manufacturing. Demand for pig iron by smaller foundries also increased. By the early 1960s, more than 80 firms had appeared in Minas Gerais to meet the demand for pig iron. Most of these were small-scale operations with small, charcoal blast furnaces producing 20 to 40 tons of pig iron a day. All but one started operating after 1951, and all but a half dozen started operating between 1958 and 1963. Seventeen were clustered in Divinópolis alone, and nine in Itaúna. The overwhelming majority were in the Zona Metalúrgica. The severe economic crisis of the mid-1960s forced nearly two-thirds of the companies to close down, leaving just 30 percent of plant capacity in operation.[16]

All of the major iron and steel producers (and most of the small pig iron producers) were located in the Zona Metalúrgica in or around Belo Horizonte. The most distant plants were Usiminas (Ipatinga), Acesita (Coronel Fabriciano), and Belgo Mineira's Monlevade operations, all located in what had become known as the Valley of Steel (Vale do Aço), although all three companies were headquartered in Belo Horizonte. The emergence of these plants and the role of the capital as the commercial and business center for the region intensified the growth of the metropolitan area and the reach of Belo Horizonte into the surrounding municipios. Increasingly, the city was becoming the center of a vortex of industrial activity drawing economic activity inward to the capital.

By the mid-1960s, mineiros had finally achieved their dream of creating an iron and steel industry in the old Zona Metalúrgica. Belo Horizonte had become the economic hub of the state's most important industry. Even though politicians and technocrats had been successful in attracting and nurturing this emerging industry, mineiro entrepreneurs had been relegated to a secondary role in its operation. Once again, the massive capital requirements for industrialization had favored multinational and public capital. Small producers operated on the margin of the industry, and some prominent entrepreneurs served on the boards or in the administration of the big three, but key players in iron and steel by the early sixties were foreign investors and technocrats.

The dependence of the large iron and steel producers on foreign technology in the two decades after World War II characterizes the iron and steel industry not only in Minas Gerais, but in all Brazil. All four of the dominant firms in Minas were created by foreign capital, and they relied on their own technological expertise and traditional suppliers for the know-how and the hardware used in constructing and developing their plants. Even in the creation of the state iron and steel enterprises, the Brazilians had little choice but to turn to the leading technology, all produced in the developed economies of the North. Given the small number of firms, and the very high entry costs for any firm attempting to move into the production of iron and steel technology, the continued reliance on imported technology, and the lack of local national technological innovation should not be surprising.[17]

Electric Power

While private (and primarily mineiro) capital developed the textile industry, and a combination of private (largely foreign) and public capital built the iron and steel industry, the electric power industry began as a private venture and by the mid-1960s had become an almost entirely state-controlled industry. State control of electric power generation and distribution began to emerge in the 1950s and had become the dominant pattern by the mid-1960s. The state's role in the emergence of the electric power industry was visionary and critical to the industrialization of Belo Horizonte and Minas Gerais.

The electric power industry is the classic example of the developmentalist ideology of Kubitschek and the mineiro elite in the 1950s. Américo Giannetti's *Plano de recuperação* (1947) and Lucas Lopes's *Plano de eletrificação* (1950) both stressed the critical need to develop an integrated and dynamic electric power grid to promote industrialization and economic development. After a gubernatorial campaign that stressed the famous *binômio energia e transporte,* Kubitschek turned to Lucas Lopes to organize a state-controlled electric holding company.[18]

Even more so than textiles, the early electric power industry was fragmented and dispersed. By the end of the 1940s more than 350 power companies in Minas operated more than 400 power stations, and more than 3,000 private plants supplied fazendas and factories.[19] Much more so than in São Paulo and Rio de Janeiro, the industry was dominated by a large number of small, inefficient companies producing relatively small amounts of power. Although mineiro power plants and firms accounted for nearly one-fifth of all Brazilian plants and firms in 1940, they produced just 12 percent of the nation's electric power. (See table 4.4.) In contrast, the state of São Paulo had barely a third of the number of companies and plants while producing nearly four times as much power. Together, the three big southeastern economic powers—Minas Gerais, São Paulo, and Rio de Janeiro (including the Federal District)—produced nearly 80 percent of the nation's electric power in 1940.

The industrialization of Greater Belo Horizonte took shape in large part due to the rise of an outstanding state electric power company, and in spite of the foreign subsidiary that controlled the electric power monopoly in the municipio of Belo Horizonte. As seen in chapter 3, the Companhia de Força e Luz de Minas Gerais (CFLMG), GE's subsidiary, purchased the monopoly concession for the municipality of Belo Horizonte in 1929.[20] Over the next three decades Bond & Share boosted its generating capacity by just over 150 percent (from roughly 14,000 to 36,000 kW) while demand and consumption increased by over 1,500 percent.[21]

By the late forties it was clear to mineiro entrepreneurs and technocrats that the state was facing a power shortage that would soon increase. The growing need for electric power (primarily to serve industry) was clearly set out in both the *Plano de recuperação* in 1947 and even more starkly in a five-volume study by the Secretaria de Viação e Obras Pública, the *Plano de eletrificação de Minas Gerais* in 1950.[22] The latter attempted an energy survey of the state and showed that more than 90 percent of all energy produced came from wood and charcoal, while hydroelectric plants produced barely 3 percent. In the Zona Metalúrgica, electricity accounted for just over 2 percent of all power generated.[23] According to these studies, the state was utilizing less than 3 percent of its hydroelectric potential. Planners singled out the

Table 4.4   **Electric Power Generation in Minas Gerais Compared with Rio de Janeiro, São Paulo, and Nation, 1920**

State	Number of Firms		Number of Plants		Horsepower	
Minas Gerais	72	(24%)	91	(27%)	58,414	(12%)
São Paulo	66	(22%)	78	(23%)	211,168	(44%)
Rio de Janeiro	18	(6%)	19	(6%)	112,980	(24%)
MG + SP + RJ	156	(51%)	188	(55%)	382,562	(80%)
Brazil	306		343		475,652	

Notes: Rio de Janeiro includes the state and the Federal District. Percentages are rounded.
Source: Panorama do setor de energia elétrica no Brasil (Rio de Janeiro: Centro de Memória da Eletricidade no Brasil, 1988), 54.

Table 4.5   Electric Power Generation in Minas Gerais Compared with Rio de
Janeiro, São Paulo, and Nation, 1940

State	Number of Firms		Number of Plants		Kilowatts	
Minas Gerais	336	(21%)	423	(22%)	144,647	(12%)
São Paulo	133	(8%)	196	(10%)	564,654	(45%)
Rio de Janeiro	79	(5%)	116	(6%)	279,308	(22%)
MG + SP + RJ	548	(34%)	735	(38%)	972,913	(78%)
Brazil	1,617		1,914		1,243,877	

Notes: Rio de Janeiro includes the state and the Federal District. Percentages are rounded.
Source: Panorama do setor de energia elétrica no Brasil (Rio de Janeiro: Centro de Memória da
Eletricidade no Brasil, 1988), 111.

shortage of electric power as one of the main bottlenecks (*pontos de estran-
gulamento*) in the state's economy.[24]

The idea for the *Plano de eletrificação* came out of the head of the Secretaria de Viação e Obras Públicas, José Rodrigues Seabra, an engineer who
had held a number of important elected and appointed political posts since
the 1930s.[25] Seabra hired an engineering consulting firm, the Companhia
Brasileira de Engenharia, to do the study, a company with no prior experience in the field. Seabra offered the contract with the specific proviso that
former secretary of agriculture Lucas Lopes be appointed to lead the study.
Lopes then personally selected the key engineers who would lead the study
with him, key friends he had made in his own engineering work across
Brazil: John Cotrim, Mauro Thibau, and Mario Behring.[26] All three (as well
as Lopes) had worked for private electric power companies gaining the experience they would need to organize and run CEMIG, and all four would
go on to national careers in the major electric power companies.

The city's and state's dependence on the production of electricity by
foreign companies became even more pronounced in the thirties and forties. In the 1930s the two largest industrial corporations in the state, both
bordering on the municipio of Belo Horizonte, built or expanded their
own hydroelectric plants to guarantee the expansion of their operations.
The St. John d'el Rey Mining Company in Nova Lima had begun building hydroelectric plants in the 1890s and in the 1930s they built several
more large plants to the south of Belo Horizonte.[27] In the late forties the
company was selling excess capacity to Bond & Share to provide power
for Belo Horizonte. Belgo Mineira also built plants in the late thirties in
the municipios of Caeté and Rio Piracicaba. Each of these two industrial

Table 4.6 CEMIG Hydroelectric Plants, 1965

Plant	Zona	Inaugurated	Kilowatt Hours Generated
Gafanhoto		1946	78,425,600
Itutinga		1959	206,908,000
Salto Grande		1956	488,782,000
Cajuru		1959	36,113,900
Camargo		1958	198,219,000
Três Marias		1962	968,519,880
Tronqueiras		1955	30,929,100
Piau		1955	104,212,000
Pai Joaquim			40,048,100
Other plants			33,499,716
Total			2,185,684,296

Sources: Panorama, 158; Francisco de Assis Magalhães Gomes, *A eletrificação no Brasil* (São Paulo: Eletropaulo, 1980), 38.

concerns generated more hydroelectric power than many of the states in the North and Northeast![28]

The creation of the Centrais Elétricas de Minas Gerais (CEMIG) was the state's response to the studies of the two *planos* and the national SALTE plan.[29] The technocrats created CEMIG as a means for a rational state electric system that would overcome the highly dispersed, small-scale, and local utility companies that characterized the state in the first half of the century.[30] Originally envisioned by Américo Giannetti and his team of technocrats under the Milton Campos administration in the late forties, CEMIG was created in 1952 by Juscelino Kubitschek.[31] The creation of CEMIG demonstrates the powerful elite consensus on the importance of electric power for industrial development. Envisioned and studied under the UDN government of Milton Campos, it became a reality under the PSD government of Juscelino. It soon became the pioneer state-controlled electric utility, and one of the best run public or private enterprises in Brazil.[32] CEMIG became the model as other state-controlled companies were formed in the fifties and sixties.

By any standard, CEMIG was an extraordinary success and a major factor in the industrialization of Belo Horizonte and the state. Minas Gerais went from a power-starved state in the forties to a power surplus in the early sixties, and the availability of cheap, electric power became one of the major factors in the ability of mineiros to attract new industry, and to expand already established industries. During the same period, the states of São Paulo and Rio de Janeiro—both dominated by the Canadian electric utility known as The Light—became energy-deficient states as they were unable to keep up with the demand for electric power. Mineiro participation in national electricity production rose from 13 to 26 percent in the 1950s. By the mid-1960s, CEMIG was selling its excess power (slightly more than 50 percent of its production) to both states.[33] It also supplied the regional electric utility companies around the state including the CFLMG. By 1961 CEMIG controlled nearly 60 percent of the installed electric power capacity in Minas Gerais, and either directly or indirectly its services reached two-thirds of the state's population.[34]

CEMIG constructed five major hydroelectric plants in the fifties (see table 4.6) raising consumption of electric power from 22,374 kWh in 1952 to just over 2 million kWh by 1965, and to over 4 million kWh by 1970.[35] In addition, CEMIG also became a major partner in the construction of the Furnas power plant on the western border of the state with São Paulo. When it was built in the early 1960s, Furnas was the largest hydroelectric plant in Latin America, and it was built to supply the growing energy demands of the São Paulo, Rio de Janeiro, and Belo Horizonte industrial complexes. By the mid-1960s Furnas was generating 1.2 million kilowatts of power. John Cotrim, one of the original board members of CEMIG, became the president of Furnas.[36] By 1963, almost entirely due to the growth of CEMIG, Minas Gerais had an electric power generating capacity of 1,291,550 kW, much larger than Rio de Janeiro (1,004,497 kW), and second only to São Paulo (2,209,621 kW).[37]

Until the 1950s nearly all the technology in the electric power industry had to be imported from the major manufacturers in the United States and Europe. As noted earlier, part of the strategy of companies like General Electric when they created Bond and Share was to guarantee patents and markets overseas. With a new phase in Brazilian industrialization taking shape in the 1950s, multinational firms began to build plants in Brazil to manufacture their products for the domestic market and export. The French firm, Schneider, with funding from the BNDE, built a plant in Taubaté in 1955 to manufacture turbines and other heavy equipment. The Swiss firm, Brown-Boveri, inaugurated a plant in Osasco (Greater São Paulo) in 1957. The Italian company, Coemsa/GIE set up in Rio Grande do Sul, and General Electric located a plant in Campinas in 1962. Siemens and Bardella also built plants in the 1960s. By the late 1960s, most of the advanced technology needed for the numerous hydroelectric projects in

Minas and the rest of Brazil was manufactured in Brazil, but by subsidiaries of foreign firms.[38]

Although the founders envisioned CEMIG as an electric utility that would eventually serve all kinds of consumers in Minas, from its inception to the 1970s its major objective was to supply the power for industrialization, especially around Belo Horizonte. As late as 1970, mineiro industry consumed *80 percent* of the electric power generated by CEMIG, and just ten industrial firms consumed 80 percent of all power supplied to industry (i.e., two-thirds of all CEMIG's power generation). Half of those companies were metallurgical plants (Usiminas, Aluminas, Mannesmann, Belgo Mineira, Companhia Siderúrgica Nacional, Morro do Níquel) and the other half were cement producers (CBCC, Companhia Cimento Portland Barroso, Companhia Cimento Portland Itaú, and Companhia Cimento Portland Cauê).[39] Along with iron and steel, electric power had become one of the pillars of mineiro industry by the mid-1960s.

Mining and Minerals Processing

The mining and processing of minerals were intimately linked to the growth of the iron and steel industry, and also became a major pillar of mineiro industrialization in the postwar decades. Iron mining grew dramatically, especially in the region around Belo Horizonte, to supply both the local iron and steel industry and plants in Rio de Janeiro and São Paulo. The aluminum and cement industries also grew at an impressive rate as new companies transformed bauxite and limestone in the Zona Metalúrgica into industrial inputs. These key mineral resources provided the raw materials that drove the industrialization of central Minas.

Iron ore mining was the most visible and dramatic evidence of the role of local minerals in the industrialization of Belo Horizonte and its hinterland. After the debates and disappointments of the prewar years, iron mining finally became a major force in the mineiro economy. By the mid-1960s, iron ore had become a major export, and the exploitation of mineiro deposits would make Brazil a world leader in iron ore production by the beginning of the 1970s. The creation of the Companhia Vale do Rio Doce was the major stimulus to the expansion of the industry after 1940.

World War II fundamentally changed iron ore mining in Minas Gerais and Brazil. With the expansion of the Axis powers after 1939, England lost its access to European iron ore. Together with the United States, the British looked to Latin America as a guaranteed source of natural resources during the conflict. Getúlio Vargas negotiated an arrangement with England and the U.S. guaranteeing them iron ore in exchange for loans that would not only develop the iron reserves of Minas, but also would help build an integrated iron and steel mill.[40]

Vargas and the mineiros shared a longstanding dream of not only exploiting the nation's enormous iron ore reserves, but also of creating a truly national iron and steel industry. To make this dream reality, Vargas created two state-controlled corporations: the Companhia Siderúrgica Nacional (CSN—in Volta Redonda, Rio de Janeiro state) and the Companhia Vale do Rio Doce (CVRD). The CVRD would control the mining of iron ore and the CSN would transform it into iron and steel. Both companies were formed with combination of Brazilian, English, and U.S. capital.[41]

With the creation of the CVRD, large-scale iron ore mining in Brazil got underway. Without the massive public investment, especially by the Brazilian government, the projects would not have been possible. The government financed the railway that carried ore to the Atlantic, and the port facilities for the export of the ore. In the case of both companies, U.S. engineering firms handled all major construction.[42]

The history of the CVRD is one of extraordinary success. When the Brazilian government created the company in 1942 iron ore mining in Minas Gerais was in the era of the shovel and pick. Mechanization and infrastructure were virtually nonexistent. The terminal for the railway in Vitória did not even have the facilities to handle the transfer of the ore from train cars to large ships.[43] By 1952, one decade after its creation, the CVRD was exporting more than 1.5 million tons of ore—70 percent to the U.S. and 23 percent to Europe. Brazilian industry consumed another 300,000 tons.[44] (In comparison, exports of iron ore in 1934 were 7,138 tons!)[45] By the beginning of the 1980s the CVRD was exporting more than 50 million tons of iron ore a year. At the same time, other iron ore exporting companies took shape, especially in the Vale do Aço around the Pico de Itabira. These firms were primarily joint ventures of foreign and national investors, and by the 1970s accounted for half of all iron ore exports. The CVRD produced the other half.[46]

The mining and processing of bauxite and limestone were also key to industrial growth. In both cases, companies located in Minas to take advantage of the abundant raw materials and the electric power of CEMIG. Much like electric power, Rio de Janeiro, São Paulo, and Minas Gerais dominated the national industry, producing three-quarters of the nation's cement during this period. The modern cement industry did not begin in Minas until 1939 when the Companhia de Cimento Portland Itaú built a factory in Itaú de Minas (present day Pratápolis) in southwestern Minas. Itaú was one of the first firms to set up operations in the Cidade Industrial in 1946, primarily due to the promise of abundant electric power for its plant. A company that was extremely well connected with the mineiro political and economic elite, Itaú in the 1940s and 1950s was controlled by the Siqueira and the Souza Meireles families. Former mayor and candidate for president in 1950, Christiano Machado was a director, and former federal interventor (1937–45) Benedito Valadares became president of the company in 1964.[47] Itaú was the largest cement plant in Minas Gerais by the early 1960s, with a capacity of nearly 500,000 tons annually. The plant used Danish technology and had a workforce of 1,600.[48]

The Companhia Cimento Portland Cauê was founded in 1952 in Pedro Leopoldo, began production in 1955, and was controlled by Juventino Dias, one of the most prominent entrepreneurs in Minas Gerais and Belo Horizonte from the 1930s to the 1960s.[49] The company was created out of bank loans from the Banco do Brasil, and the original collateral for the loan was the Dias family farm (*fazenda*). The board was dominated by members of the Dias family along with representation from the Gonçalves de Souza textile families, and Júlio Soares, the brother-in-law of Juscelino Kubitschek, and his initial political patron in the 1930s. The company began with promises of plentiful power from CEMIG, and with state-of-the-art technology from the United States.[50] Both Juventino Dias, and his son, Gerson, would serve as presidents of the ACM and both were important figures in the FIEMG.[51] Eventually, the municipio of Contagem renamed the industrial park, the Cidade Industrial "Juventino Dias" in his honor.[52]

The Companhia Mineira de Cimento (COMINCI), unlike Itaú and Cauê, was controlled by foreign capital, with 85 percent of its stock in French hands. In a manner similar to Belgo Mineira, the company had a French director and technical chief. The French built the plant on the highway to Brasília at Matozinhos. Inaugurated in 1959, the plant's production rose dramatically as the principal supplier for the construction of the national capital in the 1960s. Brasília initially consumed 80 percent of the plant's production.[53]

By the late 1960s, the number of cement plants in Minas had grown to seven, with the three largest located within 65 kilometers of Belo Horizonte: Itaú (Contagem), Cauê (Pedro Leopoldo), and COMINCI (Matozinhos). These three plants accounted for more than 50 percent of the industry's production and primarily supplied the cement market in Minas. Itaú's plant in Pratápolis, Barroso in the Mantiqueira region, and COMINCI's plant in the upper São Francisco were primarily geared toward exporting their production to São Paulo and Rio de Janeiro.[54]

The growth of the cement industry is a primary indicator of economic growth in any economy. As a crucial input for construction of plants, buildings, housing, roads, and other infrastructure, cement consumption is an indicator of development. Consumption per capita, for example, in western Europe in 1964 was 368 kilograms per capita, and 279 per capita in the USSR. In Brazil the figure reached 70 kilograms per capita, low compared with the Europeans, bur nearly four times the figure for Brazil in 1940.[55] Although Brazil had become the fifteenth largest producer of cement by the late sixties (with 29 plants), these plants were concentrated in Minas Gerais, Rio de Janeiro, and São Paulo. Sixty percent of the market was controlled by just four groups: José Ermírio de Morais's Votorantim group (22 percent), Severino Pereira (11 percent), Lone Star (11 percent), in Rio and São Paulo, and Itaú (11 percent) in Minas. This crucial industry was clearly dominated by oligopoly.[56]

Another important company that was also a charter member of the Cidade Industrial was Magnesita S/A, also well connected to the webs of political and economic power in Minas. Originally founded in Rio de Janeiro in 1941 to exploit the manganese deposits of Minas Gerais, it produced bricks and ceramics for use in industrial blast furnaces. When the company transferred its headquarters to Belo Horizonte in 1945 its first vice-president was Antônio Mourão Guimarães, one of the most important industrialists and entrepreneurs in the state. Louis Ensch, the dynamic Luxembourg-born director of Belgo Mineira, was the second vice president (Belgo Mineira owned 10 percent of the company's stock) while the industrial director of the company was Fernando Mello Viana, one of the most important mineiro politicians of First Republic.[57] The natural resources of Minas and locational advantages brought Magnesita to the Cidade Industrial. The company used local fireclay, quartzite, and dolomite while importing magnesite from Bahia and chromite from Goiás. The plant used primarily U.S. and Italian technology. Magnesita shipped about 40 percent of its refractory products to Volta Redonda, another 40 percent supplied mineiro furnaces, and the rest went to industries in the state of São Paulo.[58]

In addition to iron ore, cement, and ceramics, the exploitation and processing of gold and bauxite were key (but small) sectors of the mining and minerals processing industry. Although the exploitation of bauxite had begun in Brazil under the farsighted leadership of Giannetti in the 1940s, the industry would not really take off until the late 1960s. (See chapter 5.) Antônio Mourão Guimarães and his family controlled the small and unproductive Passagem gold mine outside Mariana. The St. John d'el Rey Mining Company, Limited in Nova Lima had been the major producer of gold in

Brazil since the mid-nineteenth century and one of the most important gold mines in the world up to the 1950s. The British-owned enterprise was the largest employer in the state (with more than 7,000 workers), the largest private corporation, and the state's largest taxpayer until the 1950s. The decline of the world gold market and the resulting crisis of gold mining worldwide after the Bretton Woods Agreement in the 1940s created a crisis for the industry in Brazil and eventually brought the end of British ownership of the mine in 1960. The Morro Velho mine continued production, and maintained a huge payroll throughout the fifties and sixties, but the mine would not become profitable again until the late 1970s.[59]

Construction

Although not an industrial sector in the same sense as textiles, iron and steel, electric power generation, and mining and minerals processing, the construction industry has also played a key role in the industrialization of Belo Horizonte and central Minas Gerais since the 1940s. Construction firms transform the inputs from other industries by turning them into finished buildings, roads, and public works. In the 1950s, mineiro construction firms were quite small. Kubitschek's road building program, as Campolina Diniz has pointed out, was an important mechanism for transferring public capital into private capital. Road building firms sprung up and grew throughout the 1950s. Mineiro construction companies also benefited enormously from the building of Brasília in the late fifties, a project created by a mineiro president who appointed Israel Pinheiro to lead the project. Novacap built Brasília and under Pinheiro it provided plenty of work for mineiro firms.[60]

Two of the firms that emerged in the 1950s eventually became the largest construction companies in all of Latin America: Mendes Júnior and Andrade Gutierrez. Originally from Juiz de Fora, José Mendes Júnior was a field engineer for the Secretaria da Agricultura trained at the Escola de Minas. In 1942 he formed the Construtora de Estradas Ltda. along with some fellow engineers, and in 1953 he founded the firm that carries his name. Andrade Gutierrez was founded in 1948 as a road-building firm by Gabriel Andrade, a graduate of the Escola de Engenharia of the Universidade de Minas Gerais along with two brothers Roberto and Flávio Gutierrez. Largely due to the phenomenal growth of these two firms in the 1960s and 1970s, the construction industry in Belo Horizonte mushroomed. Although privately held, family enterprises, both companies depended heavily for their growth and development on government contracts, for roads, bridges, and large public works projects.[61]

The industrial surge in Minas Gerais, in essence, was built on a foundation of textiles, iron and steel, and mining and minerals processing that predated World War II. In the 1950s, however, as the nation's industry surged forward, especially under the presidency of Juscelino Kubitschek, iron and steel, mining and minerals processing, and construction became the pillars of mineiro industrialization. The leadership and vision of politicians, along with the urging of entrepreneurs, and the management of technocrats converged during this period to propel this process of industrialization forward.

The Technocrats

The notion of an increasingly influential technocracy in Minas Gerais is not a new one. Important studies by Campolina Diniz and Andrade in the early 1980s firmly established the importance of technocrats in the process of mineiro industrialization.[62] In fact, social scientists have produced a substantial literature on the rise of technocrats and technocracy in the post-1964 military regime.[63] In a some ways, the literature on the rise of the mineiro technocracy under the post-1945 republic parallels studies of political elites during the Old Republic. Both genres are concerned with identifying the power brokers in Brazilian politics. Both have a tendency to place individuals in a single category, be it politician or technocrat. Even the work of Hagopian, in key ways a counterargument to the studies of Campolina Diniz and Andrade, classifies individuals into a single career category.[64]

As I argue throughout this book, quite often individuals pursue more than one career in their lifetime.[65] The effort of social scientists to fit everyone into a single category simply does not do justice to the complexity of the mineiro past. Christiano Guimarães (in the early twentieth century), for example, trained as an engineer, became a very successful businessman, and exerted important political influence. Américo Renê Giannetti, also trained as an engineer, became an entrepreneur, a classic technocrat, and then a prominent politician. In the postwar years, José de Magalhães Pinto would epitomize the man of many careers. A businessman who experienced phenomenal success, he became one of the most prominent political figures in Brazil in the decades after World War II. Furthermore, even when individuals did largely pursue a single career as a politician, technocrat, or entrepreneur, other family members built parallel careers providing a single family with members operating simultaneously in a variety of spheres of influence. Kinship often connected the three overlapping and interlocking webs of power.[66]

One of the major objectives of this chapter (and this book) is to move beyond the aggregate vision of the mineiro economy, and of the reduc-

tionist analysis of a single group controlling economic growth. An influential technocratic elite did emerge in Minas Gerais, especially after 1950,
and it played a crucial role in the industrialization of Belo Horizonte and
the rest of the state. A detailed analysis of the major actors in the process
of industrialization, however, makes it clear that politicians and entrepreneurs also played key roles, and that key actors quite often do not fit into
neat categories.

As Campolina Diniz points out, it was not until the 1930s that the conditions for the formation of a technocracy began to take shape in Minas
Gerais and Brazil. The shock of the depression, its devastating effects on
Brazil's agro-exporting economy, and the increasing influence of authoritarian politics, converged to nurture the formation of technocrats. In his words,
"technocracy is the direct child of authoritarianism."[67] Increasingly in the
1930s, politicians turned to the experts for advice on how to move the
Brazilian and mineiro economy forward. Principally, they turned to engineers for the answers.[68]

In Minas Gerais, the Escola de Minas de Ouro Preto played a very prominent role in the formation of technocrats, ironically, because of the underdevelopment of the private sector. Since its formation in the 1870s the Escola
had been producing engineers—mining, civil, metallurgical, and mechanical.
Unable to find employment in the private sector, nearly three-quarters of the
Escola's graduates went into the public sector. They built roads, railways, public buildings, dams, power plants, and bridges across the state. Many of them
moved into appointed positions in the state bureaucracy.[69]

The most influential group of young technocrats took shape in the Secretaria da Agricultura, Indústria, Comércio e Trabalho in the 1930s. The Secretário da Agricultura from 1933 to 1942 was Israel Pinheiro da Silva, one
of the most important figures in the industrialization of Belo Horizonte into
the 1970s. Born in 1896 in Caeté, his father, João Pinheiro, was governor
(1906–1908) and one of the legendary figures in mineiro politics. Trained
in civil and mining engineering at the Escola de Minas, he finished first in
his class in 1919. In the 1920s he ran the family ceramics business in Caeté,
and helped build forges and blast furnaces for three different companies.
(The family business supplied the paving stones for the streets of Belo Horizonte, including what would eventually become the Avenida João Pinheiro.)
Like many mineiro political figures, his initial training was in municipal politics, first as a *vereador,* and then as the *agente executivo municipal* (equivalent to *prefeito* today). He was named Secretary of Agriculture (Secretário da
Agricultura) in 1933, and served in that position until 1942 when Getúlio
Vargas named him the first president of the Companhia Vale do Rio Doce.[70]

The technocrats in the Secretaria da Agricultura, and those who would follow them in the decades afterward, were frustrated and driven by the relative backwardness of the mineiro economy when compared with that of Rio de Janeiro, and especially with the paulista economy. Giannetti vividly expressed the sentiments of these technocrats in the 1930s and 1940s:

> Although it possesses potential riches and recognized possibilities, Minas is a state with an unbalanced economy. Its geographic location and the disorder with which its most important economic problems have been confronted have been giving to its neighboring states the opportunity to achieve their own progress at a rhythm that is now well accelerated, clearly demonstrating an economic imbalance that is fatal to Minas and also in the future to all Brasil.[71]

The central theme of those promoting mineiro industrialization since the 1930s has been the desire to overcome this relative backwardness and, in Giannetti's words to be treated "fairly."[72] The technocrats of the thirties did not have a central plan or even a notion of regional planning. They sought to promote the state's economy by finding ways to modernize agriculture, to promote industry, and to develop basic infrastructure. One of their principal objectives was to end the pattern of exporting the state's raw materials (iron ore, coffee, sugar, beef) only to see them transformed into manufactured products elsewhere—in Rio, São Paulo, or overseas.[73] As Pinheiro put it in his plan for the development of the state in 1937, "protectionism is not only industrial, it is our economic independence."[74] They also wanted to stem the export of human capital from Minas to other states, especially São Paulo.[75] "The progress and stability of the national economy," Giannetti argued, "are intimately linked to the industrialization of the country." The exploitation of mineiro natural resources and the development of hydroelectric power were crucial to mineiro industrialization. This should be done in Giannetti's view, through "private enterprise with the State merely supporting or acting directly in those cases in which private enterprise was shown to be unable or entirely incapable" of acting.[76]

They either failed or fell far short of expectations in nearly every project they attempted. After sending Américo Renê Giannetti to Europe and the United States to study aluminum production, his efforts to build an aluminum industry eventually collapsed in 1945. Plans to build a plane factory stayed on the drawing board. The state lost out to Rio de Janeiro in its efforts to build the CSN mill in Minas Gerais. Two projects did achieve some success, and would blossom in the 1950s: the creation of the CVRD to the east of Belo Horizonte and the Cidade Industrial on the outskirts of the capital.[77]

The creation of the CVRD epitomizes the central problem of mineiro entrepreneurs—the mobilization of capital. Throughout the first half of the century, mineiro politicians, technocrats, and entrepreneurs had pushed for the creation of an iron and steel industry to take advantage of the state's enormous iron ore reserves. It seemed, however, that only foreign capital would make this possible. European capital funded the Companhia Siderúrgica Belgo Mineira in Sabará, and the firm became the dominant force in the industry, especially after it constructed a new plant in João Monlevade in the mid-1930s. Mineiros had fought tenaciously against the efforts of Percival Farquhar to develop the iron ore around Itabira in the 1920s and 1930s.[78]

In the 1940s, the Vargas regime bargained with the United States and the United Kingdom to cofinance the CVRD. The five-member board of directors would include two members chosen by the United States and the United Kingdom, and Israel Pinheiro became the first president of the CVRD. At the end of the war, both the United States and the United Kingdom backed out of the arrangement, and the company survived only with new capital generated by the state and federal governments. In the late 1940s, the future of this long-awaited mineiro project was still very much in doubt.[79]

The Cidade Industrial was the brainchild of the technocrats at the Secretaria da Agricultura. They hoped to create an industrial pole by using state investment to provide all the infrastructure necessary to attract new industries. After years of fruitless efforts to convince Bond and Share to develop a larger power grid, the government chose to place the Cidade in the município of Contagem, adjacent to Belo Horizonte. That placed the project outside Bond and Share's monopoly in the capital. Although the Cidade was the pet project of Israel Pinheiro, it was inherited by Lucas Lopes when Pinheiro left the Secretaria to head the CVRD in 1943. Benedito Valadares appointed Lucas Lopes to head the Secretaria with specific instructions to inaugurate the Cidade Industrial. (In addition to Lopes's excellent technical credentials his brother-in-law had married Interventor Benedito Valadares's daughter Lúcia.)[80]

In 1941, the government expropriated 270 hectares of land as the location for a hexagonal-shaped industrial park. Pinheiro simply copied the design of the industrial park in Canberra, Australia.[81] The Plan called for the paving of a 35-meter-wide avenue (Avenida Amazonas) to connect the Cidade with the rail terminal in downtown Belo Horizonte. The state government leveled the ground, laid out the streets, and constructed a hydroelectric plant (Gafanhoto) on the Rio Pará some 90 kilometers away to provide the Cidade with 10,000 horsepower. The project achieved only small success in the 1940s. In 1947, there were only ten industries operating with just 1,000 workers. The Companhia de Cimento Portland Itaú was the largest of the firms with a capital stock of some 20,000 contos.[82] By 1960, some 82 industrial firms operated in the Cidade Industrial employing 15,000 workers. By 1967 the number of firms had passed 100 with more than 16,000 employees. By the late 1960s the Cidade had, in effect, become completely saturated with no space left for any new industries.[83]

By the late 1940s, however, the growing influence of mineiro technocrats was pronounced. The *Plano de recuperação econômica e fomento da produção* (1947) represents the first major effort by the mineiro technocracy at economic planning.[84] Technocrats at the Secretaria da Agricultura drew up the *Plano*. Governor Milton Campos had appointed a group of highly qualified technocrats to state offices. Américo Renê Giannetti headed the Secretaria.[85] The *Plano* blamed the backwardness of the mineiro economy on lack of access to the sea, dependence on financial and commercial institutions outside the state, difficult topography, deficiencies in transport systems, increasing infertility of the soils, and highly dispersed industrial production. According to the technocrats, Minas reproduced the general Latin American economic pattern on a small scale: it exported raw materials at low prices and imported expensive manufactured goods. They saw economic centralization and industrialization around Belo Horizonte as the way out of this "colonial economy."[86]

With funds generated by a special tax, the Secretaria sought to implement a series of projects to promote industry and economic growth. As the planners saw it, the keystone to growth was the construction of a hydroelectric power system, and an articulated road system.[87] Cheap electricity and good roads would attract industry and promote economic integration.[88] The *Plano* also called for the creation of agencies to develop fertilizer plants, slaughterhouses for the cattle ranchers, and an industrial park in Santa Luzia (23 kilometers north of Belo Horizonte). Despite serious problems in the implementation of each of the major objectives, the *Plano* established an agenda for economic planners, and it represented the first sustained effort to stimulate industrial concentration around Belo Horizonte.[89]

The Politicians

The emergence of an influential corps of technocrats would not have been possible without the support of the political leaders who brought them into the government, and then increasingly came to accept their vision for the fu-

ture. The long, slow process of the emergence of technocrats and the gradual acceptance of their vision was a journey that began to take shape in the
last decade of the nineteenth century, and did not come to fruition until the
1950s. The process in Minas paralleled a larger process in Rio de Janeiro and
São Paulo. In effect, as the Brazilian coffee exporting economy suffered serious reversals in the first three decades of this century, a small but vocal lobby
emerged arguing for a greater emphasis on industrialization and diversification of the economy. The economic and political crisis of 1929–1930 added
strength to this argument, and brought to power politicians who were increasingly sympathetic to it.[90]

In the 1930s, Getúlio Vargas and his authoritarian republic offered the
first opportunities for intellectuals and technocrats to serve in positions of
influence and power. The impact of World War II on Brazilian trade, the
continuing crisis of the coffee sector, and a growing industrial base shifted
the balance of influence in government by the end of the 1940s. By the
1950s, the country had embarked on the path to full-scale industrialization,
a process stimulated by Vargas, and consolidated by Juscelino Kubitschek in
the late fifties.

The process in Minas paralleled and accompanied the larger shift in the
federal government. When the first Congresso de Agricultura, Comércio e
Indústria met in Belo Horizonte in 1903, it was dominated by the state's
agricultural interests. The backers of industry, however, made a strong case
for promoting industrialization, especially to develop mineiro natural resources. Their cause was greatly helped, no doubt, by the persuasive efforts
of one leading industrialist, João Pinheiro, soon to become the governor. At
the time of the second Congresso in 1924, the industrialists made similar arguments, and their numbers were larger. In 1927, the major business leaders of the state converged on Belo Horizonte for the Congresso das Classes
Conservadoras. These "conservative classes," or "productive classes," as they
liked to call themselves, brought together commercial, agricultural, and industrial leaders in an effort to forge a common set of economic proposals for
the state government, a true sign of the corporatist mentality of the business
elites.[91] The leadership for these congresses was drawn from the Associação
Comercial de Minas and the Sociedade Mineira de Agricultura.

By the fourth Congresso in 1935, the influence of the technocrats in the
Secretaria da Agricultura had become visible.[92] They carefully argued for the
industrialization of agriculture and manufacturing. In a sense, they argued
for the industrialization of mineiro products, whether produced by cattle
ranchers, sugar and coffee planters, or by mining iron ore and bauxite. The
congress declared that "at this moment when we will present many problems

for the consideration of the state government it would be just to give the congress our wholehearted support so that it will be strengthened with the solidarity of the productive classes that may with all rights request the collaboration of the Union and take upon itself the measures within its reach and that are dependent on its deliberation."[93] Business leaders clearly believed that economic development in the state would arise out of a close relationship between the state government and the business elites.

Vargas's handpicked interventor in Minas, Benedito Valadares, played a crucial role in the promotion of industry, a role that has often been overlooked. Between 1933 and 1945, Valadares modernized and reformed the administrative structure of state government, in part to assist Vargas in his efforts to centralize power and weaken the regional power bases of the Old Republic. Israel Pinheiro and his technocrats clearly had the ear of Valadares who once stated that the industrialization of Belo Horizonte was the best place for the "natural development" (*desdobramento natural*) of an active center of commerce. Valadares and Pinheiro, as Dulci has pointed out, believed that agricultural modernization would gradually lead to less imports in the agrarian sector, and then modernization would gradually extend into the industrial sector. They tried to direct government support and resources to those nontraditional areas that needed development in both agriculture and industry. It was Valadares who signed the decree-laws in 1941 to create the Cidade Industrial.[94]

Perhaps the single most important politician in mineiro and Brazilian industrialization in the 1940s and 1950s was Valadares's protege, Juscelino Kubitschek. Born in Diamantina in 1902, Kubitschek is one of the greatest figures in twentieth-century Brazilian politics. The great-grandson of a Czech immigrant on his mother's side, his grandfather, João Nepomuceno Kubitschek, was a prominent political figure in the later imperial period and the first years of the republic. He was elected vice president of the state in 1896. Kubitschek's father died when his son was just two years old, and he and his sister were raised by their mother, a schoolteacher. In his teens, he was educated in a seminary, before attending medical school in Belo Horizonte during World War I. He put himself through medical school working at nights as a telegrapher. A number of the friends he made during medical school in the 1920s would become key political figures in Minas in the succeeding decades. He received his medical degree in 1927.[95]

In the 1920s and 1930s Juscelino practiced medicine in Belo Horizonte, largely in government-appointed positions. When a revolt broke out in São Paulo in 1932 he served as a medical officer in Minas for the government forces. During his service he befriended Benedito Valadares, then an obscure politician from Pará de Minas. Between 1934 and 1937, Kubitschek built a political base in Diamantina and served as a federal deputy. After the 1937 coup imposing the Estado Novo, he returned to full-time medical practice. Much against Kubitschek's wishes, Valadares appointed him *prefeito* of Belo Horizonte in April of 1940. Thus began the career of Juscelino Kubitschek the builder.[96]

"To build is to govern" describes the political career of Juscelino Kubitschek. First as *prefeito* of Belo Horizonte in the forties, then as governor and president of Brazil in the fifties, Kubitschek became the nation's principal industrial promoter. In his presidential campaign in 1955, he announced that during his administration the nation would advance "fifty years in five." In some ways, the career of this remarkable politician can be seen as a lifelong effort to bring together politicians, technocrats, and entrepreneurs, first in Minas, and then in Brazil. Juscelino Kubitschek, in many ways, was the pivotal figure in the creation of a modern, industrial Brazil.

His annual message as governor in 1953 clearly lays out his views on the importance of industrialization.

> Industrialization is the guiding force for the economic development of a populous state with a large potential internal market and endowed with adequate natural resources. . . . State intervention to stimulate the acceleration of industrial investment is thus a logical requirement for underdeveloped regions. . . . When the state works to overcome [bottlenecks], it tends to create "germination factors" capable of stimulating private enterprise on a scale that would not have been possible before the state stepped in. The concentration of state resources, obtained via special taxes and applied in programs of energy and transport, will strengthen the level of investment in basic sectors of the economy, and at the same time, liberate private enterprise of this burden providing it with the incentive for growing investment in industry and agriculture.[97]

During his term as governor in the early fifties (1951–56), his administration concentrated on the famous *binômio energia e transporte*.[98] Taking his cue from the *Plano,* he helped create the Centrais Elétricas de Minas Gerais (CEMIG). With funds from the *Plano's* tax fund CEMIG coordinated and developed the state's electrical energy network. A state enterprise led by an outstanding group of directors with extensive political and business experience, CEMIG became a training ground for technocrats, and quickly gained an international reputation for its high level of technical and political competence. By the late fifties, the company had built up an excess capacity and became a major promoter of industrial development in order to insure continued growth of both supply and demand.[99]

Kubitschek's push to create an integrated state road system not only laid the base for greater economic integration, it also shifted enormous amounts of public resources into the hands of mineiro entrepreneurs. Private companies were given lucrative road-building contracts that allowed them to import machinery and equipment at very favorable exchange rates. The state road-building program was a powerful stimulus in the growth of private construction companies in Minas Gerais. Among the contractors, for example, were Mendes Júnior and Andrade Gutiérrez, both relatively small mineiro enterprises then, but by the 1980s, among the very largest of privately-owned corporations in Latin America. The construction companies built nearly double the 2,000 kilometers of roads projected by the government.[100] The construction of Brasília by Kubischek in the late fifties also helped integrate Belo Horizonte and the Minas transport system with their strategic location midway between the new national capital and Rio de Janeiro and São Paulo.

Kubitschek and the technocrats also made significant efforts to promote industrial investment in the state. In view of the historical shortage of capital investment by local entrepreneurs, they sought to increase investment by the government and by foreign capital. In addition to traditional government spending, the state eventually (1962) created the Banco de Desenvolvimento de Minas Gerais (BDMG). Modeled after the Banco Nacional de Desenvolvimento Econômico, the BDMG would become one of the principal tools for channeling capital to local entrepreneurs, and for attracting foreign investment. Along with the CEMIG, it became a major center for the formation of mineiro technocrats in the 1960s and 1970s.[101]

The Technocrats Again

Long famous (or perhaps notorious) for their political acuity and entrepreneurial failings, the emergence of a technocracy provided mineiros with new opportunities for their talents. Many of the technocrats, particularly those in prominent positions, became "public entrepreneurs."[102] Rather than exerting their influence via elected office or through business in the private sector, these mineiros could shape public policy and the business environment through their appointive positions. Although some prominent figures did spend most or all of their careers as technocrats, others also had careers in business or politics, or both.

Israel Pinheiro da Silva is an outstanding example. One of the original technocrats as Secretário da Agricultura in the 1930s, president of the CVRD in the 1940s, and head of the commission that built Brasília in the

1950s, Pinheiro was also a successful businessman, and was elected governor of Minas Gerais in 1965. José de Magalhães Pinto forged a successful career in banking in the 1930s and 1940s before going into politics. He too was elected governor of Minas (for the term before Pinheiro). In short, just as it is overly simplistic to categorize individuals as members of an economic *or* political elite during the Old Republic, it is equally reductionist and simplistic to attempt to categorize all individuals after the 1930s as politicians *or* technocrats *or* entrepreneurs.

Perhaps the most famous—and archetypal—technocrats were formed by the experience of CEMIG in the 1950s. As Campolina Diniz and Andrade have pointed out, CEMIG became something of a school for technocrats in Minas. The leadership of CEMIG came out of the planners who put together the *Plano de recuperação* in the late 1940s. Following the recommendation of the *Plano,* when Kubitschek became governor in 1951 he created four regional power companies with CEMIG as the holding company. As the first four directors of CEMIG, Kubitschek appointed Pedro Laborne Tavares (former president of the ACM), Mario Penna Bhering, John Reginald Cotrim, and Mauro Thibau. He named Lucas Lopes the company's first president.[103]

In many respects, CEMIG is the classic example of a first-rate state enterprise. This is due, in large part, to the excellence of its founders and to guarantees given to Lucas Lopes that they would be able to operate the company with a minimum of state intervention. Lucas Lopes and his directors became exceptional public entrepreneurs. They set out to construct and unify the electric power grid that had long been the objective of the industrial promoters. As farsighted industrial entrepreneurs they also pursued a policy of expanding power generation ahead of demand to attract new industry that would then create additional demand. In effect, they wanted to stimulate demand to keep the company expanding. CEMIG became one of the most important stimuli to industrial expansion in Belo Horizonte and Minas Gerais.[104]

Three decades of gradual—if weak—industrialization and the enormous difficulties that continued to stymie an industrial breakthrough had produced a fundamental shift in outlook among politicians, technocrats, and entrepreneurs by the early 1960s. By the late 1950s it had become clear that industry provided the route to geopolitical power in the world, and the limitations of the old coffee economy clearly left Brazil at a disadvantage in the world marketplace. This shift had begun to gain speed in the 1930s under Vargas, and accelerate after World War II. Increasingly convinced that industrialization was the only route to a prosperous future, and stimulated by a growing economic nationalism, many Brazilian politicians, technocrats, and entrepreneurs had become convinced of two fundamental notions. First, Brazil must industrialize, and, second, this would be possibly only through state intervention. Enormous differences arose over the extent to which the state should intervene. The economic liberals wanted the state to unleash productive forces by using its power to open up the economy. The nationalists argued that this would quite simply lead to foreign control of all major sectors of the Brazilian economy. They wanted the state to step in and promote key sectors of the economy, through state corporations and protectionism.[105]

In Minas, the weakest link in the most industrialized region of the nation, the interventionist sentiment was even more pronounced. Mineiros not only saw the need for national protection against foreign competition, they also argued for state level protection and intervention to counter the power of Rio de Janeiro, and especially São Paulo. Part of the political genius of Juscelino Kubitschek was his ability to balance the contending forces in this debate. He took the side of the liberals arguing for more foreign investment and greater trade, but sided with the interventionists on the need to protect and foster Brazilian industry.

In many ways, Kubitschek carried out on a national scale in the late fifties the programs he had promoted in Minas in the early fifties. As president, he turned to technocrats to draw up plans for the nation, just as they had done for Minas. The *binômio energia e transporte* became a more ambitious and sweeping *Plano de metas* during his presidency (1956–61). Development banks and state enterprises would provide the public capital for industrialization while foreign capital (primarily from multinational corporations) would also stimulate key industries. Kubitschek became Brazil's great industrial promoter, and the arrival of Volkswagen in the late fifties was his most visible triumph.[106] By the early 1960s, an alliance had emerged—in Minas Gerais and Brazil—among a powerful group of politicians, technocrats, and entrepreneurs. The principal objective of this alliance was to mobilize the capital for industrialization—through public funds or foreign investment, or a combination of the two.

The Entrepreneurs

Despite the powerful emergence of technocrats acting in alliance with politicians, Brazilian and mineiro entrepreneurs did not disappear from the scene. In Minas, even more so than Rio and São Paulo, the historical weakness of entrepreneurs (that is, their inability to mobilize capital) presented them with few options in the 1950s. As the state took an increasingly larger role in the process of industrialization, and as multinational corporations began to enter their territory, mineiro entrepreneurs had four choices: join forces with the state, or with foreign capital, with both, or go it alone. As the amounts of capital needed for the next phase of industrialization increased, few mineiro entrepreneurs could afford to go it alone.

Perhaps the greatest entrepreneur in Minas, Américo Giannetti, became a powerful negative symbol for others who might choose to enter into competition with foreign capital without the support of the federal or state government. Américo Renê Giannetti is one of the legendary figures in the Minas business community. The child of Italian immigrants, Giannetti was born in Rio Grande do Sul. When he was a small child, his father moved the family to Rio Acima, in what would become the municipio of Nova Lima (bordering Belo Horizonte). His father built an iron and steel foundry, Metalúrgica Santo Antônio S.A. Giannetti attended *colégios* in Belo Horizonte, and then graduated from the Escola de Minas in 1923.[107]

More so than any other figure of his era, Giannetti combined the three careers of politician, technocrat, and entrepreneur. From the 1920s to the 1950s he founded and ran a paper factory (Fábrica de Papel Cruzeiro S.A.), a ceramics factory (Cerâmica Santo Antônio), a real estate firm (Imobiliária Mineira S.A.), a construction firm (Companhia Mineira de Estradas e Construções S.A.), a chemical company (Eletro-Química Brasileira S.A.), as well as his father's foundry. At the same time, he built roads and participated in the elaboration of the Plano Rodoviário de Minas Gerais. He formed part of Israel Pinheiro's team of technocrats at the Secretaria da Agricultura in the 1930s, and then served as Secretário under Governor Milton Campos (1947–52). It was under his direction that the *Plano de recuperação* was put together. As if two careers were not enough to keep him busy, Giannetti also took part in electoral politics. He was elected vereador, first in Nova Lima, and then in Belo Horizonte. In 1951 he became the first elected *prefeito* in the city's history.

From 1939 to 1947 he was president of the Federação das Indústrias do Estado de Minas Gerais (FIEMG). Along with Roberto Simonsen and Euvaldo Lodi (a fellow graduate of the Escola de Minas), he served in the Conselho Nacional de Indústrias playing a key role in the creation of the Serviço Social da Indústria (SESI) and the Serviço Nacional de Aprendizagem Industrial (SENAI).[108] During the 1930s and 1940s he also served as a director in the Associação Comercial de Minas (ACM), and as its vice president, and he was president of the Sociedade Mineira de Engenheiros.

Clearly, Giannetti was one of the most active figures of his era, and perhaps no one else of his generation could match his combination of entrepreneurial, technocratic, and political experience. Giannetti's story, however, ends tragically. In the late thirties and early forties, he traveled in Europe and the United States at the request of the federal government to study aluminum production. During the war, he built an aluminum foundry powered by three electric power plants in Rio Acima capable of generating 17,000 horsepower. He accomplished this feat despite constant gasoline and cement shortages and having his original shipment of equipment sunk by a German torpedo in 1943. The plant began operations in March 1945, just as the end of World War II began to reshape the global marketplace. With the end of the war, the price of aluminum dropped abruptly. The administration of Eurico Dutra, for reasons that are not clear, refused to back the company. After several months, Giannetti was forced to halt operations while incurring huge debts. His domestic political enemies (he was a prominent figure in the União Democrática Nacional or UDN) persuaded the Banco do Brasil to block all access to credit over the next decade. Alcoa (Alcan do Brasil) took over the plant and began operating it in 1952 under the name Alumínio Minas Gerais S.A.[109] Giannetti died of a massive heart attack in September 1954 while serving as mayor of Belo Horizonte.[110]

The lesson for mineiro industrial entrepreneurs could not have been any clearer. In the postwar years, attempting to go it alone without government or multinational partners—especially in heavy industry—presented obstacles and challenges beyond the means of most entrepreneurs. If someone with the entrepreneurial talents, technocratic expertise, and political connections of a Giannetti could not go it alone, how could they? Mineiro entrepreneurs would have to associate with government or multinational capital or move into areas that did not challenge multinational corporations.

The careers of Christiano França Teixeira Guimarães offer an equally full life in business, and to a lesser extent in politics. Guimarães is the quintessential figure in the transition from small town Minas in the 1890s to metropolitan Belo Horizonte in the 1970s. As we saw in chapter 3, the Guimarães family from Sete Lagoas originally accumulated its wealth from landholdings, and Christiano's father (Américo) then became one of the pioneers in the textile industry in central Minas Gerais. Born in 1895, Christiano attended the Colégio Mineiro in Ouro Preto and Belo Horizonte, and then graduated from the Escola de Minas in 1909. After several years in Rio learning about the industrial machinery business in Rio, he returned to Belo Horizonte to manage the family's Companhia Industrial de Belo Horizonte.[111]

With the capital accumulated in the textile industry, Guimarães branched into other businesses. In 1917, he was one of the founders of the Companhia Siderúrgica Mineira, the precursor of Belgo Mineira.[112] In 1923, he joined with Sebastião Augusto de Lima and other investors to form the Banco Comércio e Indústria de Minas Gerais, one of the two most important banks in Minas in the next few decades.[113] Along with Oswaldo de Araújo he founded the Companhia de Seguros–Minas Brasil, which Araújo would serve as president for many years. (Araújo was also a founder of the Banco da Lavoura and served on the board of the Banco de Minas Gerais. From 1938–40 he served as the *prefeito* of Belo Horizonte.)[114] Guimarães, in short, was one of the most powerful figures in banking, textiles, and the iron and steel industry, and he remained active in the business community until his death in 1970.

Christiano Guimarães also became the mentor for one of the most successful businessmen and politicians of the postwar period: José de Magalhães Pinto. His is the classic story of the ambitious, bright, hardworking young man who rises through the ranks to extraordinary success. Born in a small town in the Zona da Mata in 1909, his father was a merchant and his mother a schoolteacher. After attending high school in Juiz de Fora, Magalhães Pinto graduated from a business college in 1923 with training in accounting. (In the 1940s he would get a law degree from the Universidade do Brasil.) In 1926 he began working as a clerk in the Banco Hipotecário e Agrícola de Minas Gerais in Juiz de Fora. In 1929 he moved to the Banco da Lavoura de Minas Gerais (today the Banco Real) and was soon promoted to manager of the branch in Belo Horizonte. He was the director of the bank from 1935 to 1943 when he was removed after signing the famous *Manifesto do Mineiros* calling for the return of electoral democracy in the country. Not one to be deterred, Magalhães Pinto then organized his own bank in 1944, the Banco Econômico de Minas Gerais (later Banco Nacional) serving first as director and then later as its president for many years.[115]

Success in banking would be Magalhães Pinto's platform to political and technocratic prominence. He served as president of the ACM in 1938–39, and he was elected a federal deputy four times (1946–63). During the Campos administration he served as Secretário de Finanças (1947–50). Throughout the forties, fifties, and early sixties, Magalhães Pinto fought to reform the state's financial system (especially taxes), and he was a strong advocate of planning. Elected governor in 1960, during his administration he created the Conselho de Desenvolvimento de Minas Gerais (Codemig), which eventually became the Secretaria de Estado do Desenvolvimento Econômico. It was under Magalhães Pinto that the Banco de Desenvolvimento de Minas Gerais (BDMG) was created.

The role of Magalhães Pinto in promoting planning and the creation of state agencies to promote development deserves emphasis. It clearly demonstrates how the ideology of *desenvolvimentismo* transcended political parties.

Magalhães Pinto (like Giannetti) was one of the most powerful and prominent members of the União Democrática Nacional (UDN), which represented the right in postwar Brazilian politics. A banker and successful businessman, he was vehemently opposed to the politics of the left in general, and Getúlio Vargas and João Goulart in particular. Yet, his experience in Minas had convinced him of the need for state planning, and government investment in the economy to stimulate economic growth. In short, many on both the right and left in mineiro and Brazilian politics in the postwar decades agreed on the need for planning and state intervention. They recognized that, for good or bad, the state offered the principal source of capital for investment. In the words of one president of the FIEMG in the late 1940s, "This is our great evil. Credit is conceded as a function of politics and this must stop."[116]

Perhaps the best example of this interventionist mentality was his work to promote the iron and steel industry in Minas. In 1961 he created Metamig (Metais de Minas Gerais), with a combination of public and private capital. The objective of Metamig was to promote the exploitation of the mineral resources of the state, especially iron ore. The idea was one long shared by the mineiro economic and political elites: keep the iron ore in Minas and transform it locally rather than simply exporting it. The state government imposed a tax on iron ore exporters to finance Metamig as well as an Instituto de Minérios e Tecnologia. Magalhães Pinto also strongly pushed state government control of the CVRD, Acesita, and Açominas. Under this political conservative in the early sixties, state planning and state intervention reached unprecedented levels. Politicians and technocrats guided the state's economy with tools that would have astonished their predecessors in the prewar decades.

These men represent the most successful mineiro industrialists of their generation. Some, like Christiano Guimarães, came from well established families, and built on that wealth and success. Others, like Magalhães Pinto, had humbler origins in the commercial class, and rose to national political (as well as state) prominence, and enormous business success. Although the mineiro business elite was almost entirely Brazilian by birth, and overwhelmingly mineiro, immigrants and their children did play an important, if secondary, role in the industrialization of Belo Horizonte and the state. Arthur Haas at the turn of the century, Louis Ensch at midcentury, and Stefan Salej (see Conclusion) at the end of the century are prominent examples of successful immigrant industrialists. Giannetti, Lunardi, and Lodi, three of the greatest names in the process of industrialization, were children of Italian immigrants. Nevertheless, these few prominent examples are the exception to the rule. Belo Horizonte and Minas Gerais are strikingly different than the experience in Rio de Janeiro, and more importantly, São Paulo, where immigrants (and their children) play a central, if not *the* central role in the process of industrialization. Mineiro industrialization is much more insular and much less cosmopolitan than that of its coastal neighbors.

The rise of state and multinational participation in the mineiro economy limited the opportunities of entrepreneurs who wished to go it alone, or even those who allied with foreign and state capital. In the first case, they faced huge obstacles in mobilizing capital and making sure not to compete with more powerful interests. In the second case, they ran the risk of becoming the weakest partner in the public-private-multinational alliance. This may explain why some of the most successful entrepreneurs in Belo Horizonte were in the commercial sector, especially in the retail sector. Many of Belo Horizonte's most prominent businessmen made their fortunes in supplying goods and services, sectors that did not face the initial problems of huge capital investment. The supply of consumer nondurables had long been in the hands of local producers and suppliers, and in the years after World War II, a few prominent businessmen seized opportunities to create large enterprises that dominated the local market. These men provide a striking example to counter the notion of a lack of entrepreneurial skills or ability on the part of mineiros.

Although born in Galicia, Ignacio and Severino Ballesteros settled in Minas and became part of the community. They emigrated to Nova Lima in the 1920s and early 1930s. Both worked in the family bakery and then selling goods at the Morro Velho gold mine. Both eventually moved to Belo Horizonte, Severino in the food processing business, and Ignacio in the shoe business. In the postwar decades Severino built the largest food products company in Minas Gerais, Aymoré, and Ignacio's company (Elmo) became the largest shoe retailer in the state. Both demonstrated that those outside the powerful *tradicionais famílias mineiras* could forge business successes.[117]

The success of Gil Nogueira in the retail grocery business is similar. Born in São José da Varginha in 1931, Nogueira arrived in Belo Horizonte in 1948. After the death of both parents, he and his siblings started a small store that led the creation of other stores. In the early 1960s, he became a pioneer in the creation of supermarkets. His chain of stores, Epa, became the largest food retailer in the state of Minas Gerais.[118] Like the Ballesteros brothers, Gil Nogueira moved into supplying retail goods, beginning small and building capital until he was able to construct a large firm. Both the Ballesteros and Nogueira had the advantage of not having to compete with large, highly capitalized firms from outside the state or nation.

Another equally important opportunity for those with entrepreneurial skills was the public sector. The rise of state enterprises provided business opportunities, if without some of the risks of the traditional entrepreneur. Public entrepreneurs, after all, were not risking their own capital, but that of the state, and should they fail, they could move on without facing complete personal financial disaster. Nevertheless, these men were entrepreneurs. They created or directed corporations, they took risks, and some failed and some succeeded. Arguably, some of these "public" entrepreneurs are among the most successful in the state in this century.

Lucas Lopes is perhaps the quintessential public entrepreneur and technocrat. Born in Ouro Preto in 1911, he went to the Colégio Arnaldo in Belo Horizonte, and then graduated from the Escola de Minas in 1932. He spent a number of years building roads in Minas Gerais, Rio de Janeiro, and western Brazil. Benedito Valadares appointed him Secretário da Agricultura, Indústria, Comércio e Trabalho during the last years of the Estado Novo (1943–45). In the late forties he participated in the construction of the Usina Gafanhoto, the power plant for the Cidade Industrial. When Kubitschek formed the CEMIG in 1952, he called on Lucas Lopes to serve as its first president. Lopes insisted on considerable autonomy for the new directors of the company, and under his guidance the company became one of the most successful corporations in Brazil in the 1950s. He helped establish a corporate culture (albeit a public corporate culture) of entrepreneurial expertise. The CEMIG became a moving force in consolidating the power grid in Minas, and creating excess capacity. In order to keep the company growing, the directors had to create demand, and the most important form was promoting industrial expansion—public and private.[119]

Israel Pinheiro is an equally important example of the public entrepreneur. A successful businessman in the private sector, Pinheiro's leadership at the CVRD and Novacap (the organization to construct Brasília), demonstrated his skills, not only as a technocrat, but also as a public entrepreneur. Many others, not as well-known as Lopes and Pinheiro, would guide the CEMIG, CVRD, Usiminas, and other state corporations in the 1950s and 1960s. With a limited range for movement at the level of big business, the role of public entrepreneur in state-controlled enterprises became an important vehicle for developing the managerial and business skills of the mineiro elite.

Webs of Power

By the mid-1960s, the relationship among politicians, technocrats, and entrepreneurs looked very different from the mid-1940s. The small political elite that had dominated mineiro politics under the Old Republic and the Vargas era had been forced to adjust to mass politics. Across the political spectrum, a powerful nationalism, and more specifically, a powerful developmentalism, permeated the political, technocratic, and business elites. A strong sense of mineirismo inclined even the Right toward government intervention to protect and nurture the state's economy. The small technocratic elite of the 1930s blossomed in the 1950s into a very influential and powerful actor in state politics and the state's economic growth. Their alliance with politicians produced a sustained drive to industrialize Belo Horizonte as the economic center of the state. Entrepreneurs—more specifically industrialists—who could not mobilize sufficient private capital in the prewar years now allied with politicians and technocrats to build the industry that they could not build in earlier decades.

During the postwar decades the ACM and the FIEMG continued to be the most important corporate interest groups for businessmen and industrialists. These two associations served as the principal mechanisms for bringing together the business community and for presenting their grievances to the state and federal governments. The FIEMG was, in the words of one of its original founders, "an institution to defend entrepreneurs when confronting the Government."[120] Although the major political struggles of the century sometimes divided the membership of the associations, they generally refrained from taking public political positions before 1964. In the late 1930s and early 1940s the animosity between Magalhães Pinto and Benedito Valadares led to a major upheaval in the elections within the ACM.[121] Generally, however, the two entities simply cultivated those in power regardless of regime type. In 1938, for example, the leadership of the ACM (including president Magalhães Pinto) fawned over Getúlio Vargas when he appeared at their meeting only months after imposing the Estado Novo dictatorship.[122] With the fall of Vargas in 1945, FIEMG proudly took up the cause of "redemocratization" in its publications.[123]

From the 1940s to the 1960s, the ACM and the FIEMG annual reports and the minutes of the directories generally are filled with very specific grievances—obstacles to economic growth and business operations that the leadership wants the state and federal governments to eliminate. The litany of complaints remains consistent throughout the first six decades of the century: scarcity of key goods such as cement, gasoline, and electricity; high freight rates and poor railway service; inadequate highways and roads; too many taxes; not enough credit; and a constant shortage of currency.[124] In the 1950s, the business community also took up the call for the construction of a pipeline to Belo Horizonte from Rio de Janeiro to end fuel shortages and high gasoline prices. By the end of the decade, rising inflation and currency stabilization also entered the list of key grievances.[125] These became more pressing issues as industry grew and the pursuit of export markets intensified. In 1960, mineiro business and economic leaders came together at the I Congresso Mineiro de Exportação sponsored by the ACM. In many ways, this congress was the successor to the agricultural, commercial, and industrial congresses before 1945.[126]

The influx of multinational capital acted as a further powerful stimulus in conjunction with state capital driving the industrial surge of the 1950s.[127] Multinational corporations became a fourth actor in the state's industrial economy. The so-called triple alliance of multinational, private, and federal capital in Minas took on a fourth partner, state capital. Minas, in effect, forged a quadruple alliance. The activist role of the state government became the critical factor behind the state's growing economic and industrial power in relation to São Paulo and Rio de Janeiro.

Although the state's political leadership had grown larger and more diverse in the era of mass politics, a relatively small elite continued to dominate state politics. The same was true of the state's and the city's business elite. The business elite had grown, but a relatively small group of enterprises dominated the key industries (textiles, iron and steel, construction, mining and minerals processing) and the financial network of public and private banking. In turn, a relatively small elite dominated those key enterprises and industries. The technocracy drew on the families and individuals who in earlier decades had manned the ranks of the political and business elites. It offered an additional career path for the sons of the elite. (Women were still very rare in this select group.)

In many ways the convergence of these three elites is even more pronounced than the convergence of economic and political elites in the Old Republic. As the multiple careers of men like Américo Renê Giannetti and Israel Pinheiro da Silva demonstrate, talented individuals moved easily within the ranks of all three groups. The convergence was sometimes summed up in the careers of a single individual. Even in those who forged single path careers in politics, the technocracy, or business became part of the influential webs of power in Minas Gerais. The elites were not static. They were constantly self-renewing and renovating. The quickest way, however, for newcomers to consolidate their own success was through intermarriage into the older elite families.[128]

In the postwar decades the webs of power became more intertwined quite simply because each of the three groups needed the others. Politicians needed the expertise of the technocrats and the experience of the entrepreneurs. The technocrats needed the politicians to support their programs and ideas, and the entrepreneurs to provide valuable support. Entrepreneurs now understood that they could not survive in the era of interventionism and multinational capital without the support (or at a minimum, the lack of opposition) from the politicians and technocrats who now played the dominant roles in the industrialization of Minas Gerais. The webs of power extended their influence as they grew larger. The converging efforts of politicians, technocrats, and entrepreneurs produced the impressive economic surge in the 1950s, putting Minas Gerais on the path to large-scale industrialization.

By the early sixties, the state had begun to put into place integrated transport and electric power systems, programs and agencies to promote industrial development, and a large industrial park in Belo Horizonte. This industrial park and its surrounding hinterland had become an important producer of intermediate goods, especially steel and cement products, primarily for markets in São Paulo and Rio de Janeiro. In spite of an impressive industrial surge in the fifties, Minas remained heavily dependent on the export of its products to these industrial giants. Furthermore, its industrial growth, while impressive when measured against the state's past, continued to lag behind that of São Paulo and Rio de Janeiro. In the 1950s, the state's share of the value of the nation's industrial production declined (along with that of Rio de Janeiro and Rio Grande do Sul) as São Paulo's own industrial boom left the rest of the country behind. Finally, at the very moment when it seemed that Belo Horizonte and Minas Gerais were ready for a major industrial "takeoff," Brazil entered into the severe political and economic crisis of the 1960s. The city and state would have to wait until a repressive military regime imposed political stability, and until the extraordinary economic surge of the late sixties, before it could resume its industrial expansion at an even more impressive rate.

Chapter 5 ◈

The "Quadruple Alliance," 1960s–1990s

After the 1964 coup d'etat the Brazilian military made industrialization a top priority of the regime. This right-wing, nationalist regime pursued industrialization as a crucial means for making Brazil a "middle power" by the late twentieth century.[1] To ensure economic expansion, the State extended its control over vital sectors of the economy, and assiduously courted foreign investment. In the 1970s, the so-called "triple alliance" of state, local, and foreign (multinational) capital emerged as a powerful force in the Brazilian economy.[2] The convergence of a technocratic regime bent on industrializing the nation and multinational corporations seeking to establish manufacturing subsidiaries in the Third World produced the so-called Brazilian "miracle" of the late sixties and early seventies.

In Minas Gerais this alliance was complicated by two factors. The state government, more so than the national government, played an increasingly prominent role in the economy, and the weakness of local capital was more pronounced than in São Paulo or Rio de Janeiro. The historical capital shortages and later industrial development placed mineiro entrepreneurs behind their counterparts in São Paulo and Rio de Janeiro. As a result, the mineiro state government and multinationals dominated the process of industrialization, and local capital was a very weak leg in the alliance. Despite this weakness, the state and multinationals converged to produce an impressive industrial surge in Minas Gerais in the 1970s, largely concentrated around Belo Horizonte.[3]

In fact, the Minas economy grew at rates exceeding those of the nation and the states of São Paulo and Rio de Janeiro and, by the early 1980s, Minas Gerais was on the verge of surpassing Rio de Janeiro as the second most important industrial state in the nation. By 1990, Minas Gerais had become the second largest state economy surpassing Rio de Janeiro, with each state accounting for about 12.5 percent of the gross domestic product of the nation.[4] In 1960, Minas Gerais was still a largely agrarian state with a growing and dynamic industrial sector. Agriculture still employed 3 out of 5 mineiros and contributed half of the state's income, and 60 percent of the population still lived in rural areas. By 1994, Minas had become a state in full industrialization and 75 percent of the state's inhabitants lived in urban areas.[5]

As Frances Hagopian has pointed out, Minas may be the "purest case of 'state-led capitalist development' in Brazil" during the years of military rule. Selective intervention by the state government into key sectors of the economy guided and managed by a technocratic elite built up the intermediate and capital goods industries. By 1980, Minas Gerais had more state enterprises than any other Brazilian state. All of this in a political system that continued to employ personalism, clientelism, and regionalism, despite the rise of a technocracy.[6]

From the 1960s to the 1990s Greater Belo Horizonte grew at a rapid pace as the city's industrialization and the massive internal migration from rural to urban areas transformed Brazil. The municipio's population nearly doubled between 1960 and 1970, from just under 700,000 inhabitants to more than 1.2 million. The metropolitan area grew from just over 900,000 to nearly 1.7 million.[7] By 1991, the municipio had passed two million inhabitants and the metropolitan area some 3.4 million. One of every five inhabitants of the state lived in Greater Belo Horizonte. The official Região Metropolitana de Belo Horizonte spanned 20 municipios, and its economic pull reached out even farther into central Minas Gerais. By the early 1990s, only the megalopolises of São Paulo (15 million inhabitants) and Rio de Janeiro (10 million inhabitants) surpassed Greater Belo Horizonte in size.[8]

A series of factors converged in the 1970s to produce the rapid industrial expansion that mineiro politicians, technocrats, and entrepreneurs had so anxiously pursued for decades. The state continued to attract industry interested in utilizing its vast resources, especially minerals (iron, bauxite, limestone, uranium). With the expansion of transport, communications, and energy systems after 1950, these resources had become more accessible and easier to exploit. The growth of the metallurgical and cement industries provided basic infrastructure for transforming the raw materials locally for capital goods producers. In addition, the growing market in Minas, and Belo Horizonte's central location between Brasília and the Rio de Janeiro-São Paulo markets also gave the state important locational advantages over other industrial centers. Just as important, mineiro politicians and technocrats aggressively promoted industrialization, offering attractive fiscal incentives and stressing the growth of regional markets. They played on the desire of investors and national policymakers to seek alternatives to the excessive concentration of industry around São Paulo and Rio de Janeiro. In short, basic infrastructure was in place by 1970, and the mineiros did an excellent job selling their state to politicians and investors.[9]

Ironically, the industrial surge in Belo Horizonte and Minas Gerais began at what seemed to the mineiro technocracy to be an extraordinarily unfavorable historical conjuncture. Although the state had built up industry around Belo Horizonte and had made great strides in the expansion of infrastructure in the fifties, the national economic and political crisis of the sixties seemed to have thwarted the technocrats at the very moment the state was poised for takeoff. Technocrats in the Banco de Desenvolvimento de Minas Gerais (BDMG), Centrais Elétricas de Minas Gerais (CEMIG), and two new agencies—the Institute for Industrial Development (INDI) and the Industrial Development Council (CDI)—had achieved broad influence in the government during the sixties culminating in the publication of a comprehensive analysis of the state economy in 1968. Compiled by a team of technocrats at the BDMG, the *Diagnóstico da economia mineira* brought the technocracy to new heights of prestige and influence despite its somber analysis.[10]

The *Diagnóstico* reemphasized the vision of Minas as a colonial economy exploited by São Paulo and Rio de Janeiro, a longstanding complaint of mineiro elites. Minas continued to produce raw materials (and intermediary goods) for Brazil's two major industrial centers, the state continued to lag in the expansion of infrastructure, and mineiro entrepreneurs appeared to be less numerous and less dynamic than their paulista and carioca counterparts. The *Diagnóstico* drew such a bleak portrait of the state's economy that the authors became known as the "prophets of catastrophe."[11] They made a series of recommendations, particularly to centralize and rationalize the state budget, and to promote industrialization through fiscal incentives, measures that would be very successful in the seventies. They also believed that industry had become too densely concentrated around Belo Horizonte, and recommended a program of deconcentration and the creation of additional industrial poles.[12] The drive to make Belo Horizonte a growth pole had become too successful.

Although the "prophets" did not realize it, their pessimistic analysis came at the very moment that Belo Horizonte and Minas Gerais were about to embark on their most impressive phase of industrial expansion yet. Between

1970 and 1977 industry in Minas grew at an annual rate of 16.4 percent compared to 6.9 percent per annum during the 1960s. For the first time in this century, São Paulo's share of national industrial production dropped while the mineiro share rose. This rapid industrial expansion was propelled forward by strong state intervention and multinational investment. More than 70 foreign firms invested a total of $1.25 billion in plants in Minas between 1970–77. The state probably received a quarter of all foreign industrial investment in Brazil during these years, even though at the beginning of the decade Minas accounted for just seven percent of Brazil's industrial production. The state government probably provided close to 65 percent of all industrial investment, foreign capital another 20 percent, and private local capital 15 percent.[13]

Despite the warnings of the technocrats, the concentration of industry around Belo Horizonte continued and intensified. By 1974, the region around Greater Belo Horizonte accounted for 73 percent of the state's industrial output, up from 68 percent just four years before.[14] Greater Belo Horizonte absorbed more than 80 percent of all new industrial investment in the period 1970–77, and one-third of the investments handed out by INDI between 1969–80. In the 1970s, the metropolitan area of Belo Horizonte produced one-third of all new employment in the state.[15]

The growth of industry also transformed the municipios surrounding Belo Horizonte and rearranged the industrial landscape of Greater Belo Horizonte. By the late 1960s, the Cidade Industrial had finally fulfilled the dreams of Israel Pinheiro. The municipio of Contagem was second only to the municipio of Belo Horizonte in the number of industrial workers as a result of the growth of the Cidade Industrial to more than 100 firms employing nearly 20,000 workers. (91 of the 117 firms had entered Contagem between 1956 and 1967.) More than half of these workers were concentrated in the metallurgical, mechanical, and electrical industries. Another 25 percent were employed in construction and the textile industries. This workforce was also overwhelmingly masculine, some 17,393 of 18,748 (or 93 percent!) of the workers were men.[16]

The arrival of Fiat in the neighboring muncipio of Betim (analyzed below) also transformed that small and rural area into an industrial city that would surpass both Belo Horizonte and Contagem in the value of its industrial production in the 1990s. By the 1990s, Belo Horizonte, Betim, and Contagem had become the powerful industrial heartland of Greater Belo Horizonte and the state of Minas Gerais. São Paulo may have its famed industrial heartland in its ABC (Santo André, São Bernardo, São Caetano) paulista. The industrial heartland of Minas is its BBC (Belo Horizonte, Betim, Contagem).

As table 5.1 shows, Belo Horizonte's share of the state's industrial production nearly doubled between 1949 and 1980. In some industries (non-metallic minerals, chemicals, and "all other") more than half of all production came from the Belo Horizonte metropolitan area. The structure of industry in the city and state also shifted between 1949 and 1980 (see table 5.2) from production of predominantly nondurable consumer goods (such as food and clothing) in the forties, to the production of intermediate, capital, and durable goods (such as auto parts, automobiles, and machinery). Dozens of foreign corporations from the United States, England, Italy, France, Germany, Japan, Canada, Denmark, Sweden, Switzerland, and Belgium built plants in Minas Gerais attracted by the state's fiscal incentives and infrastructural improvements.

In the most prominent example, Fiat built an industrial complex in Greater Belo Horizonte (Betim), the Italian company's first automobile assembly plant outside of Europe. Governor Israel Pinheiro had begun to woo Fiat in the late sixties, and this process continued under Governor Rondon Pacheco in the early seventies.[17] In 1973 the state government gave the company two hundred hectares of land at rock bottom prices, did the

Table 5.1 **Participation of Greater Belo Horizonte in the Industrial Production of Minas Gerais (in percent)**

	1949	1959	1980
All industrial	19.7	29.7	34.5
Food processing			6.8
Textiles			17.1
Mining			19.7
Leather, wood, clothing			20.8
Metallurgy			29.0
Nonmetallic minerals			46.1
Chemicals			52.7
All other			65.7

Notes: Greater Belo Horizonte includes the municipios of Belo Horizonte, Betim, Caeté, Capim Branco, Contagem, Esmeraldas, Ibirité, José de Melo, Lagoa Santa, Matozinhos, Nova Lima, Pedro Leopoldo, Prudente de Morais, Raposos, Ribeirão das Neves, Rio Acima, Sabará, Santa Luzia, Taquaraçú de Minas, and Vespasiano.
"All other" includes mechanical, electrical, transport, furniture, paper, rubber, pharmaceuticals, plastics, drinks, tobacco, perfume, soap, publishing, and the census category "diverse."
Sources: Censo industrial [de 1950], v. III, t. 1, 93–94; *Censo industrial de 1960,* v. III, t. IV, 91–92; *Censo industrial: dados gerais. Minas Gerais,* v. 16, 66–74.

Table 5.2 Structure of Manufacturing Industries in Minas Gerais, 1949–1980
(in percent)

	1949	1959	1970	1980
Nondurable consumer	76.0	60.2	37.4	29.1
Intermediate consumer	20.5	33.7	50.4	55.1
Capital and durable	2.4	5.0	8.9	13.5
Diverse	1.1	1.1	3.3	2.3
Totals	100.0	100.0	100.0	100.0

Sources: *Censo industrial [de 1980],* v. 16, 2–3; *Minas Gerais: indicadores sócio-econômicos, 1950–1980* (Belo Horizonte: SEPLAN, 1983), 260.

Table 5.3 Ten Largest Firms in Minas Gerais, 1987

Firm	Ranking in Brazil	Dominant Type of Capital
Aço Minas Gerais S.A. (Açominas)	14	State
Cia. Energética Minas Gerais (Cemig)	19	State
Usinas Siderúrgicas Minas Gerais S.A. (Usiminas)	32	State/Japanese
Cia. Siderúrgica Belgo Mineira	34	Luxembourg
Construtora Andrade Gutiérrez S.A.	35	Private
Alcoa Alumínio S.A.	45	U.S.
Construtora Mendes Júnior S.A.	47	Private
Cia. Aços Especiais Itabira S.A. (Acesita)	48	State
Fiat Automóveis S.A.	71	State/Italian
Mannesmann S.A.	72	German

Note: Rank by book value of 200 largest firms in Brasil.
Source: "As 200 maiores empresas do Brasil," *Visão* (2 September 1987), 61–2.

earthmoving work for the company, built connecting roads, installed an electric power plant, a water system, telephone lines, and sanitation systems. In addition, the state provided 46 percent of the Brazilian subsidiary's capital, and extended a wide range of tax breaks and fiscal incentives. The combined value of the state's incentives and direct investment was around $350 million.[18] The state liquidated its financial interest in Fiat in 1988, ironically for just $150 million, or much less than the initial investment.[19]

In effect, the state government acted as the promoter and guarantor of foreign capital in new industries, especially in the Zona Metalúrgica around the state capital. Entrepreneurs in Minas Gerais played an important role in the industrial surge, but took a back seat to the state and foreign capital. Of the ten largest firms in Minas Gerais in the late 1980s, three were state controlled, two were jointly controlled by state and multinational capital, and three were controlled by multinationals. Just two, both construction firms, were controlled by private capital. (See table 5.3.) Of the 50 largest firms in the state, 31 had their headquarters in Belo Horizonte, and another 6 in the surrounding municipios (Sabará, Caeté, Pedro Leopoldo, Betim, Contagem).[20]

The patterns of industrialization from the mid-1960s to the mid-1990s are clear. After the economic slowdown of the sixties, the mineiro economy surged in the seventies, before the debt crisis of the eighties once again pushed the Brazilian economy into stagnation, recession, and inflation. In the 1990s the Brazilian and mineiro economies rebounded and experienced growth, although not the clear industrial surge of the fifties and seventies. Furthermore, as we shall see in the concluding chapter, the nineties mark a shift to a new economic era with neoliberal economic policies including privatization of state-controlled corporations, a new and massive influx of foreign direct investment, and reduced government intervention.

The industrial surge of the seventies arose out of the combined efforts of politicians, technocrats, and (to a much lesser extent) entrepreneurs to mobilize public and multinational capital. Technocrats, with the strong support of politicians under an authoritarian military regime, played perhaps the central role in planning and promoting this industrial surge.

They had their greatest successes in developing sectors of the economy that built on Minas's natural resource advantages: iron and steel, cement, automobiles and auto parts, and construction. The electric power industry continued to play a vital role in economic growth. Textiles and food processing remained important, but increasingly less so to the core of the state and city's economy. The industrialization of the seventies did not fundamentally reorient the Minas economy, it accelerated the trends of previous decades. In the words of Andrade, the process did not alter the "character of the state industrial structure but its rhythm of growth."[21] Finally, despite important efforts to decentralize industrialization by creating secondary industrial poles, Greater Belo Horizonte and its hinterland increased its dominance and importance as the heart of the state's industrial economy. The industrialization of the seventies heightened the regional disparities within the state.

Banking and finance grew and expanded, both in the private and the public sectors. The traditional mineiro banks became more prominent and powerful, the state created a development bank, and the federal government also provided new sources of capital. These private and public banks provided much of the capital for the key industries, which ranged from state-controlled to mixed private and public capital to privately-owned (by either Brazilian or foreign capital). At the one end of the capital continuum was the electric power industry dominated by CEMIG, a state controlled enterprise. At the other were food processing, textiles, cement, and banking, which were overwhelmingly in the hands of local entrepreneurs. In between were the iron and steel corporations and the automotive industries that combined both private foreign capital and state participation.

Key Industries

Five traditional industries continued to play key roles in Belo Horizonte and Minas Gerais into the 1990s: textiles, iron and steel, electric power, mining and minerals processing, and food processing. Two other industries rose to prominence in these years, one with roots in the expansion of the 1950s (construction) and the other building on the successful iron and steel industry (automotive). By the 1980s metallurgical industries accounted for 31.8 percent of the value of all industrial production, up from 12.6 percent in the 1960 census, and easily the single largest sector in the mineiro economy. Food processing and textiles, two of the longstanding key sectors of the state's economy, continued to lose ground in relative terms. The former had accounted for nearly half of the value of all industrial production in 1960, but had dropped to 20.9 percent by 1980, still the second largest sector of the industrial economy. Textiles, the second largest industry in 1960, had dropped to 6.5 percent by 1980, the sixth largest industrial sector. (Leather, wood, and clothing production also continued to decline in size.) In contrast, industries linked to the state's natural resources base flourished after 1960—chemicals, nonmetallic minerals, and mining each accounted for seven-nine percent of all industrial production. In essence, these shifts reflected a move away from the textile and food processing economy of the early twentieth century to a more diversified industrial economy by the end of the century, but one based on the transformation of natural resources: iron ore, bauxite, manganese, limestone, phosphates, gold, and other minerals.

The seven key industrial sectors that dominated the city and the state's economy were, in turn, dominated by a relatively small group of firms in each sector. In 1984, of the 25 largest (nonfinancial) firms with their headquarters in Belo Horizonte, six were metallurgical companies, four mining companies, another four construction firms, and another five were state en-

Table 5.4 Industrial Structure of Minas Gerais, 1919–1980 (percent of value of
         production by industry)

Industry	1919	1940	1960	1980
Food processing	51.5	34.1	48.9	20.9
Textiles	29.7	14.4	15.5	6.5
Metallurgy	2.3	20.0	12.6	31.8
Leather, wood, clothing	9.9	7.9	7.0	2.5
Chemicals	1.3	1.9	1.1	8.9
Non-metallic minerals	—	3.3	4.4	7.2
Mining	—	5.0	2.8	7.4
Other	5.3	13.4	7.7	14.8
Totals	100.0	100.0	100.0	100.0

Sources: Recenseamento de 1920, v. 5, pt. 1, pp. 394–5; *Censo industrial [de 1940]*, pt. XIII, t. 3,
p. 475; *Censo industrial [de 1960]*, v. III, t. IV, p. 69; *Censo industrial [de 1980]*, v. 16, p. 2.

terprises such as CEMIG and TELEMIG (the state telecommunications
monopoly).[22] The industrial surge of the seventies and the economic growth
of the nineties reinforced the longstanding pattern of concentration within
each industry. Well into the 1990s the electric power industry was essentially
the domain of a state enterprise—CEMIG. Until the privatization wave of
the nineties, the iron and steel industry was dominated by a handful of state-
controlled firms (Usiminas, Acesita, Açominas, CVRD) and multinational
corporations (Belgo Mineira, Mannesmann). Fiat quite clearly dominated
the automotive industry.

Mining and minerals processing, textiles, construction, and food processing were dominated by a small group of firms under the control of
mineiro or Brazilian entrepreneurs. The textile industry in both Minas
Gerais and the old Zona Metalúrgica was still dominated by a small group
of firms, most of whom had their origins in the late nineteenth century and
continued to be family owned. With a few exceptions, the "newer" firms had
been founded before World War II. Eight of the 14 largest firms in the state
had their roots in the Zona Metalúrgica, and they accounted for more than
half of the revenue of the industry. At the state level a shift had occurred with
the decline of the old industry in Juiz de Fora and the rise of modern plants
in the Norte, primarily to take advantage of tax breaks given to firms investing in the blighted São Francisco River Valley region.[23]

The mining and minerals processing industry is even more exclusive,
with a handful of firms dominating the sector. One oddity of this industry

is that two of the giants, the CVRD and Minerações Brasileiras Reunidas (MBR), both have their headquarters in Rio de Janeiro although most of their operations take place in the iron ore fields of Minas Gerais. They are the two largest iron mining operations in the country. Until the 1990s, the CVRD was a state enterprise. The other two major firms—Samitri and Socoimex—both are a combination of Brazilian and multinational capital. Samitri was a subsidiary of Belgo Mineira and Socoimex was formed in the early 1950s by private capital to carry iron ore for the CVRD.[24] Three large, private firms control the production of cement in central Minas—Portland Itaú, Cauê, and Soeicom. Magnesita, another privately held family firm, controls the heat resistant ceramics industry.[25]

Although there are a large number of construction firms in central Minas, the huge family-owned multinational, Andrade Gutierrez, accounts for one-third of the revenues of 65 largest firms in the state. The second largest firm, Construtel, has revenues that are just a quarter of those of Andrade Gutierrez. Likewise, in the food processing industry, one that has historically been pulverized into hundreds of small firms producing for local markets, concentration has taken place in the last three decades. In central Minas, the family controlled Aymoré has become the giant, with several bottling companies accounting for the other major firms (Antarctica, Kaiser, Refrigerantes Minas).[26]

The economy of both the state and Greater Belo Horizonte in by the 1980s and 1990s was more diverse, but a few sectors formed the core of the industrial economy, and a small number of firms dominated each of these sectors. Consequently, a relatively small business and technocratic elite ran the major industrial enterprises in Greater Belo Horizonte and its surrounding region. Remarkably, most of the private firms remained under family control into the 1990s. In the cases of the most powerful firms controlled by the state and by multinational capital, the leadership of these firms still came primarily from elite mineiro families. Executives of state and multinational firms often came from the same pool of people circulating through technocratic, political, or corporate positions.

Electric Power

The principal industry with the most direct state participation in this period was, again, electric power generation. Juscelino Kubitschek's creation from the early 1950s had become a fundamental piece of the process of industrialization by the early 1960s. By 1960, CEMIG was generating just over 1,000,000 Gwh, exactly one-third of all electrical power generated in the state. This figure tripled by 1970 to 3,500,000 Gwh, again, one-third of state production. Slightly more than another third of production came from a CEMIG spin-off, Furnas Centrais Eletricas S/A. By 1986, CEMIG was generating nearly 26,000,000 Gwh, Furnas another 26,000,000 Gwh, accounting for virtually all electrical power generated in the state.[27] By 1994, CEMIG had 31 generating plants on rivers across the state.[28] In early 2000, CEMIG hooked up its five millionth consumer.[29]

Part of this expansion came from the continual construction of new hydroelectric plants, and, to a lesser extent it came from swallowing up preexisting privately-owned companies. In 1967, CEMIG took over the Companhia Sul Mineira de Eletricidade. In 1972, it took over the old and infamous Companhia Força e Luz de Minas Gerais, and finally began supplying power to Belo Horizonte after more than 40 years of dissatisfaction with the electric power supply in the municipio. In 1981, CEMIG swallowed up Bernardo Mascarenhas's old Companhia Mineira de Eletricidade.[30] In effect, the state constructed an electrical holding company in the fifties and sixties, and in the seventies and eighties used it to consolidate control of virtually all electric power generation. This approach guaranteed control over a vital input for industrialization, and eliminated the possibility of problems like those created by Força e Luz in the 1930s and 1940s. It also meant that the company pursued the policy of building generating plants rather than focusing on the distribution of electrical power.[31]

Mineiro politicians and technocrats were acutely aware of the importance of electric power for industrial development, and of the relative backwardness of the state's power grid in comparison with Rio and São Paulo. In 1953, then-Governor Kubitschek justified the creation of CEMIG partly to solve the "chronic scarcity of power" in the state, and partly in anticipation of growing power shortages in its two neighboring states. Juscelino played to mineiro pride, arguing that the "creation of a strongly based electric power system" in Minas would eventually allow Minas to sell power to its neighbors. In short, the state of Minas Gerais and CEMIG pursued what Judith Tendler has called "pre-emptive power development." By the late 1960s, the growing supply of electric power was attracting industry to Minas, CEMIG was selling excess power to its neighbors, and its rates were among the lowest in Brazil.[32]

Although the company had more than 40 hydroelectric plants by 1986, four (Tres Marias, Jaguara, Volta Grande, and São Simão) accounted for 80 percent of all power generated.[33] Industry continued to be the principal consumer of electric power generated by the state. In 1960, industry consumed 65 percent of all electric power and commercial operations another

9 percent. By 1970, these figures were 68 and 7 percent, and, by 1980, 77 and 5 percent. Furthermore, the ten largest industries in the state accounted for around 80 percent of all industrial consumption (Usiminas, Aluminas, Mannesmann, Belgo Mineira, the Companhia Siderúrgica Nacional, and several cement producers).[34] In short, over these years the state consolidated its position as the producer of huge amounts of hydroelectric power primarily for a handful of metallurgical and cement enterprises. The vision of politicians (principally Kubitschek) and technocrats (such as Lucas Lopes and João Camilo Penna) had come true by the 1980s—the state had created the electric power generating system needed to spur industrialization.

CEMIG had achieved such success by the 1970s for two important reasons: the state recruited an outstanding group of technocrats and then largely left them alone to build their company. The careers of the five original managers are indicative of the quality of CEMIG's technocrats. John Cotrim later became president of Furnas, Flávio Lyra its technical director, and Benedicto Dutra its commercial director. Mauro Thibau became the military regime's first Minister of Mines and Energy in 1964 and Dutra his chief of staff. Mário Bhering became president of Eletrobrás in 1967, and Lucas Lopes served as Minister of Finance under Kubitschek (among other important posts in the 1970s and 1980s).[35] Again, according to Tendler,

> In Brazilian power circles there was one point on which opposing sides always agreed. The Light and the anti-foreign-company nationalists, the *privatistas* and the *estatistas* (those against and in favor of state-sponsored power), the World Bank and the Brazilian Development Bank—all said that Minas Gerais' state power company, CEMIG, was one of the best run enterprises in Brazil.[36]

Much like the CVRD, CEMIG stands out as preeminent example of a successful state enterprise. Its constant process of expansion since the 1950s has been one of the driving forces in mineiro industrialization. Without the guarantees of increased power generation from CEMIG, the state government would have had a very difficult time over the past 40 years trying to attract foreign capital and industry to the state. Like the CVRD, despite its success and excellence, the state government decided in the early nineties to privatize CEMIG. Although one-third interest was sold to Southern Electric in 1998 under Governor Eduardo Azeredo, the government of Governor Itamar Franco (1999–) has blocked efforts to pass control of the company to a foreign corporation.

Iron and Steel

Much of the energy produced supplied the most important industry in Minas Gerais, iron and steel production. By the 1960s, a handful large state-controlled firms and multinationals that supplied big manufacturers (such as auto plants) dominated the iron and steel industry. A handful of small producers (founded primarily in the early 1950s) supplied smaller, regional firms. (See table 5.5.) Usiminas and Acesita (both state enterprises), Belgo Mineira, Mannesmann, and the Companhia Ferro Brasileiro (all foreign owned), along with Queiroz Júnior (local private capital) accounted for 96 percent of the workforce in the industry. Four smaller, locally-owned firms in the area around Belo Horizonte employed the other 4 percent.

The industry grew at a rapid pace after the military coup. The regime's push for domestic industrialization and the growing demand for iron and steel products that arose out of the new economic model promoted growth in the industry, and reinforced the predominance of state and foreign capital. In the late seventies and early eighties, Brazil's iron and steel industry experienced phenomenal growth. The country moved from its status as a net importer to a net exporter in most iron and steel products. By the late 1980s, the Brazilian steel industry consisted of some eight state-controlled firms and 31 private companies. The state firms produced 68 percent of all crude steel, and two foreign-owned firms produced another 9 percent (Mannesmann and Belgo Mineira). Mineiro plants (Usiminas, Acesita, Açominas, Pains, Mannesmann, Belgo Mineira, and Mendes Júnior, Itaunense) accounted for one-third of Brazil's crude steel production.[37]

Some 70 firms produced pig iron in Minas Gerais in the late 1980s, with two-thirds of production concentrated in the region around the município of Belo Horizonte. Five of the firms were in Greater Belo Horizonte, and another 52 were in the surrounding region (Metalurgica and Campos das Vertentes). Sete Lagoas alone was home to some 20 firms, accounting for nearly 40 percent of the state's production. Another 15 firms in Divinópolis comprised 12 percent of production. The largest firms in central Minas, as measured by installed capacity, were located in Pitanguí, Sete Lagoas, Contagem, Betim, and Itaúna.[38] Minas produced 29 percent of Brazil's pig iron, and nearly 90 percent of the production was concentrated in the Zona Metalúrgica. The mineiro foundries produced primarily auto parts and other types of machine parts.[39]

The powerful construction firm, Mendes Júnior, had bought up the old Queiroz plant that dated from the late nineteenth century, and Belgo Mineira was the fruit of the first venture of foreign capital into Minas in the

1920s. Usiminas, Mannesmann, Pains, and Acesita were the fruits of state and foreign investment from the 1950s and 1960s.[40] Usiminas, in particular, represented the merger of state and multinational capital. Nippon Steel Corporation designed the plant in Ipatinga in the late 1950s and early 1960s, and continued to provide technical assistance over the next three decades. The technology at the plant was on a level comparable to Japanese plants of the same scale. From its construction in the 1950s to the 1980s, 70 to 80 percent of all machinery and equipment were imported.[41]

By the 1980s Usiminas supplied 80 percent of the flat steel used in the production of railway cars in Brazil, and 60 percent of that used in automobiles and shipbuilding. The company transformed iron ore from the old Itabira Mine (Farquhar's old holdings) some 100 kilometers away, and purchased manganese ore and dolomite from areas around Belo Horizonte some 225 kilometers from Ipatinga. Japanese participation in the company (both in capital investment and management) decreased throughout the 1970s and 1980s as Brazilian technocrats developed the company into the largest integrated iron and steel operation in Brazil.[42]

In the 1970s and 1980s the process of state and multinational capital was reinforced with the expansion of state enterprises (Usiminas, Açominas, Acesita) as well as growth of Mannesmann and Belgo Mineira. With the move toward privatization and neoliberalism in the 1990s, the state government auctioned off Usiminas, Açominas, and Acesita, ending 40 years of state intervention in the iron and steel industry.

Usiminas is a classic example of the importance of political and kinship networks, and the convergence of foreign and state capital to produce a very successful state-controlled enterprise. Since the beginning of the century mineiro elites had yearned for the construction of an iron and steel mill in Minas. The founders of the Companhia Siderúrgica Mineira (Christiano Teixeira Guimarães, Amaro Lanari, Gil Guatimosim, and Ovídio de Andrade) had tried to make this dream a reality, but had to settle for handing over control of their young firm to foreign capital and Belgo Mineira in the 1920s. Vargas's decision to locate the Companhia Siderúrgica Nacional in Volta Redonda angered and disappointed the mineiro elites, and they clearly believed that Vargas's help in bringing Mannesmann to Belo Horizonte in the early 1950s was his way of settling accounts with them.[43] Yet, these elites, especially the business and technocratic elites pushed hard in the 1950s for the construction of a large-scale, integrated iron and steel mill in Minas. The FIEMG asked Dermeval José Pimenta (the second president of the CVRD) and a young economist, Jayme de Andrade Peconick, to produce a study on the feasibility of building such a mill.[44]

The proposed company, Usinas Siderúrgicas de Minas Gerais S.A., became a reality when Nippon Steel was persuaded to put up 40 percent of the investment. (Most of the rest came from the Banco Nacional de Desenvolvimento Econômico.) To head the new company, Juscelino Kubitschek, by now the president of Brazil, chose Amaro Lanari Júnior, the son of one of the founders of the CSM. The elder Lanari was born in Argentina of an Italian father and a mother from Rio Grande do Sul. He married into the Andrada family in southern Minas, one of the most traditional and powerful families in the state. (Governor Antônio Carlos was its most prominent representative in the mid-twentieth century.) Like his father, Lanari Júnior was trained as an engineer at the Escola de Minas and his early training came building roads in western Brazil, alongside Lucas Lopes, his brother-in-law. His great-uncle was Carlos Wigg, the founder of an early iron foundry. Throughout his long career, Lanari Júnior was perhaps the most entrepreneurial technocrat of his generation. Kubitschek named Lanari to the presidency of Acesita in 1957 to provide him some experience in running a steel company so he would be ready when Usiminas became a reality. In 1958 Kubitschek personally selected him to become the first president of Usiminas, a position he would hold until 1976, when he was succeeded by Rondon Pacheco, the former military-appointed governor of Minas Gerais. According to Lanari, the project would never have been possible without the support and encouragement of Juscelino.[45]

Usiminas officially came into existence in April 1956 with a list of founders that is a virtual list of the mineiro and *belorizontino* business, technocratic, and political elite. Among others the original board of directors included Lídio Lunardi (president of FIEMG), João Ewerton Quadros (president of the Banco Mineiro da Produção), Antônio Mourão Guimarães (Magnesita), Júlio Soares (brother-in-law of Juscelino Kubitschek), Gil Guatimosim (a founder of Belgo Mineira), José de Lima Barcelos (later state secretary of public works under Israel Pinheiro), Gabriel Janot Pacheco (a key figure in Usiminas), and Paulo Macedo Gontijo (a former president of FIEMG). And the list goes on and on.[46]

A commission of Japanese technicians chose to locate the plant in the iron ore zone at Ipatinga, some 200 kilometers to the east of Belo Horizonte on the route of the CVRD's railway to Vitória. Two factors (in addition to the location of the ore reserves) determined the location of the plant: the railway that would bring coal in from abroad, and, more importantly, the proximity of CEMIG's Salto Grande hydroelectric plant. CEMIG would provide the electricity, and the CVRD would be able to fill up empty railway cars with coal shipments after delivering its iron ore to ships in Vitória.

Unlike CEMIG, rather than build the plant using a foreign construction firm, Lanari and Usiminas contracted Brazilian firms to build the plant under Japanese guidance. All the important technology came from Europe, Japan, and the United States. Although Usiminas did create a research and development department (Centro de Pesquisas) in the 1970s, it focused on adapting the foreign technology to local conditions.[47] Like Lanari Júnior and Rondon Pacheco, most of the directors, and the presidents of Usiminas (while under state control) came from the small mineiro technocratic and political elites.[48]

Açominas and Acesita were also the creations of the state and federal governments, and eventually became substantial producers, but never achieved the financial and managerial stability of Usiminas. Both companies arose out of the longstanding mineiro dream that created Usiminas, the desire to convert the state's natural resources into manufactured products on local soil rather than exporting ore to be transformed in Rio de Janeiro, São Paulo, or abroad. Although created by the military regime in 1966, Açominas faced enormous difficulties building its first mill, despite large loans contracted abroad. It was not until the mid-1980s that the company inaugurated its plant in Ouro Branco near the colonial capital, Ouro Preto. In the early 1990s, Açominas was producing two million tons of steel, about one-fifth of national production, and exporting 60 percent to 25 countries on five continents. The company was privatized in 1993.[49] It was under the presidency of Miguel Augusto Gonçalves de Souza that Açominas became a reality. Part of the Gonçalves de Souza clan from Itaúna that had helped build and dominate the textile industry in central Minas, Miguel Augusto held several cabinet positions during the governorship of Magalhães Pinto, was president of the ACM (1963–65), president of Credireal (1975–79), and president of Fiat (1979–83) before assuming the presidency of Açominas in 1984. He also managed the family textile and iron and steel businesses. In short, he combined the careers of entrepreneur and technocrat.[50]

As we have already seen, Acesita (Aços Especiais Itabira) began as a private enterprise in the 1940s largely out of the initiative of the much maligned Percival Farquhar. In the early 1950s financial problems led the Banco do Brasil to take over control creating another state-owned iron and steel firm. Like all the other major industrial firms, electric power played a crucial role in its location and development. The company built an enormous hydroelectric plant (Sá Carvalho) in 1951. As with the other firms, Acesita was built and rebuilt over the decades with European, U.S., and Japanese technology. Like the Belgo Mineira works at João Monlevade, and the Usiminas mill (later) in Ipatinga, Acesita set up operations in the iron ore zone, along the Vale do Rio Doce (to capture its hydroelectric potential), and on the railway from Belo Horizonte to Vitória to take advantage of the transportation corridor.[51]

Acesita began to expand and thrive only after President Vargas named Edmundo Macedo Soares e Silva to run the company. Born in the old federal district of Rio de Janeiro in 1901, Macedo Soares was a classic combination of technocrat and politician. Trained as an army officer, he participated in the lieutenants' (*tenentes*) revolt in 1922 and eventually went off into exile in France where he trained as a metallurgical engineer. With the triumph of Vargas in the 1930s, Macedo Soares became a key figure in the iron and steel industry, as the first technical director of the CSN and later as its president. He served on the boards of many iron and steel firms including Mannesmann and Belgo Mineira. Elected the governor of Rio de Janeiro (1946–51), he later became the minister of industry and commerce in the late 1960s under the military regime.[52] Macedo Soares also turned to German and U.S. technical assistance and technology.

Financial problems plagued the company from the late fifties to the early seventies. Under the leadership of Amaro Lanari Guatimosim (Amaro Lanari's nephew and Amaro Lanari Júnior's cousin) in the seventies. Acesita experienced its most impressive expansion. Like Belgo Mineira, Acesita used charcoal for its operations and had to embark upon a massive forestry program to supply its plant. The leadership of Acesita, following the old pattern, generally came from the mineiro elites. After Macedo Soares stepped down as president in 1957, Amaro Lanari Júnior assumed the presidency. Between 1958 and 1961 two political appointees served as president. Dermeval José Pimenta (1961–64), one of the founders of the CVRD and key figures in the creation of Usiminas, ran the company. Guatimosim (1972–81) continued his family's tradition of leadership in the industry. Francelino Pereira dos Santos, the military-appointed governor of Minas (1979–83), took over in 1983–84 to be followed by Oswaldo Pieruccetti (1984–85), the former military-appointed mayor of Belo Horizonte (1971–75). Clearly, it was a small world of technocrats and politicians who cycled through these key state firms.[53]

By the mid-1970s the iron and steel industry in Minas was not only at the heart of the state's economic expansion, but at the core of Brazil's industrial development. Mineiro plants accounted for two-thirds of all pig iron production, half of all iron bars (*ferro-ligas*), and 40 percent of steel bars and plates.[54] By the early nineties the state produced 42 percent of all raw steel and 47 percent of the nation's steel plate. Usiminas and Açominas alone accounted for two-thirds of the raw steel production.[55]

Table 5.5 Largest Iron and Steel Firms in Minas Gerais, 1998

Firm	Revenue (in $1,000)	Ownership
Usiminas	1,806,496	Brazilian
Açominas	615,450	Brazilian
Acesita	583,704	Brazilian
Mannesmann	451,688	German
Belgo Mineira	451,237	Luxembourg
Total revenue	3,908,575	
Total for 41 largest metalurgical firms	6,451,591	
Share of top 5	60.6%	

Sources: Balanço anual, Minas Gerais 5:5 (October 1998: 69–70.

Textiles

Textiles remained the most traditional of all mineiro industries into the 1990s. Cedro e Cachoeira, Santanense, and Itaunense alone—three firms dating back to the end of the nineteenth and the beginning of the twentieth century—accounted for 35 percent of the revenues of the 31 largest textile firms in the state. All three remained in the hands of the original families (Mascarenhas and Gonçalves de Souza). The Mascarenhas family also controlled Cedronorte, Estamparia, and Cachoeira Velonorte. Even the companies in the North, despite the location of their factories, were controlled by families in Belo Horizonte. The number of firms had dropped by nearly half since the 1960s and would continue to decline in the 1990s with increased foreign competition coming from reduced tariff barriers.[56]

As the Brazilian economy opened up and globalization spread in the 1990s, the textile industry faced a serious shakedown. Between 1989 and 1994 the number of textile firms in Brazil declined by 12 percent. The Southeast (Minas Gerais, Rio de Janeiro, and São Paulo) dominated the national industry, accounting for three-quarters of all firms. (The South was a distant second with under 20 percent of all firms.) Textiles remained an industry with an enormous number of small, highly dispersed, and specialized enterprises. Virtually all the large firms with a significant market share were integrated firms combining spinning and weaving (less than 100 firms). The vast majority of these firms consumed cotton or polyester.[57]

In Minas Gerais and the rest of Brazil the restructuring required the importation of the latest technology from Japan and Europe, and a massive reduction of the labor force. Between 1989 and 1994 the number of workers in the industry dropped from more than a million to around 500,000, a massive readjustment. Textile entrepreneurs increased their installed capacity by nearly 50 percent in the same period. They pointedly complained of the high interest rates they paid for new technology, as well as the import duties they faced. The largest companies in Brazil and Minas Gerais experienced a profound process of integration of all phases of spinning, weaving, and clothing production to achieve economies of scale.[58]

Although part of the robust industry in the Southeast, by the mid-1990s Minas produced just 8 percent of the national production, and largely for the domestic market. Some 53 companies accounted for most of the industry's production in Minas Gerais. Thirty-six of these firms were controlled by local capital, another sixteen by other Brazilian corporations, and just one was controlled by foreign capital. As in the late nineteenth century, most of these key firms and their factories were located in the region around Belo Horizonte and in the Zona da Mata. Some two dozen were in Greater Belo Horizonte and its economic zone of influence.

The most aggressive and dynamic of the firms in the 1990s was Coteminas, formed in the 1960s by José Alencar Gomes da Silva. A native of Muriaé, he came from a merchant family and was the eleventh of 15 children. (His paternal grandfather was Portuguese and his maternal grandfather a Spaniard.) In the 1950s he began merchandising cloth goods, and in 1964 opened his own factory. He formed Coteminas in Montes Claros in 1967 as well as another firm (Cotene) in Natal.[59] In this period he, and other entrepreneurs, took advantage of tax incentives to build factories in the underdeveloped North of Minas. Silva built very modern plants in this zone and his company quickly became the second largest firm in the state. He also became the president of the FIEMG and a major player in state industrial policy. Although his factories were located in the North, his business enterprises were all based in Belo Horizonte.

This oldest and most traditional of mineiro industries faced a major transition at the end of the twentieth century as family-controlled firms faced stiff foreign competition from imports. Technological restructuring (through imported machinery) and managerial innovation were the biggest issues facing the mineiro textile industry. As the 1990s came to a close, even the largest and most traditional firms, such as those controlled by the Mascarenhas and Gonçalves de Souza families, were moving toward the hiring of professional managers and association with foreign capital (or both). With the end of more than a century of protection and the opening of the national economy, the textile industry faced a serious restructuring at the beginning of the twenty-first century.[60]

Table 5.6 Major Textile Firms in Minas Gerais, 1998

Name	Revenues (R$ milhões)	Region
Cedro e Cachoeira	128,026	Metalúrgica
Coteminas	107,351	North
Santanense	90,321	Metalúrgica
São José Tecelagem	47,229	Metalúrgica
Itaunense	38,379	Metalúrgica
Cataguases	33,676	Mata
Renascença	32,494	Metalúrgica
Cedronorte	30,375	North
Estamparia	27,865	Metalúrgica
Santa Helena	27,447	North
Manufatora	25,536	Mata
Divinópolis	18,134	Metalúrgica
Cachoeira Velonorte	14,739	Metalúrgica
Itabirito	14,255	Metalúrgica
São Joanense	13,138	Metalúrgica
A = total revenues (top 15)	648,965	
B = total revenues (top 30)	715,817	
A / B	91%	

Source: Balanço anual, Minas Gerais 5:5 (October 1998: 66–7.

Mining and Minerals Processing

Although companies mine more than three dozen minerals in Minas Gerais, generating some 30,000 jobs and accounting for a third of the value of the nation's mineral production, iron mining dominates the industry, especially in central Minas around Belo Horizonte. About three dozen iron mining firms account for 80 percent of the value of all mineral production and nearly 100 percent of all minerals exports from the state. Within the iron mining industry, the CVRD, MBR, Samitri, Ferteco, and Samarco dominate. In 1998, the 20 largest mining firms in the state accounted for nearly all production, and three firms—Samarco, Samitri, and Fósfertil (a fertilizer producer)—accounted for more than 80 percent of all the industry's revenues. The two iron mining companies—Samarco and Samitri—brought in nearly 55 percent of the industry's revenues. In the early 1990s, the CVRD produced nearly two-thirds of all iron ore exports, MBR close to 20 percent, with Samarco, Ferteco, and Samitri accounting for virtually the rest of all iron ore exports.[61] Although the CVRD, MBR, and Ferteco have the core of their mining operations in Minas Gerais, and are the three largest operations, their headquarters are in Rio de Janeiro. Ferteco (R$318,281,000) is slightly larger than Samarco (R$274,398,000) in revenue, MBR (R$474,049,000) is almost twice as large, and the CVRD dwarfs the other major firms with more than R$3 billion in revenue in 1998![62]

The CVRD, MBR, and Ferteco have long drawn their leadership from both Minas and other regions of Brazil, especially São Paulo and Rio de Janeiro. As private corporations, MBR and Ferteco have combined the capital and expertise of Brazilian entrepreneurs (the Antunes family in the case of MBR) with foreign managers. Samarco and Samitri, both firms based in Minas have drawn primarily on their parent corporations for leadership. Joseph Hein, for example, the head of Belgo Mineira, also headed the board of directors for Samitri, its subsidiary.

Cement dominates the mineral processing industry in Minas, and a small group of private firms control the production of cement in Minas—Portland Itaú, Cauê, CIMINAS, and Soeicom. As pointed out in the last chapter, the Companhia de Cimento Portland Itaú was one of the first to set up operations in the Cidade Industrial. Controlled by a small group of families, the company began operations in Itaú de Minas, Passos in 1937. In the 1950s, Itaú expanded under the leadership of José Balbino de Siqueira and the Souza Meireles family. The prominent politician and ex-presidential candidate, Christiano Machado, became a board member in 1952, and Benedito Valadares became the president of the board in 1964. In the late 1970s, the paulista entrepreneur, José Ermírio de Morais, gained control of the company and moved its headquarters to São Paulo. In the 1980s and 1990s, the Gonçalves de Souza family (of textile fame) controlled the board of directors.[63]

The Companhia de Cimento Portland Cauê is one of the classic family-owned industrial firms in Minas Gerais and Belo Horizonte. Founded by Juventino Dias in the 1940s, it began operating in the early 1950s, and today is the second-largest cement producer in the state (with revenues about a third of those of Itaú). From humble rural origins, Dias embarked on a career in retail commerce in Paraopeba, then Sabará, Caeté, and Santa Bárbara before moving to Belo Horizonte in the 1920s. Along with Sebastião Augusto de Lima, Christiano Guimarães, and José de Castro Magalhães he helped found the Banco de Comércio e Indústria de Minas Gerais. He was also one of the founders of the Banco de Minas Gerais. In the 1930s he was one of the cofounders of the Companhia Renascença Industrial. In 1938 he joined with the most powerful businessmen—Christiano Guimarães, Benjamim Ferreira Guimarães, José de Magalhães Pinto—in Belo Horizonte to form the Companhia de Seguros Minas-Brasil. (Today the company controls about 80 percent of the insurance coverage issued by mineiro firms.)[64] For his entrepreneurial achievements in the postwar period, the state government named the Cidade Industrial after Dias.

CIMINAS (Cimento Nacional de Minas S/A) has a factory in Pedro Leopoldo to the north of Belo Horizonte. Inaugurated in 1975, the factory uses technology imported from Denmark (by F. L. Smidth). Like the rest of the industry, the factory was built to supply not only the demand in Minas Gerais, but also São Paulo, Rio de Janeiro, the Federal District, and Goiás. As with the cement industry in Minas in general, CIMINAS took advantage of the locational advantages of the state—minerals, plentiful electricity, rail and road connections to the southeastern markets, and a state government anxious to promote industrial development.[65] By 1975 the cement industry in the state was producing over four million tons of Portland cement. By 1994, this figure had risen to more than six million tons or one-quarter of the nation's production. São Paulo (5 million tons) and Rio de Janeiro (2 million) and Paraná (2 million) account for nearly 40 percent of Brazil's cement production.[66]

The other major firm in the minerals processing industry is Magnesita, another privately-held family firm, that controls the heat-resistant-ceramics industry.[67] Magnesita produces one-third of national exports in the refractories industry. Originally founded in Rio de Janeiro, in 1945 Magnesita moved its headquarters to Belo Horizonte to take advantage of the mineral deposits in the region. The company built the first factory in Latin America to produce refractory materials. The central figure in the company's development was Antônio Mourão Guimarães, another major figure among mineiro entrepreneurs. His father, Benjamim Ferreira Guimarães (1861–1948), came from humble origins, and like Juventino Dias began his career in retail commerce. Beginning in Valença, Rio de Janeiro, Ferreira Guimarães founded a series of textile firms throughout Minas Gerais and Rio de Janeiro. He also founded a navigation company on the São Francisco River, and purchased control of the Passagem gold mine in Mariana.[68]

Antônio Mourão Guimarães was born in Bom Successo in 1888 and studied pharmacy in Ouro Preto and medicine in Rio de Janeiro before returning to open a medical practice in Belo Horizonte. He served as secretary of agriculture, industry, commerce, and labor briefly in 1945–46. In the late 1940s he was elected to the state legislature. Most of his life, however, was dedicated to business enterprises, principally Magnesita. In addition, he helped run a series of family businesses, including a real estate firm (Companhia Predial Ferreira Guimarães), the Renascença textile factory, the Companhia Seguros Minas-Brasil, and a series of cinemas (Companhia Cine-Brasileira). He and his son, Flávio Pentagna Guimarães, ran the family's principal financial enterprise, the Banco de Minas Gerais. Like his father, Flávio served as secretary of industry and commerce (1988–90).[69]

Automobiles

From the 1970s to the 1990s the concentration in the automotive industry is more dramatic and pronounced than any other large sector of mineiro industry. In essence, Fiat was the automotive industry in Minas until the late 1990s, and the Italian company had become the largest and most important industry in the state, and the largest foreign corporation in Brazil (overtaking Volkswagen).[70] What had begun as a joint venture between Fiat of Italy and the state government of Minas Gerais in the 1970s, had become a hugely successful industry without any government participation by the 1990s. Fiat's enormous plant in Betim has spun off more than 40 plants that manufacture and supply Fiat with auto parts. Most of these plants are in the Greater Belo Horizonte region.[71]

When Fiat began building its plant in the municipio in 1974 Betim had a population of less than 40,000. Today the plant employs some 20,000 people and the municipio is approaching 300,000 inhabitants. Betim has also become the mineiro municipio with the highest industrial production in the state, surpassing both neighboring Contagem and Belo Horizonte.[72] In 1999, Fiat produced 400,000 vehicles accounting for 32 percent of automobile production in Brazil making it the largest automaker in the country. The company exported 103,000 of these vehicles, or nearly half of all Brazil's automobile exports. Revenues approached US$3 billion. Between 1998 and 2000 Fiat invested more than US$2 billion expanding its operations, most notably a light truck plant in a joint venture with Iveco in Sete Lagoas and the addition of a new motor factory at its Betim plant.[73] As with auto plants around the world, the Betim plant has spawned dozens of smaller plants in the surrounding region to supply auto parts to the plant with its "just in time" philosophy. Clearly, Fiat has been the greatest success of the industrial recruiters, creating a multibillion dollar industry concentrated in Greater Belo Horizonte.

Although controlled by the parent corporation in Italy, Fiat in Minas has drawn on the regional business elite for its leadership since its inception in the 1970s. Until the withdrawal of the state government from financial participation in the company in the 1980s, Fiat always selected prominent members of the local elite to serve as president of the board of directors. The first president (1973–79), Adolfo Neves Martins da Costa, for example, came from a traditional mineiro elite family, and twice served as president of the Associação Comercial de Minas (1969–70 and 1971–72). Trained as a civil engineer, he had broad experience in the construction industry in the 1950s and 1960s.[74] Miguel Augusto Gonçalves de Souza, the second president (1979–83), was a member of the venerable textile family from Itaúna, in between stints as president of Credireal Bank (1975–79) and Açominas (1984–85).[75]

Cássio José Monteiro França, president in 1986–87 is a classic example of the intertwining of local business, political, and technocratic networks with this major multinational. A native of Belo Horizonte (b. 1926), França began his business career as the head of the Rio office of the venerable Companhia Industrial de Belo Horizonte in the 1940s and 1950s. Director-superintendent of the União Brasileira Distribuidora de Tecidos (1958–81), he also became a director of Credireal (Banco de Crédito Real de Minas Gerais S.A.) in the late seventies. Governor Francelino Pereira dos Santos named him president of Credireal in 1982. He was also president of the Banco de Desenvolvimento de Minas Gerais in 1986, before assuming the presidency of Fiat.[76] França is the epitome of the late twentieth-century mineiro business executive working for private, public, and multinational firms.

Politicians and Technocrats

Clearly, the most important fact of political life in Minas Gerais and Brazil until the mid-1980s was military rule. From the coup that overthrew João Goulart in 1964 until the inauguration of José Sarney in 1985, the military dominated political and economic affairs. Frustrated with traditional politics and political parties, the armed forces turned to what some scholars have called the "politics of anti-politics."[77] Central to their drive to remake the national polity, the generals wanted to replace clientelism, personalism, and regionalism with a depoliticized system built on planning, technocracy, and efficiency. Many observers, including critics of the dictatorship, believed that an authoritarian regime offered the best chance to put into place a technocracy, and to eliminate traditional politics.

The military's efforts stimulated scholars to produce a sizable literature on so-called bureaucratic-authoritarian regimes (especially in the southern cone), and the rise of a technocratic elite.[78] In Minas, two of the technocratic elite wrote important works analyzing the changing nature of the state economy and the rise of a technocracy.[79] In particular, Luís Aureliano Gama de Andrade's unpublished dissertation traces the rise of a technocratic elite in Minas. Andrade asserts that, "It is only against the background of increasing technocratization of the state—concentrated in the so-called indirect sector—that the transformation of the Minas economy can be apprehended and fully understood."[80]

Although the technocrats clearly came into their own under the military regime, and Andrade is right about the importance of the emergence of an influential technocratic elite, Frances Hagopian very effectively demonstrates that the traditional politics of clientelism and personalism survived and thrived. She shows that "traditional politicians survived in top state posts to an even greater extent than did politicians without roots in traditional families." The state political elite was "subtly reconfigured" and "modernized" under military rule. The political elite "was better educated and qualified at the end of the authoritarian regime than it was at its outset; sons of oligarchical families became engineers, and its traditional politicians were willing to work with the technical elite to manage the affairs of state. The elite, like clientelism, underwent some necessary degree of 'modernization.'"[81]

In short, by the mid-1980s, after two decades of authoritarian politics and state-led economic growth, a modernized version of clientelism, elite family networks, and regionalism characterized Minas Gerais. Andrade was right to trace the rise of technocrats to roles of increasing prominence by the 1980s, but Minas Gerais was not a technocracy. Clientelistic politicians continued to make the most important decisions, most importantly, who would fill the crucial technocratic posts. Mass politics after World War II, and military rule from the mid-1960s to the mid-1980s had transformed Minas, but regionally-based elite family networks employing clientelism continued to dominate a "modernized" state politics.

An important shift had taken place, however, in the training and professionalization of the technocrats. In the 1930s and 1940s key technocrats were overwhelmingly trained as engineers, especially in the Escola de Minas. Beginning in the 1950s, and increasingly after the 1960s, the technocrats were trained in economics.[82] In the early 1940s, prominent local entrepreneurs and politicians founded two schools of economics as offshoots of local schools of commerce. The two schools merged in 1945 to form the Faculdade de Ciências Econômicas e Administrativas (FACE). Among the founders of the Faculdade were Américo Giannetti (then president of the FIEMG), Antônio Mourão Guimarães (president of the Banco de Minas Gerais), Sandoval Soares de Azevedo (president of the Banco de Crédito Real), Cristiano Guimarães (president of the Banco do Comércio e Indústria de Minas Gerais), Caetano de Vasconcelos (president of the Federação do Comércio and past president of the ACM), and Paulo Macedo Gontijo (president of the ACM).[83] In 1948, the Faculdade was incorporated into the Universidade Federal de Minas Gerais (UFMG). The FACE became *the* intellectual and academic center for the training of economists in the fifties and sixties, and created "a cohesive and aggressive group, aware of its special condition as an elite."[84]

The FACE trained the majority of the technocrats who would staff the Banco de Desenvolvimento de Minas Gerais, created under the Magalhães Pinto administration in 1962. The Banco had been created by politicians after businessmen—especially industrialists from the FIEMG—had grown increasingly frustrated with the Banco do Brasil and the Banco de Desenvolvimento Econômico (BNDE). The mineiro business community had been unsuccessful in convincing the BNDE to establish a branch office in Belo Horizonte in the late fifties. Governor Magalhães Pinto, in fact, had been one of the key businessmen in the fifties who had complained about the lack of public financing available for mineiro entrepreneurs.[85]

The Banco de Desenvolvimento had three vague principal objectives. The first was "to influence the creation of a new mentality—objective and achievement-oriented—so that the insufficiencies related to the entrepreneurial aptitude in the state can be overcome."[86] The second was to pursue planning and research on the mineiro economy, while the third was to invest directly, primarily in small and medium-size businesses. In 1963 and 1964, the bank organized *Jornadas de Desenvolvimento* in three dozen cities across the state. These "journeys" aimed to identify entrepreneurs, make them aware of the bank's programs, and awaken "entrepreneurial vocations." The bank's strategy clearly aimed at fostering economic growth in Minas by focusing on the small enterprise and the mineiro entrepreneur.[87]

The bank did not become an important and crucial force in mineiro industrialization until the appointment of Hindemburgo Chateaubriand Pereira Diniz as its president in 1967. His career is the epitome of the importance of kinship to politics and the technocracy. Although born in Paraíba, Diniz had married the daughter of Governor Israel Pinheiro, providing ties of kinship that would give him exceptional access to state power during his presidency.[88] Ambitious and young (35), Diniz reoriented the bank's programs away from the small business and toward the large enterprise. Furthermore, the bank increased its role in the state economy through the creation of new initiatives.

In partnership with CEMIG, the BDMG created the Instituto de Desenvolvimento Industrial (INDI).[89] Along with the new Conselho de Desenvolvimento Industrial (CDI) and the Instituto Latinoamericano de

Planificación Económica y Social (ILPES), the bank signed an agreement to work together to promote comprehensive planning for the state. Finally, Diniz created the Fundação João Pinheiro (FJP), an institute to undertake research and planning for the state and the private sector. In 1970, Diniz left the presidency of the BDMG to become the first president of the FJP.[90]

While concentrated in the Secretaria da Agricultura before the fifties, thereafter state agencies became the training ground of technocrats. The CEMIG in the fifties and the Banco de Desenvolvimento de Minas Gerais after 1962 were the principal training grounds for the elite technocrats. By the 1970s they were key players in many government agencies, especially the Gabinete de Planejamento e Controle of the CDI, the INDI, the FJP, and the Secretaria da Fazenda.

Andrade's study astutely analyzes a revolution in state government and planning that takes place in the late sixties and early seventies. This revolution was built on the decades of work done by earlier generations of technocrats—from the Secretaria da Agricultura in the 1930s and 1940s, to CEMIG in the 1950s, the BDMG in the 1960s, culminating in the creation of the state Finance Department in 1971. By the 1970s, a series of institutions formed the nuclei of the technocratic elite: CEMIG, INDI, the CDI, and the BDMG. Ultimately, two tendencies emerged. Economists on the CDI who advocated comprehensive planning, and what Andrade labels as "opportunistic planners" centered in the Finance Department with allies at INDI, CEMIG, and the BDMG.[91]

Planners at the BDMG had originally made the most powerful case for comprehensive planning with their *Plano Mineiro de Desenvolvimento Econômico e Social* in 1971. Heavily influenced by the consulting assistance of the Instituto Latinoamericano de Planificación Económica y Social (an offshoot of the United Nation's Economic Commission for Latin America—ECLA—in Santiago, Chile), the *Plano* became the first true comprehensive document in the state's long history of planning. In effect, it echoed the earlier analyses of the *Plano de recuperação* (1947) and the *Diagnóstico* (1968). Like those documents, it stressed the historic backwardness of the mineiro economy relative to São Paulo and Rio de Janeiro, emphasizing the disadvantages of geography, the tendency to export resources, or barely transform them. It noted the low integration of the state's industrial structure, the decline of agriculture, and the enormous regional disparities within the state. Most importantly, the *PMDES* called for a complete overhaul of state government institutions to promote industrialization and economic growth. The planners singled out the need to increase exports of iron ore, coffee, livestock, and to promote Minas as an alternative to the industrial concentration of the southeastern coast.[92] Minas Gerais in 1970, although the fourth largest exporter of all Brazilian states, accounted for less than 10 percent of Brazil's exports, while São Paulo accounted for more than a third.[93]

The state Finance Department took a different approach, one that ultimately triumphed over the calls for comprehensive planning. Created in 1971 to bring order to the longstanding chaos in state finances, the Department quickly asserted central control over state revenues and spending under the direction of Fernando Reis. Like so many of the technocrats, Reis had been trained at the Faculdade de Ciências Econômicas (FACE) of the Universidade Federal de Minas Gerais (UFMG). He became an economist for the Associação Comercial and the BDMG in the sixties. As the editor of the *Diagnóstico,* he was one of the "prophets of catastrophe." Newly-appointed Governor Rondon Pacheco named him to be Secretário da Fazenda in 1971 (at the age of 38).[94]

Rather than attempting the task of remaking the state's institutions, and facing the possibility of bruising bureaucratic infighting with so many interest groups and institutions, Reis and his team sought "to gain access to the state resources and control their use. The reform of the Department, and not the restructuring of the entire *mineiro* public sector, was their ultimate institutional goal."[95] As Andrade points out, this was politically realistic and a viable form of strategic planning that helped produce the enormous successes of the industrial surge of the seventies. Comprehensive planning failed. It simply had too many adversaries, and the technocrats did not have the power to assert control over all sectors of the bureaucracy.[96]

Although technocrats exerted growing and powerful influence over the formulation and implementation of economic policy after 1964, they owed their power and influence to politicians. Without the support of politicians to create new institutions and to implement the policies in the various plans, the technocrats would not have been able to emerge and thrive. As Hagopian points out, however, despite the emergence of a technocratic elite, Minas was not run by a technocracy in the seventies. The technocrats reached the height of their influence in the first half of the seventies, but they never created a true technocracy. While the technocrats exerted enormous influence within the state agencies, especially those that formulated economic policy, the politicians retained control over patronage. Traditional politics and politicians survived the efforts of the military regime to install a technocracy. Rather than creating a technocracy, the new technocratic elite emerged and developed in conjunction with the clientelism of traditional politics.

The military regime did change politics in important ways in Minas Gerais. By weakening parties and the electoral process, the generals concentrated power in the hands of the technocrats and the executive branch. Governors became even more powerful than in the previous two decades. In some ways, the regime represented a return to the centralization of the 1930s and early 1940s under Vargas. Although family ties and kinship networks diminished in importance after 1945, they remained important determinants of power and influence. Of the 14 governors between 1946–99, ten had ties or direct roots in the traditional elite families, and the other four were newcomers. (Francelino Pereira dos Santos and Newton Cardoso were natives of the Northeast who had married into local families and become proteges of powerful political and economic figures.) The election of Eduardo Azeredo in 1994 and Itamar Franco in 1999 hearkened back to traditional mineiro state politics. Azeredo's family has deep roots in Sete Lagoas and Belo Horizonte, while Franco's political base is in Juiz de Fora. Despite political changes, a diversification of the elites, and economic globalization, these two elections are symbolic of the continuing persistence of the political power of traditional families with roots in mineiro politics dating back to the mid-nineteenth century.

Although law remains the usual training for the political elite, including governors, a subtle change did take place beginning in the mid-1960s. Three of the governors between 1966 and 1999 were trained as engineers (Israel Pinheiro, Aureliano Chaves, and Eduardo Azeredo). Although they both eventually completed law degrees, José de Magalhães Pinto and Newton Cardoso both essentially received their professional training in the world of business. Roughly half of the governors during this half-century era were out of the traditional law and politics career pattern.

Even more so than the years of the First Republic, governors were men of multiple careers, even when politics was their primary career. Kubitschek worked as a physician well into his political career. Pinheiro, as already noted, moved between the worlds of the entrepreneur, technocrat, and politician. Garcia has coffee and construction firms. Newton Cardoso, in particular, has been so deeply engaged in both politics and business that he has frequently been accused of using his public offices and influence for private gain. Finally, Eduardo Azeredo worked for IBM throughout the seventies as a systems analyst before spending most of the eighties as a technocrat running a variety of data processing agencies for the state. His political career did not really begin until he turned 40.

Furthermore, many politicians and technocrats moved back and forth between the two careers. Hagopian found that 27 percent of the members of

Table 5.7 Governors of Minas Gerais, 1946–1999

Name	Term of Office
Milton Soares Campos	1946–51
Juscelino Kubitschek de Oliveira	1951–56
José Francisco Bias Fortes	1956–61
Jose de Magalhães Pinto	1961–66
Israel Pinheiro da Silva	1966–71
Rondon Pacheco	1971–75
Antônio Aureliano Chaves de Mendonça	1975–79
Francelino Pereira dos Santos	1979–83
Tancredo de Almeida Neves	1983–85
Hélio Carvalho Garcia	1985–87
Newton Cardoso	1987–91
Hélio Carvalho Garcia	1991–95
Eduardo de Brandão Azeredo	1995–99
Itamar Franco	1999–

Note: Does not include names of those who served as interim governors for brief periods.
Source: "Lista de governadores de Minas Gerais e prefeitos de Belo Horizonte, 1897–1992,"
APCBH.

the mineiro political elite in the three decades after 1964 "served at some point as directors, presidents, or board members of state banks."[97] Positions in state agencies became an effective means of patronage, a temporary reward for a political ally who had lost an election and was in need of a new base of operations. The age-old clientelistic practice of *empreguismo,* in fact, not only did not disappear with military rule, it flourished, and would even more so after the return of civilians to power in 1985. Between early 1984 and early 1988, for example, expenditures for "employees of the direct public administration increased 90 percent in real terms."[98] Politicians throughout Brazil turned to *empreguismo* with such gusto in a time of numerous elections in the late eighties that some states in the Northeast found themselves with personnel payrolls that surpassed their total state revenues.[99]

The careers of the mayors (both appointed and elected) of Belo Horizonte also demonstrate the ease with which members of the elite moved between politics, business, and the technocracy. Some, like Oswaldo Pieruccetti, were primarily politicians. When the military regime removed the elected mayor, Jorge Carone Filho, in 1965, they replaced him with Pieruccetti. Although he completed high school in Belo Horizonte at the very traditional Ginásio Mineiro, Pieruccetti moved to Araguarí in the

Table 5.8 Mayors of Belo Horizonte, 1947–1997

Name	Term of Office
Elected	
Otacílio Negrão de Lima	1947–51
Américo Renê Giannetti	1951–54
Sebastião de Brito[a]	1954–55
Celso Melo de Azevedo	1955–59
Amintas de Barros	1959–63
Jorge Carone Filho[b]	1963–65
Appointed	
Oswaldo Pieruccetti	1965–67
Luís Gonzaga de Sousa Lima	1967–71
Oswaldo Pieruccetti	1971–75
Luiz Verano	1975–79
Maurício Campos	1979–82
Júlio Laender	1982–83
Elected	
Hélio Garcia	1983–84
Rui Lage[c]	1984–85
Sérgio Ferrara	1986–88
João Pimenta da Veiga Filho	1989–90
Eduardo Azeredo[d]	1990–92
Patrus Ananias de Sousa	1993–96
Célio de Castro	1997–

Notes: [a]Finished out term after sudden death of Giannetti.
[b]Removed from office.
[c]Named to finish term of Garcia who became governor.
[d]Completed term of Pimenta da Veiga when he stepped down to run for governor.

Triângulo where he became mayor (1948–51). He entered the state legislature in the 1950s for the UDN. He became president of the UDN in Minas
and under Governor Magalhães Pinto was named Secretary of the Interior
and Justice and then president of Credireal. He was a key figure in the con-
spiracy in Minas to bring down the Goulart government. Pieruccetti served
two terms as mayor (1965–67 and 1971–75).[100]

Luiz Verano and Rui Lage, on the other hand, moved among all three
worlds with careers in business, technocracy, and politics. From Itajubá in
southern Minas, Verano (b. 1912) was trained as an engineer, worked for
Acesita in the 1950s before going to work for Amaro Lanari Júnior at

Usiminas in 1958. He became a major figure on the Usiminas board before becoming state secretary of industry under Governor Aureliano Chaves, and then mayor of Belo Horizonte (1975–79).[101] Lage is a native of Belo Horizonte, and made his fortune in the financial world and real estate. When Hélio Garcia was elected governor in 1984 he stepped down as mayor of Belo Horizonte and named Lage to finish out his term. He then served terms as president of Agrimisa (Banco Agrícola de Minas Gerais S.A.) and Copasa (Companhia de Águas e Saneamento de Minas Gerais), both important state-controlled firms.[102]

The rapid growth and urbanization of Belo Horizonte, and the era of mass politics, had diminished the role of elite family networks in the two decades after World War II, but these networks remained strong—both in the economic and political arenas. Likewise, traditional clientelism with its rural roots in the small towns of Minas had been transformed with the growth of cities and communications, but had taken on modern, urban forms. Technocrats had become more prominent and influential, but the state was still run using updated forms of traditional politics. The role of entrepreneurs had also changed.

Entrepreneurs

Long the weakest and most maligned link in the industrialization of Belo Horizonte, entrepreneurs saw their world transformed with the rise of military rule in Brazil. They both gained and lost by the influx of multinational capital. On the one hand, their inability to mobilize the resources needed for the next stage of industrialization made them welcome the influx of both public and private funds, even if the latter were foreign. The perspective of Nansen Araujo in an editorial in the FIEMG's official monthly magazine sums up a commonly held view among mineiro industrialists.

> The simple example of Volkswagen is indisputable testimony to the value and fertility produced by non-Brazilian funds sent here to stay. It is known that the factory does not return to Germany even the smallest fraction of the fabulous quantities that are invested in São Paulo. Its 25,000 workers represent bread for 100,000 persons as each worker feeds four persons.[103]

Mineiro entrepreneurs very often benefited enormously as foreign corporations turned to local businesses for joint ventures, or even just Brazilian nationals as convenient front men for their subsidiaries. Some entrepreneurs would become true partners of foreign capital shaping the contours of the industrialization of Belo Horizonte and Minas Gerais. On the other hand, the secondary role played by these allies of foreign capital provided eloquent testimony to the failure of mineiro entrepreneurs (for whatever reasons) to achieve the next level of industrialization on their own. In other words, foreign capital filled the economic space that mineiro entrepreneurs had long hoped to create and occupy.

The mineiro business community wholeheartedly embraced the military coup of 1964, and many key figures actively worked to bring down the Goulart presidency.[104] The ACM "manifested its applause and solidarity with the armed forces" and supported "the principles of the Revolutionary High Command" in aftermath of the coup.[105] The FIEMG, in collaboration with the army, formed a "group for industrial mobilization" to work jointly with the military so solve the nation's problems.[106] Yet, the mineiro business elite quickly became disillusioned with national leadership and the perception that Rio de Janeiro and São Paulo were being favored in the regime's drive to industrialize.

As we have seen throughout this study, this sense of inferiority and backwardness in comparison with its two powerful neighborhoods has long plagued Minas Gerais. In the early sixties, one member of the ACM summed up elite dissatisfaction when he said that

> In Brazil, there had been created, as in many other stagnated countries, a developmentalist mentality. We are no longer a backward or stagnant country, but we are underdeveloped . . . Minas Gerais suffers from the polarizing action of its powerful neighbor, the state of São Paulo. . . . We need to definitively fix an industrial base in our state and now, more than ever, to defend without yielding the installation of an automobile and petroleum industry [in Minas Gerais]."[107]

Within months of the coup the ACM had formed a "Front for the Defense of the Minas Economy" saying that the Front had "arrived thirty years late." The main of objective of the Front was to "convince the federal high command (*cúpula*) to treat us as we are and not as it thinks we should be." The high command, from the perspective of these business leaders included the Instituto Brasileiro de Geografia e Estatística, the Fundação Getúlio Vargas, the Ministério de Planejamento, the Banco Nacional de Desenvolvimento Econômico, as several other federal agencies (CACEX, SUMOC, IAA, SUNAB, IBC) that set prices, exchange rates, and fiscal policies.[108] This dissatisfaction intensified and by 1966, the ACM was publishing angry speeches critical of federal economic policies. One ACM official bitterly complained that "Minas Gerais was an economy in the process of economic decline, suffering hemorrhages of all sorts on all sides, treated with certainty and a strange indifference by the authorities who should be giving to the state a greater portion of its economic programs." He complained of capital flight, that Minas was no more than a supplier to other states' industrial parks, and that Minas was being drained of its human capital and its electric power, simply to become dependent on other states.[109] At the FIEMG, Nansen Araujo, one of the key figures among mineiro industrialists, fulminated against "internal imperialism" and "the powerful industrial groups of São Paulo who decided that their interests meant the interests of Brazil."[110]

The complaints of mineiro entrepreneurs and industrialists in the 1960s were more advanced versions of the old complaints of the 1930s: better transportation, transferring the headquarters of the CVRD to Minas, the need for a large iron and steel complex, a better banking network, and access to credit, and lower taxes.[111] They also divided over the issue of state enterprises. While nearly everyone agreed on the value and excellence of CEMIG and the BDMG, powerful business leaders railed against state enterprises such as the National Motor Factory as examples of "*empreguismo*" and disorganized planning.[112]

The relative weakness of entrepreneurs in Minas Gerais most likely originated with its peripheral role in the coffee economy beginning in the nineteenth century. The phenomenal boom in coffee production and exports, first in Rio de Janeiro and then São Paulo in the late nineteenth century, generated enormous amounts of capital that the paulistas (in particular) reinvested in the region to produce Latin America's most dynamic industrial park by the 1930s and 1940s.[113] Although southern Minas formed part of the coffee economy, it formed part of the hinterland of its two neighboring states, and mineiro coffee revenues did not flow into the rest of the state. Unlike Rio de Janeiro and São Paulo, the coffee export economy did not create an economic growth pole in the state.[114]

Physically isolated in the interior, and without access to the capital resources found in the cities of São Paulo and Rio de Janeiro, Belo Horizonte (and Minas) was late in generating the entrepreneurial dynamism that characterized these two cosmopolitan coastal centers. Not until the massive capital infusions of the postwar decades, and especially the seventies, could Belo Horizonte begin to generate similar dynamism. By then, however, mineiro entrepreneurs faced competition that paulista and carioca entrepreneurs had not encountered at the turn of the century. How could they compete with the resources and economies of scale that the State and multinationals were able to amass? In short, late entry into the game faced mineiro entrepreneurs with even greater challenges than those their paulista and carioca counter-parts had encountered 50 to 75 years earlier. Mineiro entrepreneurs paid a very high price for their historical lag.

Location is not an entirely satisfactory explanation, however.[115] Banking in Minas Gerais provides another angle on the problem of historical lag. As noted earlier, banking in Minas was late to develop and in the early twenti-eth century most certainly formed an important obstacle to industrialization in contrast to the development of banking and industry in Rio de Janeiro and São Paulo. Nonetheless, by the 1930s and 1940s mineiros had begun to show great skill at forming and expanding the banking and credit system. By the outbreak of World War II the state had become the third most impor-tant financial center in the country. By the 1950s, the mineiro banking sys-tem had become the largest in the country as measured by the volume of deposits, and the three largest private banks in the country had their head-quarters in Minas Gerais (Banco da Lavoura, Banco Nacional, Banco Mor-eira Salles).

The 1960s and 1970s, however, witnessed a profound transformation and decline of mineiro banking as the largest banks moved their head-quarters to São Paulo, or became insolvent. The Banco da Lavoura, cre-ation of the mineiro financier Clemente de Faria and the training ground of José de Magalhães Pinto, moved its headquarters to São Paulo in 1971 and became Credireal.[116] Magalhães Pinto's Banco Nacional moved its headquarters to Rio de Janeiro and in the 1990s entered into financial col-lapse after it was mismanaged by his children. The Banco Moreira Salles, begun in a tiny town in the south of Minas in the 1920s, had become the second largest private bank in Brazil by the 1960s. In the late sixties, the Moreira Salles family transformed the bank into Unibanco with its head-quarters in São Paulo.[117]

Studies of this profound transformation of the state's private banking sys-tem have all severely criticized the managerial expertise of mineiro bankers. Perhaps this is justified, but it overlooks the success of "mineiro" banks that migrated to the financial heartland of the nation—São Paulo. In a sense, the "smartest" entrepreneurs were those who recognized the continued success required them to move the center of their operations to the nation's finan-cial center. Even the major banks in Rio de Janeiro migrated to São Paulo in the 1970s and 1980s. (Rio de Janeiro was the headquarters of 155 banks in 1970s. By 1994 the number had dropped to just 18!)[118] In a sense, these banking entrepreneurs eventually gave in to the enormous gravitational pull of the paulistano economy leaving the financial systems in Rio de Janeiro and Minas Gerais weaker and more dependent on their powerful neighbor.

Mineiro entrepreneurs by the 1970s and 1980s had to turn increasingly to private capital outside the state for their survival and success.

In each of three phases of industrialization we have seen certain entrepreneurs stand out and serve as exemplars of the era. In the decades before 1950, Christiano Teixeira Guimarães is perhaps the greatest entrepreneurial figure of his era. In many ways he represents the shift from the landed and commercial elites of the late nineteenth century who accumulated the capital that their sons then invested in industry and banking. Guimarães moves into textiles (in the family firm), pools his assets with his kin and allies, and then branches out into banking, insurance, iron, and steel. All this in an age of pronounced capital shortages both in the private and public sector. He is the closest mineiro equivalent to the captains of industry in the late nineteenth-century United States or to Mauá in São Paulo.

In many ways the golden age of the mineiro entrepreneur was from the mid-1940s to the mid-1960s. This is the era of Américo Renê Giannetti, Israel Pinheiro, and José de Magalhães Pinto. These powerful figures of the mineiro business community, however, combined their entrepreneurial talents in the private sector with careers in the technocracy and political arena. All three circulated within all three elite sectors, demonstrating the error of seeing powerful elite figures through a single lens and a single career trajectory. They benefited from greater private capital opportunities (primarily from foreign sources) as well as the expanding role of the state (and State) as financier of industrial development, a process they helped create and promote.

The generation of the 1960s to the 1990s is also indicative of the shifting nature of industrialization. With the full-scale consolidation of the quadruple alliance, the role of the state and foreign capital became so dominant that industrialists found themselves in a weak position. There are no towering entrepreneurial figures in the private sector in these decades comparable to Guimarães, Giannetti, or Magalhães Pinto. The major figures who immediately come to mind in these decades are best known for their technocratic careers as (what I have called) public entrepreneurs—Amaro Lanari Júnior, Lucas Lopes, João Camilo Pena. Lanari Júnior is perhaps the epitome of the era; a man who led Usiminas as a state enterprise, he moved easily between the public and the private sector, as an executive for public or multinational firms.

Clearly, there were successful entrepreneurs in Belo Horizonte and Minas Gerais during these years, but those in the industrial elite often controlled family firms that paled in size and capital when compared with the largest and most successful firms. Nansen de Araújo and Fábio de Araújo

Table 5.9 Presidents of the Federation of Industries of Minas Gerais, 1933–2000

Term of Office	Name
1933–34	José de Moraes
1934–39	Alvimar Carneiro
1939–47	Américo Renê Giannetti
1947–52	Newton Pereira
1952–54	Hamleto Magnavacca
1954–56	Lídio Lunardi
1956–58	Theódulo Pereira
1958–60	Lídio Lunardi
1960–83	Fábio de Araújo Motta
1983–89	Nansen Araújo
1989–94	José Alencar Gomes da Silva
1995–	Stefan Salej

Source: FIEMG Archive.

Motta, two of the most important leaders of the industrial elite, ran an instruments manufacturing firm and a textile company.[119] Both men were dominant figures in the FIEMG and the business community in Belo Horizonte and Minas.[120] For nearly the entire period, the two of them controlled the presidency of the FIEMG. Despite their prominent leadership roles in the business and industrial community, their entrepreneurial talents and influence were vastly overshadowed by the likes of Lopes, Lanari Júnior, and Pena. This was truly the era of the public entrepreneur and not the private entrepreneur.

Yet a shift had begun to take place by the 1990s with privatization, globalization, and the opening of Brazilian markets. The age of the public entrepreneur was coming to an end. As public capital receded, the role of multinational capital expanded, and private mineiro capital remained weak. A new era of industrialization had begun and the relationship among entrepreneurs, technocrats, and politicians began to shift once again as Belo Horizonte's industrialization moved into the twenty-first century.

Conclusion ▨

Webs of Power—A Century
of Industrialization

By the end of the twentieth century Belo Horizonte had grown far beyond the wildest dreams of its creators. The industrial expansion at
the end of the twentieth century culminates a century of industrialization that began with the construction of Belo Horizonte in the 1890s. By
any measure, the industrialization of the city has been impressive. The second largest industrial center in the eighth largest economy in the world—a
metropolis of some 20 municipios approaching four million inhabitants—
now sits on a plateau where one hundred years ago a small hamlet of a few
thousand scratched out a living on the land. The turn-of-the-century political and technocratic elites succeeded in creating the economic and political
capital they envisioned for Minas Gerais.

The industrialization of Belo Horizonte, especially after 1950, drew hundreds of thousands of Brazilians into this growing economic pole. Belo Horizonte produced, on a state level, the megacephalic pattern of many Latin
American countries. Nearly a quarter of the state's inhabitants now live in
the capital's metropolitan region, and the second largest city in the state
(outside of this region) is Juiz de Fora with some 400,000 inhabitants—a
tenth of the population of Greater Belo Horizonte. One of the great tasks
facing politicians, technocrats, and entrepreneurs in the coming decades, in
fact, is how to deconcentrate industrial growth in Minas Gerais and to develop other industrial zones in the state.

After the debt crisis and recessions of the 1980s, the Brazilian and
mineiro economies have resumed growth again in the 1990s. In the recur-
ring pattern of the last half century, a decade of economic slowdown has
been followed by industrial and economic growth (albeit not as impressive

or as sustained as growth in the 1950s and 1970s). In Minas Gerais, Brazil, and Latin America, however, the resumption of economic growth this time around has been accompanied and stimulated by a profound shift in economic policy and practice. In the aftermath of the disastrous 1980s, governments across the region have taken up the banner of neoliberalism and the free market. Democratically elected governments from North America to Argentina (to widely varying degrees) have reversed a half-century of state intervention to pursue pragmatic policies of trade liberalization, downsizing the role of the state, and privatizing their economies.[1]

As always, the Brazilians have followed a more pragmatic and cautious path than many of their Latin American neighbors. While the Chileans and Argentines have led the way in reconstructing their economies along neoliberal lines, the Brazilians have moved more slowly and cautiously. The essential processes of the transition—reducing trade barriers, selling off state enterprises, downsizing the state apparatus—have moved forward more slowly in Brazil than in any of the other large economies in Latin America. In the early 1980s, by one estimate, nearly 60 percent of the Brazilian gross domestic product was in state hands.

The shift toward neoliberalism began under the brief administration of Fernando Collor de Mello (1990–92), paused during the presidency of Itamar Franco (1992–94), and has moved slowly forward under the leadership of President Fernando Henrique Cardoso (1995-). At both the national and state levels, governments have sold off assets and enterprises in a dramatic fashion. The original and prime symbols of state-led industrialization and nationalism—state-controlled iron and steel companies—have been privatized in the past decade, along with electric utilities and telecommunications systems. Perhaps the greatest symbol of the end of the era of state-directed growth was the sale of the Companhia Vale do Rio Doce in 1997.[2]

Although the nineties have not seen the phenomenal expansion of the early 1970s, the Brazilian and mineiro economies have experienced growth. The turning point was the implementation of the Real Plan in mid-1994. After more than a decade of failed efforts to end astronomical inflation and rolling recessions, the Real Plan stabilized the economy, ending 15 years of high inflation, and a half-century of chronic double-digit inflation. Over the past six years the annual inflation rate in Brazil has hovered in the single digits, an economic situation unprecedented in the lifetime of the vast majority of Brazilians.[3]

Over the last four years, low inflation and the move to more open trade and capital flows has once again attracted foreign capital, but at unprecedentedly high levels. During the debt crisis of 1980s the influx of new capital into Brazil essentially halted. Since 1994, more than $150 billion in foreign capital has flowed into Brazil, revitalizing the economy and financing a massive industrial and commercial restructuring. In 1999 alone $30 billion of foreign investment flowed into Brazil, the highest foreign investment flow into any country in the world.[4] Like much of the developing world, the Brazilian economy is becoming more tightly integrated into a global economic system where national political boundaries have become more and more problematic.[5]

Minas Gerais has received a major portion of this massive capital inflow. As it did in the 1970s, the government of Minas has been an industrial promoter and capital recruiter experiencing tremendous success. The recent economic revival has also been accompanied by the sale of most of the key state enterprises in Minas Gerais: the CVRD, Acesita, Açominas, Usiminas, and CEMIG. Investment has been directed not only at Greater Belo Horizonte, but also other regions of the state (Pouso Alegre, Santa Luzia, Juiz de Fora) to develop other regional industrial poles, most notably in the automobile industry. Many of the traditionally powerful mineiro firms have also been bought up by foreign corporations, or they have had to associate with powerful foreign firms in order to survive.[6]

The 1990s have been a difficult time for Brazilian and mineiro firms. The opening of the national market has created intense competition with global conglomerates, the inflation of the early nineties, and the overvalorization of the real in the late nineties have made national firms less competitive and more vulnerable than at any time in the past century. The textile industry, the oldest and most traditional industry in Minas Gerais and Belo Horizonte, faces serious questions about its ability to survive. The old family firms—Santanense and Cedro Cachoeira, for example—will not survive in their present form. They will have to modernize their management and seek alliances with foreign capital.[7] Even in the already highly internationalized iron and steel industry, Belgo Mineira and the CVRD have been repositioning themselves through ventures with other international firms, and through the reorganization of their operations within Minas Gerais and Brazil.[8] Even President Fernando Henrique Cardoso has publicly recognized the need for Brazilian firms to merge on an unprecedented scale to allow them to compete with multinational corporations. As he put it in 1999, "We cannot imagine a Brazil isolated from the world."[9] Some of the leading mineiro firms will not survive long, as has been the case with the collapse of the construction giant, Mendes Júnior.[10]

Fiat, the newest entry into the industrial economy of Belo Horizonte, appears to be its strongest and best positioned enterprise. The company's management in Turin has begun to invest several billion dollars into the expansion of its operations in Betim, and dozens of suppliers in the surrounding region are expanding. The central plant now employs some 20,000 workers around its daily operations, and production is at record levels. In the late 1990s, Fiat surpassed Volkswagen as Brazil's largest automobile manufacturer, and is now the single largest exporter in Minas Gerais. With revenues of $6 billion in 1998, the Grupo Fiat do Brasil has become Brazil's largest industrial conglomerate, comprised of some 16 firms and more than 25,000 employees.[11] Fiat do Brasil has become a classic example of the latest stage of globalization: European capital investment in manufacturing in Brazil to manufacture for the growing Brazilian market (and Mercosul), and to produce exports. The company has become a major player in the world automotive industry's search for new markets outside the traditional North Atlantic economies. It has done this pursuing the production of automobiles for the lower end of the market—the so-called "world car."

Mining and minerals processing and the electric power industries are also increasingly drawn into a global economy. With the sale of the CVRD, Brazilian and foreign capital have combined to modernize what is one of the most successful state enterprises ever created. In the Brazilian industrial economy of the early twenty-first century, minerals have joined automobiles as the most important exports of the nation. The electric power industry has moved haltingly toward privatization, a process that is gradually moving this most central of public utilities into the hands of large multinational corporations. Under the administration of Governor Eduardo Azeredo, CEMIG, another extraordinarily successful state enterprise, was partially auctioned off to foreign investors. Governor Itamar Franco, a bitter opponent of privatization, has blocked the process, probably only for the short term. Most likely, the complete privatization of this exceptional state enterprise is only a matter of time.

Despite the recent criticism of state intervention, Belo Horizonte owes its creation, growth, and impressive industrialization primarily to the role of the state government, and the mineiro elites. The city is a classic case of state-led economic growth. This growth was made possible by the convergence of three key groups: politicians, technocrats, and entrepreneurs. As we have seen, the politicians provided the political support, the technocrats (especially after the 1930s) shaped the process, and the entrepreneurs found in the other two groups the means to promote economic growth and industrialization.

It was the sweat and blood of hundreds of thousands of workers, especially migrants from the countryside into the city, whose muscle and energy built this industry. They were, however, primarily shaped by industrialization and only secondarily were they the shapers of the city's industrial destiny. The industrialization of Belo Horizonte has been primarily shaped and directed from above, and not from below, despite the continual efforts of the lower and middle classes to participate in the process.[12] That is why this book has been unabashedly a history of elites. For despite the give and take among the different groups and social classes in twentieth-century Brazil, it remains a country with an enormous socioeconomic divide where powerful elites continue to dominate the direction of national life. It is precisely because of the importance of the hierarchy and power inequities that define twentieth-century Brazil that I have chosen to place so much emphasis on political patronage and clientelism. They are at the center of political and social life in Brazil.[13]

Clientelism and political patronage made possible the economic transformation. The often converging and interconnected webs of political and economic power lay behind Belo Horizonte's impressive industrialization over the past century. The construction of the political center for Minas Gerais brought together the regional networks of political patronage around the city that they would shape (however fitfully) into the economic center that their state so badly lacked. Even more acutely than the mineiro elites' sense of political rivalry with Rio de Janeiro and São Paulo was their full awareness of their state's economic backwardness in comparison to their two political rivals.

Clientelism and patronage mobilized the resources of the state government, and the most important resource was capital. The greatest obstacle to economic growth, and more specifically, industrialization, in Minas Gerais was a shortage of capital. Like most of Latin America in the century after independence, the scarcity of capital held back economic growth. This scarcity was even more acute in Minas than in Rio de Janeiro and São Paulo. The coffee economy transformed Rio, and then even more dramatically São Paulo. The scarcity and fragility of financial institutions in Brazil handicapped economic development. When compared to its two powerful neighbors, Minas had even weaker financial institutions and its ability to generate capital for growth was even weaker.

By the 1930s it had become clear in Minas Gerais and Brazil that only foreign and public capital could make up for the inability of domestic entrepreneurs to mobilize capital for growth. First the state government (beginning in the 1940s), and then multinational corporations (beginning in the 1950s), stepped in to finance the industrialization of Belo Horizonte. For nearly 50 years the state government acted as the midwife of economic growth. In this new age of downsizing the state and reducing state intervention, foreign capital has become the principal stimulus for mineiro (and Brazilian) industrialization.

Mineiro elites are divided over these trends, just as they had been over foreign capital and nationalism in the 1950s. Although some powerful political leaders such as Governor Itamar Franco resisted the privatization of CEMIG, FURNAS, and other public utilities, the dominant ideology was clearly to reduce the role of the state in the economy and to unleash the forces of private capital, both foreign and domestic.[14] Governor Hélio Garcia summed up the prevailing view in a speech to the FIEMG in 1991 when he said, "The path is precisely this one, the State must get out of businesses in which it is not competent, make itself smaller and efficient. . . . What we have to do is create a new State."[15] The language of nationalism and development supported by public and private capital with an interventionist state, the discourse that had dominated discussion among the elites in the 1950s, 1960s, and 1970s, had evolved by the 1990s into a view of development through globalization driven by private capital. The role of the state in the 1950s was to attract, create, and direct new capital investment for industrialization. By the 1990s, mineiro economic and political elites saw the role of the state as one of attracting private investment through the sale of state enterprises and assets and by removing obstacles to private capital flows. Developmentalism had given way to globalization.[16]

The "Lessons" of the Mineiro Model

This study of Belo Horizonte is one of the few book-length works on the industrialization of Latin American cities that are not national capitals or the primary economic center of the nation. The relatively sparse literature on Latin American industrialization focuses overwhelmingly on national capitals, logically enough, since the capital is usually the major national industrial center. São Paulo is the great exception to the rule once it surpasses Rio de Janeiro as the principal industrial park of Brazil in the 1930s. Brazil is unusual in Latin America in the quantity of large cities outside the capital (even before the construction of Brasília). Even in Mexico and Argentina, the second and third largest economies of Latin America, the national capital dwarfs the second-largest city, as well as other cities. Despite the growth of "secondary" cities in both countries in the last half-century, both Argentina and Mexico continue to suffer from a historic process of megacephalia.[17]

The impressive growth of secondary industrial centers calls for more scholarly attention. Belo Horizonte, as I have stressed from the beginning of this study, has barely been studied, yet it has a population of nearly four million. A few studies have been done on other secondary centers in other Latin American countries, but the list is short.[18] Monterrey, Mexico and Medellín, Colombia immediately stand out as the most comparable parallels to the industrialization of Belo Horizonte. As provincial cities that arise in (conscious) competition to the national capital, all three are known by their very similar cultural stereotypes: a relatively isolated people, politically conservative, economically astute, and bound by tight family networks.[19] In all three cases, the strong regional competition within the countries has marked a struggle between the political and economic heartland and the regional elite in the provinces. The so-called traits of *mineiridade* mirror the prevailing stereotypes of *regiomontanos* and *antioqueños*.

The fascination with the national industrial centers has skewed our vision of Latin American industrialization. Just as all politics is not the story of what transpires in the capital, all economics do not radiate outward from one center. This study of Belo Horizonte barely begins to reorient our view of the national economy of Brazil as a series of regional economies that slowly become one national economy by the late twentieth century. We need a clearer understanding of industrialization and economic growth in Salvador, Porto Alegre, and Curitiba—just to name a few other important regional economic centers. We must decenter our view of Brazilian economic growth and industrialization.

What this study also clearly demonstrates is the persistence and power of clientelism and political patronage as Brazil moves into the twenty-first century.[20] Despite the fascination with bureaucratic modernization and rationalization under the military regime, and declarations of the death of clientelism in the 1970s and 1980s, political patronage and clientelism are alive and well, not only in Minas Gerais, but also in national politics. Once seen as primarily of rural origins, and representing an outmoded form of traditional politics, clientelism has continually been refashioned and adapted to a "modern," urban, industrial Brazil. It has survived government and regime changes throughout the last century and has now become an integral feature of contemporary democratic, civilian politics.[21]

The "old boy" networks of nineteenth-century Minas Gerais converged on the new capital after 1897, eventually becoming a web of regional networks. The political and business networks—reinforced by the bonds of families—are at the heart of the industrialization of Belo Horizonte in the twentieth century.[22] The persistence of family enterprises into the late twentieth century is one of the more striking characteristics of Brazilian industrialization. In the 1990s, 287 of Brazil's 300 largest firms were controlled by families.[23] The rise of the modern business enterprise in the United States, Europe, and Japan gradually divorced ownership and management and brought about the decline of the family firm in the late nineteenth and early twentieth centuries. Although modern business enterprises did arise in Minas in the twentieth century, the process was much later and slower than in these other regions. Furthermore, the most modern of the business enterprises were usually foreign or state corporations.[24] In the future, we will probably look back on the 1990s as the decade when the era of family enterprise began to come to a close with globalization and the opening of Brazil's markets. These elite kinship networks—in politics, state government, and business—forged the path of industrialization and economic growth. The state government promoted and led this process. Politicians, technocrats, and entrepreneurs were the vanguard in it.

The FIEMG and the ACM, to cite the most prominent examples, were the vanguard organizations of the elites. Through these two corporate entities these elites came together, debated, discussed, and then lobbied the state and federal governments, as well as foreign capital. It is worth restating once again that the leadership of these organizations, the major politicians, and the technocrats, were almost universally males from a relatively small group of regional elites. Although immigrants and those from humble beginnings did achieve success and enter into the upper echelons of power, the continuity of elite families and their networks is impressive. Equally striking is the almost complete absence of women from these elites, even in the business world. One looks almost in vain in the 1990s, for example, for prominent female business leaders, and the few that appear are nearly always in smaller retail and consumer-oriented industries.[25]

Created to provide the state with a political and (to a lesser extent) economic capital, Belo Horizonte drew the regional elites together in fitful, but powerful, alliances. The dominance of the idea of the state (Minas Gerais) gradually won out over the regional interest groups. Belo Horizonte became the political and economic vortex of Minas Gerais pulling the powerful inward and together. Thus, paradoxes unfolded: Clientelism and patronage survived and thrived in a mass democratic polity, and a strong sense of regionalism continues to prevail in a state that has forged a well-defined sense of identity and unity.

As Peter Evans has pointed out in his comparative study of the information technology, states intervene in a variety of ways to promote industrialization and economic growth.[26] The key to successful intervention is the ability to create the right conditions for industrialization, and not necessarily to attempt to control and direct the process. As in the case of the computer industry in South Korea, the state of Minas Gerais has been very successful at nurturing new industry. Politicians have created the conditions for technocrats and entrepreneurs to promote industry in the state. They have not always been successful, but they have created some important "islands of excellence"—state enterprises that have thrived. The state has also fostered the development of successful private industries through the efforts of both politicians and technocrats.[27]

The state and federal governments today have moved toward a model that relinquishes direct control of key sectors of the economy, but continues to promote industrial investment and development. The focus is on developing the economy to produce more jobs, more export revenue, and greater government tax revenues. On the state level, Minas Gerais pursues the same export-led growth model as the federal government in Brasília. The dilemma facing both the state and the State is how to continue to shape the process of industrialization and economic develop as they relinquish their traditional tools of influence, public investment, and state-controlled enterprises. Neoliberalism, if carried through to its ultimate logic, will weaken the power and influence of the government to guide the economy while increasing the power and leverage of global corporations.[28]

As I have pointed out throughout the last half of this study, the technocrats who created and directed such enterprises as CEMIG, the CVRD, and Acesita served as public entrepreneurs investing and building capital, not for themselves in the private sector, but for the state government. One of the foremost characteristics of mineiro industrialization has been the role of the state in nurturing and developing these public entrepreneurs. As Barbara Geddes has argued in her work, bureaucrats, politicians, and technocrats are the human side of the so-called State.[29] They are rational and self-interested actors whose combined choices become the choices of the state. In Minas Gerais, these actors drove forward the process of industrialization making rational choices that they believed would benefit the state by promoting economic growth and industrialization.[30]

Tropical Capitalism

The history of the industrialization of Belo Horizonte and Minas Gerais has primarily been the story of the choices and decisions of politicians, technocrats, and entrepreneurs. Despite the important contributions and contestations of other sectors of society, especially the working class, this industrialization was driven, and continues to be driven, by the power and policy decisions of elites. As I have pointed out repeatedly, these three groups have not been mutually exclusive, and at times, individuals have been part of all three categories at different stages of their careers. The relationships among the groups have not always been smooth, but all three have needed each other to attain their joint goals of industrialization and economic growth for the state. Their efforts have rarely been altruistic, and more often than not, private benefit has come from the public policies. After all, success in this political and economic system has long hinged on the ability to create new resources to strengthen one's portion of the patronage system. Economic growth and industrialization, ironically, have reinforced clientelism.

The weakest link in the elite groups driving forward industrialization has been mineiro entrepreneurs in the private sector. Their inability to mobilize capital on a large scale has historically been the greatest obstacle for Brazilian and (especially) mineiro entrepreneurs. Even more so than their counterparts in São Paulo and Rio de Janeiro, entrepreneurs in Minas Gerais faced daunting challenges. Located in the mountainous interior and isolated from the coastal ports for centuries because of inadequate roads, railways, and communications systems, mineiro entrepreneurs faced even greater obstacles than paulista and carioca industrialists. Consequently, they were even more dependent on public and foreign capital than their neighbors.

Beginning in the 1920s, mineiro entrepreneurs forged alliances with multinational corporations (Belgo Mineira) and by the 1940s, with the state (CVRD). As state-led industrialization began to take shape in Brazil after 1930, São Paulo and Rio de Janeiro reinforced their traditional dominance in the Brazilian national economy. Frustrated mineiro politicians and entrepreneurs increasingly used the state government to make up for what they perceived as the federal government's inability or unwillingness to invest in Minas Gerais. The political and economic networks, especially family networks, became the principal means for channeling state resources to the private sector. This process helped maintain the traditional family networks in the state throughout the twentieth century, and to incorporate new families into these traditional webs of power.

The end result has been the development of industrial capitalism in Minas Gerais, but a form of capitalism that looks more like the European or Japanese versions than U.S. capitalism. The persistence of family-owned corporations, close relationships between the state and private corporations, and the role of technocrats in guiding the economy are all characteristics that mineiro industrialization shares with twentieth-century economic developments in Japan and Western Europe.[31]

The mineiro path to industrialization should also demonstrate the importance of analyzing the elite groups that guided the process of economic growth in Brazil. The politicians, technocrats, and entrepreneurs who shaped the process were not part of mutually exclusive or distinct groups. They did not represent specific class interests. They did pursue policies and made decisions that collectively shaped Belo Horizonte's and Minas Gerais's industrialization. Furthermore, this study has attempted to "humanize" industrialization with a sort of collective biography of politicians, technocrats, and entrepreneurs. I have tried to emphasize the need to recognize that these men (and occasionally women) were not unidimensional. They often spent portions of their careers in more than one of these groups and ties of politics, kinship, and business often overlapped.

In recent years, a number of political scientists have studied the role of business leaders in the process of redemocratization in Brazil, and in other regions of Latin America. We need to extend this analysis back in time to look at the role of business elites, not only in politics and political transitions, but also in the political economy of Brazilian industrialization. We need to bring together the studies of technocrats and entrepreneurs and extend these studies back in time.[32]

The greatest flaw in the process of industrialization in Belo Horizonte and Minas Gerais has been the lack of technological innovation. Perhaps the most distinctive feature of the process has been the continual importation of new technology but with very little indigenous innovation. Technology transfer has been a long and continual process in Minas Gerais—technology creation has not. In the classic cases of industrialization—England, the United States, Germany, Japan—technological innovation has been at the heart of the process. It has been key to creating self-sustaining growth. Mineiro—and Brazilian—industrialization remains dependent on the continual importation of new technology rather than a cycle of importation, adaptation, and innovation.[33] In a recent United Nations study Brazil was ranked forty-third of seventy-two nations on a scale of technological advance, behind Mexico, Argentina, Chile, Uruguay, and even Trinidad and Tobago! The index ranked Brazil in the third rank of development categorized as "dynamic adoption of technology," behind the first two groups— "leader countries" and "potential leaders."[34]

Mineiro economic growth has been noticeably weak in research and development. Few enterprises—public or private—have engaged in any significant research and development. Multinational corporations have relied on industrial research labs in their home countries, and large local businesses have dedicated little of their resources to creating new technology. Whether in textiles, iron and steel, electric power, mining and minerals processing, or the automotive industry (the pivotal mineiro industries), few companies have emerged that have even attempted to develop technology for the local market and local industries. This is a profound difference with the self-sustained industrialization of the powerful economies of the so-called developed or First World.[35] As Joseph Schumpeter pointed out long ago, one of the keys to economic growth is productivity, and productivity ultimately depends on constant technological innovation.[36]

Although capital mobilization has historically been the greatest obstacle to mineiro industrialization, the lack of technological innovation may be the greatest obstacle to achieving self-sustained industrialization and economic growth. In this sense, Brazil has experience rapid industrialization during the past half-century, but it has not experienced a true industrial revolution. Brazil will not enter into the ranks of the great industrial powers until industries and firms in Brazil begin to invest heavily in research and development.

This flawed process of industrialization has not only produced a highly industrialized nation that has not yet achieved self-sustained growth, it also has failed to significantly improved the historic socioeconomic inequities in Brazilian society. Belo Horizonte, despite its phenomenal growth and industrialization, has reproduced on a local scale the profound inequities of Brazilian industrialization. In the early 1990s, more than half of all Brazilians lived below the "poverty line" of roughly $100 a month income. More than 100 *favelas* (slums) had proliferated around Greater Belo Horizonte, and larger and larger numbers of the poor were being pushed into the surrounding municipios unable to afford the cost of living in the center of the city.[37] An estimated 5,000 people lived by collecting paper off the streets while seeking shelter beneath bridges and viaducts at night.[38] Industrialization, in other words, has produced great wealth, but that new wealth has been primarily controlled by the business, political, and technocratic elites in Minas Gerais. A century of industrialization has not significantly altered the income distribution of Minas Gerais, or Brazil. Capitalism and democracy in Brazil have not yet brought with them the fruits of a high-quality standard of living for the majority of Brazilians. It remains to be seen whether Brazil's tropical capitalism can, in fact, bear these fruits.

Whatever the obstacles to economic growth, this study shows the key role of the state in the industrialization of Belo Horizonte. Without intervention by the state government, mineiro industrialization would not have begun in the 1940s or surged forward in the 1950s, 1970s, and 1990s. The state has been the principal promoter and force behind industrialization. Yet, as I have argued, the state is not some abstract concept, but rather (in Weberian terms) a set of institutions and the collection of individuals in those institutions.[39] The decisions and policies these individuals made moved industrialization forward in Belo Horizonte and Minas Gerais. The principal means for implementing these decisions has been the politics of patronage and clientelism, and family networks have played a crucial role in both politics and economics.

The central question facing Brazil's economic and political leaders today is how to refashion the State (and the state) so that it facilitates economic growth, while not leaving the enormous mass of poor Brazilians to lives of continued poverty and despair. Beginning in the 1930s, the interventionist State sought to promote economic development and to construct a social safety net for poor Brazilians. Despite lagging behind the handful of powerful industrial economies in the so-called North, Brazil today is one of the most industrialized nations of the world. Yet it remains a nation with abysmal social indicators. High infant mortality rates, high illiteracy rates, lack of basic housing and health care become even more tragic in an economy that pays its corporate executives some of the highest salaries in the world.[40]

As Joseph Schumpeter pointed out long ago, capitalism is an evolutionary process that never is and never can be stationary. Keeping the "capitalist engine in motion" calls for constant pursuit of new goods, markets, methods of production, and new forms of industrial organization.[41] As a late industrializer, Brazil faces different challenges than earlier industrializing nations in the eighteenth and nineteenth centuries. This late industrialization also raises questions about the directions Brazil should go in an age that has already been called "post-industrial" and even "post-capitalist."[42]

I have tried to show in this book that the forms of industrial organization that evolved in Brazil, in Minas Gerais, and, more precisely, in Belo Horizonte, have much in common with patterns and characteristics in other industrial nations—but with a peculiarly mineiro style and structure. This is a peculiar form of late industrialization in a late industrializer. It relies heavily on State and state intervention, in particular, to mobilize the scarce capital for new industry. The key role of family networks and interconnected elite networks operating through patronage and clientelism provide this industrialization with its most distinctive characteristic. The end result is rapid and impressive industrialization in Belo Horizonte in the twentieth century, and especially after 1950, but without generating a process of technological innovation and renovation. Belo Horizonte and Brazil experienced industrialization, but not an industrial revolution. This peculiar and continually evolving form of capitalism, this "tropical capitalism," defines the industrialization of Belo Horizonte, and will continue to evolve and reshape the city as it moves into its second century.

Appendix A

Industries and Professions, Belo Horizonte, 1922

Professions		
Profession	*Individuals*	*Totals*
I. *Professionals*		*163*
Advogado	56	
Arquiteto	4	
Dentista	57	
Engenheiro	4	
Médico	42	
II. *Managers and Executives*		*21*
Banqueiro	6	
Diretor		
de banco	4	
de S.A.	4	
de Cia de Electricidade 2		
de cia têxtil	2	
Gerente		
de banco	2	
de cia têxtil	1	
III. *Office Workers*		*91*
Agentes comercial	1	
de empréstimos	35	
de leilões	1	
de loteria	1	
de seguros	1	
de transporte	4	

(continues)

Professions (continued)

Profession	Individuals	Totals
Guarda-livros	45	
Procurador	3	
IV. *Services*		*64*
Alugador de bicicletas 4		
Automoveis	44	
Carro de praça	13	
Folheiro	3	
V. *Artisans and Craftsmen*		*161*
Alfaiate	35	
Barbeiro	50	
Bombeiro	7	
Carpinteiro	2	
Colchoeiro	1	
Constructor	5	
Costureira	1	
Empreteiro	11	
Encardenador	1	
Ferreiro	8	
Fotografo	4	
Joalheiro	6	
Marmorista	6	
Modista	4	
Ourives	5	
Parteira	1	
Pedreira	5	
Quadros e molduras	2	
Relógios	3	
Seleiro	4	
Total Individuals		*500*

Industries

Industry	Individuals	Firms	Totals
I. *Commercial*	*549*	*152*	*701*
Açogue	10	1	

(continues)

Industries (continued)

Industry	Individuals	Firms	Totals
Agência			
de companhia	1		
de loteria	1		
de transporte	1		
Aguardente	3	1	
Armas e munições	1		
Artigos dentários	2		
Atelier de pintura	1		
Barbearia	3		
Bilhares	6	1	
Botequim	71	3	
Café	6	7	
Casa de armas	1		
Casa de brinquedos	3		
Casa de pasto	1		
Cereaes	2		
Chapeus e calçados	15		
Charutaria	2		
Cinema	8		
Confeitaria	4		
Deposito			
unspecified	2		
de inflamáveis	1		
Eletricidade			
unspecified	1		
artigos	3	2	
Escritório			
Cia	13		
Comercial	1		
de commissões	1		
Unspecified	5		
Farmacia	30	6	
Fazendas e armarinhos 58	27		
Ferragens	6	2	
Flores	2		
Frutas	8		
Fumos	2		
Garage	9		
Géneros	210	36	

(continues)

Industries (continued)

Industry	Individuals	Firms	Totals
Hervario	1		
Hotéis e Pensões	48	3	
Joalheiria	1		
Livraria	1	4	
Louças	1	2	
Maquinas	1	3	
Malas	1		
Mercador de cal	1		
Móveis	10	5	
Música (objetos)	1		
Optica	1		
Padaria	15	4	
Papelaria	2		
Restaurante	3		
Roupas	1		
Sapataria	6		
Seguros	5		
Sementes	1		
II. *Financial*	*2*	*3*	*5*
Banco	2		
agencia	1		
Casa de câmbio	1		
Casa de penhores	1		
III. *Factories*	*47*	*19*	*66*
Banha	1		
Bebidas	8		
Biscoitos	4		
Calçados	13	2	
Cerveja	1	1	
Chapeus	2		
Confeitos	2		
Carros	1		
Doces	2		
Ladrilhos	1		
Malas	1	2	
Manteiga	1		
Massas	2	2	
Móveis	8	1	
Oleos	1		

(continues)

Industries (continued)

Industry	Individuals	Firms	Totals
Roupas	1		
Sabão	1	3	
Salchichas	2		
Tecidos	3		
IV. *Shops*	*66*	*13*	*79*
Alfaiataria	7		
Cerâmica	1		
Commissões	3	1	
Curtume	1		
Couros	1	1	
Fundição	1	1	
Lenharia	9	1	
Maquina			
de beneficio de arroz	1		
Oficina			
de consertos	6		
de costura	2		
de móveis	1		
Olaria	13		
Serraria	12	2	
Tinturaria	10		
Typografia	5		
Totals for Industries	*664*	*187*	*851*
Totals for Industries and Professions	*1,351*		

Source: Minas Geraes, December 28, 1922, suplemento, 1–13.

Appendix B 🔳

Key Textile Firms in Belo Horizonte and Surrounding Region, Founding Directors

Firm	Municipio	Founded
Cia Cedro e Cachoeira	*Paraopeba*	*1868*
Bernardo Mascarenhas		
Caetano Mascarenhas		
Antônio Cândido da Silva Mascarenhas		
Cia União Itabirano	*Itabira*	*1878*
Ten. Antonio Camillo de Oliveira		
Cel. José Baptista Martins da Costa		
Desembargador João Baptista de Carvalho Drummond		
Cia Industrial Sabarense	*Belo Horizonte*	*1880*
Dr. Alipio da Silva Mello		
Dr. Carlindo dos Santos Pinto		
Comendador Septimo de Paula Rocha		
Ten. Cel. Antonio da Rocha Mello		
Antonio Augusto de Araujo Vianna		
(Cia Fiação e Tecelagem Minas Gerais)		*1915*
Dr. Manoel Thomaz de Carvalho Brito		
Cia Cachoeira de Macacos	*Sete Lagoas*	*1886*
João da Matta Teixeira		
Américo Teixeira Guimarães		
Antônio Vaz de Senna Mello		
Cia Fabril Mascarenhas	*Alvinópolis*	*1901*
Cel. José Maria A. Baeta		

(continues)

Firm	Municipio	Founded
Dr. Francisco A. Alvares da Silva		
Padre José Marciano de Aguiar		
Aristides José Mascarenhas		
(originally Cia Industrial Paulo Moreirense)		*1888*
João Alves Fernandes		
Ten. Cel. José Pedro Gomes		
Virgílio Domingues Gomes Lima		
Cia Fabril de Pedreira	*Itabira*	*1913*
(originally Andrade, Guerra & Cia)		*1888*
Dr. Domingos Martins Guerra		
Pedro Martins Guerra		
Cia de Tecidos Santannense	*Itaúna*	*1891*
Mardocheu Gonçalves de Souza		
José Gonçalves de Souza Moreira		
Cel. Manoel Gonçalves de Souza Moreira		
Acacio Baeta Coelho		
Cia Industrial Itabira do Campo	*Itabirito*	*1892*
Cel. José Maria Afonso Baeta		
Padre Francisco Xavier de Souza		
Alberto da Costa Soares		
José Augusto de Araujo Lima		
Arthur de Abreu Lacerda		
Pedro de Araujo		
Jorge Pereira de Lima		
Cia de Tecidos Pitanguiense	*Pitangui*	*1893*
José Gonçalves de Souza		
Sergio Mascarenhas Barbosa		
Cel. Diogo Gabriel de Castro Vasconcellos		
Cia Industrial Belo Horizonte	*Belo Horizonte*	*1906*
Américo Teixeira Guimarães		
Ignacio Mascarenhas		
Manoel Gonçalves de Souza Moreira		
Cia Renascença Industrial	*Belo Horizonte*	*1908*
Américo Teixeira Guimarães		
João da Matta Teixeira		
João de Paula França		
Herculino Francisco França		
Cia Minas Fabril	*Belo Horizonte*	*1911*
Antônio Mendes Campos		
Adolpho Braga		
Arnaud Ribeiro		

(continues)

Firm	Municipio	Founded
(originally Cezar Baccer & Cia.)		*1907*
Cezar Braccer		
Antônio Ribeiro Seabra		
José João Baptista		
Manuel Franco Ventura		
Antônio Mendes Campos		
João Antônio da Silva Cardoso		
Alfredo Pinto da Fonseca		
Cia Industrial Itaunense	*Itaúna*	*1911*
Augusto Gonçalves de Souza Moreira		
João de Cerqueira Lima		
Antônio de Mattos		
Cia Fiação e Tecidos São Gonçalvo	*Pará de Minas*	*1922*
Ferreira Guimarães family		

Source: Annual reports in *Minas Gerais* and Junta Comercial de Minas Gerais.

Notes

Introduction

1. Some of the standard works on the subject of the emergence and power of the West in modern times are William H. McNeill, *The Rise of the West: A History of the Human Community* (Chicago: University of Chicago Press, 1963); Nathan Rosenberg and L. E. Birdell, Jr., *How the West Grew Rich: The Economic Transformation of the Industrial World* (New York: Basic Books, 1986); Paul Kennedy, *The Rise and Fall of the Great Powers: Economic Change and Military Conflict from 1500 to 2000* (New York: Random House, 1987); David S. Landes, *The Wealth and Poverty of Nations: Why Some are So Rich and Some So Poor* (New York: W. W. Norton, 1998).

2. Francis Fukuyama, "The End of History?" *The National Interest* 16 (summer 1989); and, Francis Fukuyama, *The End of History and the Last Man* (New York: The Free Press, 1992).

3. See, for example, Jorge G. Castañeda, *Utopia Unarmed: The Latin American Left After the Cold War* (New York: Vintage Books, 1993).

4. See, for example, Menno Vellinga, ed., *The Changing Role of the State in Latin America* (Boulder, Colorado: Westview Press, 1998).

5. Adam Smith, *An Inquiry into the Nature and Causes of the Wealth of Nations*, R. H. Campbell and A. S. Skinner, eds., 2 v. (Oxford: Clarendon Press, 1976 [1776]).

6. Karl Marx, *Capital: A Critique of Political Economy*, v. 1, trans. Ben Fowkes (New York: Vintage Books, 1977 [1867]).

7. Joseph A. Schumpeter, *Capitalism, Socialism, and Democracy*, (New York: Harper & Brothers, 1947). For a recent reevaluation of this classic work, see Thomas K. McCraw, "The Creative Destroyer: Schumpeter's *Capitalism, Socialism, and Democracy*," EH.NET Project 2000, ehreview@eh.net.

8. Milton Friedman, *Capitalism and Freedom* (Chicago: University of Chicago Press, 1962).

9. My definition draws on Thomas K. McCraw, ed., *Creating Modern Capitalism: How Entrepreneurs, Companies, and Countries Triumphed in Three Industrial Revolutions* (Cambridge, Mass.: Harvard University Press, 1997), esp. 3–4.

10. Although the old terminology of First, Second, and Third World is inadequate, especially for the contemporary world, I still find it useful shorthand. Throughout this book I use developing world and newly industrializing countries (NICs) interchangeably. Irving Louis Horowitz, *Three Worlds of Development: The Theory and Practice of International Stratification* (New York: Oxford University Press, 1966), esp. 1- 38.

11. According to one estimate, the five largest economies in 1994 were the United States, China, Japan, Germany, and India, followed by France, the United Kingdom, Italy, and Brazil. Angus Maddison, *Monitoring the World Economy, 1820–1992* (Paris: Organization for Economic Cooperation and Development, 1995), esp. 180–92.

12. T. S. Ashton, *The Industrial Revolution* (Oxford: Oxford University Press, 1948); Phyllis Deane, *The First Industrial Revolution* (Cambridge: Cambridge University Press, 1967) are two of the "classic" accounts. Pat Hudson, *The Industrial Revolution* (London: Edward Arnold, 1992) provides a useful and thorough overview of the "industrial revolution." In particular, pp. 9–36 provide an excellent survey of the historiography. For the role of the State in this process, see Eric J. Evans, *The Forging of the Modern State: Early Industrial Britain, 1783–1870,* 2nd ed. (London: Longman, 1996), esp. chapter 12.

13. Warren Dean, *The Industrialization of São Paulo, 1880–1945* (Austin: University of Texas Press, 1969) and Wilson Cano, *Desequilíbrios regionais e concentração industrial no Brasil: 1930–1970* (São Paulo: Global, 1985). In 1907, São Paulo (16.6 percent) and Rio de Janeiro (39.9 percent) (the Federal District and the surrounding state) accounted for 56.5 percent of the value of Brazil's industrial production. By 1940, the positions of the two states had reversed (São Paulo at 38.6 and Rio de Janeiro at 27.9 percent), but they now accounted for 66.5 percent of the value of the nation's industrial production. *Recenseamento de 1920,* v. 5, pt. 1, p. vii; *Recenseamento de 1940,* v. III, p. 185.

14. James Brooke, "Inland Region of Brazil Grows Like Few Others," *New York Times,* 11 August 1994, C1; "Estado em disparada," *Veja,* 26 April 1995, 104–5.

15. Barrington Moore, Jr., *Social Origins of Dictatorship and Democracy: Lord and Peasant in the Making of the Modern World* (Boston: Beacon Press, 1966), esp. chapters 5 and 8.

16. "[T]he Industrial Revolution marked a major turning point in man's history. To that point, the advance of commerce and industry, however gratifying and impressive, had been essentially superficial: more wealth, more goods, prosperous cities, merchant nabobs. . . . It was the Industrial Revolution that initiated a cumulative, self-sustaining advance in technology whose repercussions would be felt in all aspects of economic life." David S. Landes, *The Unbound Prometheus: Technological Change and Industrial Development in*

Western Europe from 1750 to the Present (Cambridge: Cambridge University Press, 1969), 3.

17. For a very critical view of this shifting pattern see, Stephen H. Haber, "The Worst of Both Worlds: The New Cultural History of Mexico," *Mexican Studies* 13:2 (summer 1997), 363–83. Two recent collections that represent a renewal (albeit not a major one) of the economic history of Latin America are Stephen Haber, ed., *How Latin America Fell Behind: Essays on the Economic Histories of Brazil and Mexico, 1800–1914* (Stanford: Stanford University Press, 1997); and, John H. Coatsworth and Alan M. Taylor, eds., *Latin America and the World Economy Since 1800* (Cambridge, Mass.: Harvard University, David Rockefeller Center for Latin American Studies, 1998).

18. For an important recent survey of the state of business history in Latin America, and the neglect of microeconomic studies, see Carlos Dávila and Rory Miller, eds., *Business History in Latin America: The Experience of Seven Countries,* trans. Garry Mills and Rory Miller (Liverpool, England: Liverpool University Press, 1999).

19. Some important examples are Jorge Caldeira, *Mauá: empresário do império* (São Paulo: Companhia das Letras, 1995) and *A nação mercantilista* (São Paulo: Editora 34, 1999); Sérgio de Oliveira Birchal, *Entrepreneurship in Nineteenth-Century Brazil: The Formation of a Business Environment* (New York: St. Martin's Press, 1999); Eugene Ridings, *Business Interest Groups in Nineteenth-Century Brazil* (Cambridge: Cambridge University Press, 1994); Duncan McDowall, *The Light: Brazilian Traction, Light and Power Company Limited, 1899–1945* (Toronto: University of Toronto Press, 1988).

20. See, for example, Alfred D. Chandler, Jr., *The Visible Hand: The Managerial Revolution in American Business* (Cambridge, Mass.: The Belknap Press of Harvard University Press, 1977).

21. The Sociedad Latinoamericana de Historia de las Ciencias y la Tecnología was not formed until 1982. For examples of (the few available) country studies see, for example, Ramón Sánchez Flores, *Historia de la tecnología y la invención en México: Introducción a su estudio y documentos para los anales de la técnica* (México: Fomento Cultural Banamex, 1980); and Shozo Motoyama, org. *Tecnologia e industrialização no Brasil: Uma perspectiva histórica* (São Paulo: Editora da Universidade Estadual de São Paulo, 1994); Milton Vargas, org., *História da técnica e da tecnologia no Brasil* (São Paulo: Editora da Universidade Estadual de São Paulo, 1994). Among Latin American specialists in the United States, a few scholars have paid attention to technology in their studies of economic history or industrialization, but none would claim to be a historian of technology. The 1993 Society for the History of Technology *Directory of Members* lists some 30 or so individuals with an expressed interest in Latin America. On closer scrutiny, however, only a dozen reside in the U.S., and of those, only 3 have published anything about Latin America.

22. A notable exception to the lack of interest in secondary cities is James R. Scobie, *Secondary Cities of Argentina: The Social History of Corrientes, Salta, and Mendoza, 1850–1910,* completed and edited by Samuel L. Baily (Stanford, Calif.: Stanford University Press, 1988).

23. Throughout this study I will use the term "State" (with a capital S) to refer to the central Brazilian State, and "state" (with a lowercase s) to refer to the state in Minas Gerais.

24. Marshall C. Eakin, "Cultural Amnesia: Systematically Erasing the History of Brazilian Industrialization," in *Documenting Movements, Identity, and Popular Culture in Latin America,* ed. Richard F. Phillips (Austin: SALALM Secretariat, University of Texas, 2000), 229–35, goes into my efforts to find archives for this study.

Chapter 1

1. Irving Louis Horowitz, *Three Worlds of Development: The Theory and Practice of International Stratification* (New York: Oxford University Press, 1966), esp. 1–38.

2. The terms "developing countries," "newly industrializing countries," and "Third World nations" are used interchangeably throughout this chapter.

3. Tom Kemp, *Industrialization in Nineteenth-Century Europe* (London: Longman, 1969), p. 1. Industrial growth, or the aggregate expansion of industry, is a prerequisite of industrialization, but as used here, the latter term refers to a broader, transformative process that also involves social and political changes.

4. T. S. Ashton, *The Industrial Revolution* (Oxford: Oxford University Press, 1948); Phyllis Deane, *The First Industrial Revolution* (Cambridge: Cambridge University Press, 1967) are two of the "classic" accounts. Pat Hudson, *The Industrial Revolution* (London: Edward Arnold, 1992) provides a useful and thorough overview of the "industrial revolution." In particular, 9–36 provide an excellent survey of the historiography.

5. Carlo Cipolla, ed., *The Fontana Economic History of Europe,* v. 3, *The Industrial Revolution,* and v. 4, *The Emergence of Industrial Societies* (Glasgow: Fontana/Collins, 1973 and 1976); David Landes, *The Unbound Prometheus: Technological Change and Industrial Development in Western Europe from 1750 to the Present* (Cambridge: Cambridge University Press, 1969); Clive Trebilcock, *The Industrialization of the Continental Powers 1780–1914* (London: Longman, 1981); Sidney Pollard, *Peaceful Conquest: The Industrialization of Europe 1760–1970* (Oxford: Oxford University Press, 1981).

6. In particular, the notion of an "Industrial Revolution" continues to stir heated debate. See, for example, Joel Mokyr, ed., *The Economics of the Industrial Revolution* (Totowa, New Jersey: Rowman & Allanheld, 1985), and Joel Mokyr, ed., *The British Industrial Revolution: An Economic Perspective*

(Boulder, Colorado: Westview, 1993), especially David S. Landes, "The Fable of the Dead Horse; or, The Industrial Revolution Revisited," 132–170.

7. "Stripped to its bare bones, the industrial revolution consisted of the application of new sources of power to the production process, achieved with transmission equipment necessary to apply this power to manufacturing. And it consisted of increased scale in human organization that facilitated specialization and coordination at levels preindustrial groupings had rarely contemplated." Peter N. Stearns, *The Industrial Revolution in World History,* 2nd ed. (Boulder, Colorado: Westview Press, 1998), 5.

8. E. A. Wrigley and others have argued that the latter is "the distinguishing feature of the industrial revolution." E. A. Wrigley, *Continuity, Chance and Change: The Character of the Industrial Revolution in England* (Cambridge: Cambridge University Press, 1988), 9. An excellent, brief synthesis of the technological complex of changes is in Landes, "The Fable of the Dead Horse," especially 137. The classic "technological" account is Landes, *The Unbound Prometheus.*

9. Michael Adas, citing Pierre Chaunu and Fernand Braudel, estimates that "the peoples of western Europe possessed an advantage of three or four to one over the Chinese in per capita capacity to tap animal and inanimate sources of power" by the fifteenth century. Michael Adas, *Machines as the Measure of Men: Science, Technology, and Ideologies of Western Dominance* (Ithaca, New York: Cornell University Press, 1989), 21.

10. See, for example, A. E. Musson and Eric Robinson, *Science and Technology in the Industrial Revolution* (Toronto: University of Toronto Press, 1969); and, Landes, *The Unbound Prometheus.*

11. See note 21 in the Introduction.

12. As used here, technology is defined as the efforts of humans to shape or control their environment—both natural and that created by humans. It includes the knowledge, the artifacts created, and the processes involved in their creation. See, for example, Melvin Kranzberg and Carroll W. Pursell, Jr., eds., *Technology in Western Civilization: v. 1. The Emergence of Modern Industrial Society: Earliest Times to 1900* (New York: Oxford University Press, 1967), 4–5.

13. Some studies showing examples of early technological diffusion and subsequent innovation in U.S. industry are Barbara M. Tucker, *Samuel Slater and the Origins of the American Textile Industry, 1790–1860* (Ithaca, New York: Cornell University Press, 1984); and, David J. Jeremy, *Transatlantic Industrial Revolution: The Diffusion of Textile Technologies Between Britain and America, 1790–1830s* (Cambridge, Mass.: The MIT Press, 1981).

14. For one controversial and masterly handling of this topic see Barrington Moore, Jr., *Social Origins of Dictatorship and Democracy: Lord and Peasant in the Making of the Modern World* (Boston: Beacon, 1966).

15. Kemp, *Industrialization in Nineteenth-Century Europe,* p. 7. "The profit-making entrepreneur . . . was the human agent of change in industry, the actual mobilizer of the factors of production who sought out market opportunities and sank or swam according to the accuracy or good fortune with which he judged the situation."

16. Trebilcock, *The Industrialization of the Continental Powers,* especially chapters 2 and 4.

17. For an example overview of the subject, see Peter H. Smith, "The State and Development in Historical Perspective," in *Americas: New Interpretive Essays,* ed. Alfred Stepan (New York: Oxford University Press, 1992), 30–56.

18. W. J. Mommsen, *Britain and Germany, 1800–1914: Two Development Paths Toward Industrial Society* (London: German Historical Institute, 1986); M. E. Falkus, *The Industrialization of Russia, 1700–1914* (London: Macmillan, 1972); Theodore von Laue, *Sergei Witte and the Industrialization of Russia* (New York: Columbia University Press, 1963).

19. See, for example, Luiz Carlos Bresser Pereira, *Development and Crisis in Brazil, 1930–1983* (Boulder, Colorado: Westview, 1984).

20. See, for example, Riordan Roett, "Brazilian Politics at Century's End," in *Brazil under Cardoso,* Susan Kaufman Purcell and Riordan Roett, eds. (Boulder, Colorado: Lynne Rienner, 1997), 19–41.

21. For the persistence of family capitalism in Japan and the West see, Ako Okochi and Shigeaki Yasuoka, eds., *Family Business in the Era of Industrial Growth* (Tokyo, n.d.), especially 1–32 and 171–206. See also, Leslie Hannah, *The Rise of the Corporate Economy,* 2nd ed. (London: Methuen, 1983).

22. Paul Bairoch, "International Industrialization Levels from 1750 to 1980," *Journal of European Economic History* 11:2 (fall 1982): 296 and 304.

23. For one ranking system, see George Thomas Kurian, *The New Book of World Rankings,* 3rd ed. (New York: Facts on File, 1991), 68.

24. Albert Fishlow, "Brazilian Development in Long-Term Perspective," *American Economic Review* 70:2 (1980): 107.

25. See, for example, Rondo Cameron, *A Concise Economic History of the World from Paleolithic Times to the Present,* 2nd ed. (New York: Oxford University Press, 1993), esp. chapters 7–9; Nathan Rosenberg and L. E. Birdzell, Jr., *How the West Grew Rich: The Economic Transformation of the Industrial World* (New York: Basic Books, 1986).

26. Alexander Gerschenkron, *Economic Backwardness in Historical Perspectives: A Book of Essays* (Cambridge, Mass.: Belknap Press, 1962).

27. See, for example, David S. Landes, *The Unbound Prometheus;* E. L. Jones, *The European Miracle: Environments, Economies, and Geopolitics in the History of Europe and Asia,* 2nd ed. (Cambridge: Cambridge University Press, 1987); Tom Kemp, *Industrialization in the Non-Western World,* 2nd ed. (New York: Longman, 1989).

28. See, for example, Victor Bulmer-Thomas, *The Economic History of Latin America Since Independence* (Cambridge: Cambridge University Press, 1994); Celso Furtado, *Economic Development of Latin America: A Survey from Colonial Times to the Cuban Revolution,* 2nd ed. (Cambridge: Cambridge University Press, 1976).

29. See, for example, Celso Furtado, *Formação econômica do Brasil* (Rio de Janeiro: Editôra Fundo de Cultura, 1959); Werner Baer, *The Brazilian Economy: Growth and Development,* 3rd ed. (New York: Praeger, 1989); Wilson Suzigan, *Indústria brasileira: origem e desenvolvimento* (São Paulo: Editôra Brasiliense, 1986).

30. A recent interpretation of the burden of the colonial legacy on economic development is Jorge Caldeira, *A nação mercantilista* (São Paulo: Editora 34, 1999).

31. The standard history of Brazil in English is E. Bradford Burns, *A History of Brazil,* 3rd ed. (New York: Columbia University Press, 1993). For a more recent treatment, see Thomas E. Skidmore, *Brazil: Five Centuries of Change* (New York: Oxford University Press, 1999). See also Leslie Bethell, ed., *Colonial Brazil* (Cambridge: Cambridge University Press, 1987).

32. C. R. Boxer, *The Golden Age of Brazil, 1695–1750: Growing Pains of a Colonial Society* (Berkeley, Calif.: University of California Press, 1969), esp. 30–60, 162–203, and 293–325; A. J. R. Russell-Wood, "The Gold Cycle, c. 1690–1750," *Colonial Brazil,* ed. Leslie Bethell (Cambridge: Cambridge University Press, 1987), 190–243.

33. Francisco Iglésias, *A industrialização brasileira* (São Paulo: Editora Brasiliense, 1985), 24–25.

34. Alan K. Manchester, *British Preeminence in Brazil* (Chapel Hill: University of North Carolina Press, 1933); Richard Graham, *Britain and the Onset of Modernization in Brazil, 1850–1914* (Cambridge: Cambridge University Press, 1968); Irving Stone, "British Direct and Portfolio Investment in Latin America Before 1914," *The Journal of Economic History* 37:3 (September 1977); 690–722; Stephen Haber and Herbert S. Klein, "The Economic Consequences of Brazilian Independence," in Haber, *How Latin America Fell Behind,* 243–59.

35. See, for example, Richard Graham, "Sepoys and Imperialists: Techniques of British Power in Nineteenth-Century Brazil," *Inter-American Economic Affairs* 23:2 (autumn 1969): 23–37; D. C. M. Platt, *Business Imperialism, 1840–1930: An Inquiry Based on British Experience in Latin America* (Oxford: Oxford University Press, 1977); Fernando Henrique Cardoso and Enzo Faletto, *Dependencia y desarrollo en América Latina* (México: Siglo XXI, 1971).

36. Two important studies are Warren Dean, *The Industrialization of São Paulo, 1880–1945* (Austin: University of Texas Press, 1969); and, Wilson Cano, *Desequilíbrios regionais e concentração industrial no Brasil: 1930–1970* (São Paulo: Global, 1985).

37. Thomas H. Holloway, *Immigrants on the Land: Coffee and Society in São Paulo, 1886–1934* (Chapel Hill: University of North Carolina Press, 1980).
38. Robert Conrad, *The Destruction of Brazilian Slavery, 1850–1888* (Berkeley, Calif.: University of California Press, 1972); and Robert Brent Toplin, *The Abolition of Slavery in Brazil* (New York: Atheneum, 1971).
39. Two classic studies are Clarence H. Haring, *Empire in Brazil: A New World Experiment with Monarchy* (Cambridge, Mass.: Harvard University Press, 1958); and Emilia Viotti da Costa, *The Brazilian Empire: Myths and Histories,* rev. ed.(Chapel Hill: University of North Carolina Press, 2000).
40. Furtado, *Formação econômica do Brasil,* esp. part five; Baer, *The Brazilian Economy,* esp. 24–47.
41. Ibid., 47–72; and Marcelo de Paiva Abreu, org., *A ordem do progresso: cem anos de política econômica republicana, 1889–1989* (Rio de Janeiro: Campus, 1990), esp. chapters 3–8.
42. Charles Lewis Taylor and David A. Jodice, eds., *World Handbook of Political and Social Indicators* (New Haven: Yale University Press, 1983), 106.
43. On the regional growth of Monterrey see Alex M. Saragoza, *The Monterrey Elite and the Mexican State, 1880–1940* (Austin: University of Texas Press, 1988); Menno Vellinga, *Economic Development and the Dynamics of Class: Industrialization, Power and Control in Monterrey, Mexico* (Assen, The Netherlands: Van Gorcum, 1979); Mario Cerutti, *Burguesía y capitalismo en Monterrey (1850–1910)* (México: Claves Latinoamericanas, 1983). For Colombia, see Carlos Dávila L. de Guevara, *El empresariado colombiano: una perspectiva histórica* (Bogotá: Pontificia Universidad Javeriana, 1986).
44. C. R. Boxer, *The Golden Age of Brazil,* 293–325.
45. Amilcar Vianna Martins Filho, "The White Collar Republic: Patronage and Interest Representation in Minas Gerais, Brazil, 1889–1930," Ph.D. dissertation, University of Illinois, 1987, especially chapter 2. The debate over the nature of the mineiro economy in the nineteenth century has been intense. During the 1980s a debate took shape over the nature of the mineiro economy in the nineteenth century. This debate was initiated by Amilcar Martins Filho and Roberto B. Martins, "Slavery in a Nonexport Economy: Nineteenth-Century Minas Gerais Revisited," *Hispanic American Historical Review* 63:3 (August 1983): 537–68. For critiques of the article and the reply of the Martins brothers see the same issue, 569–90. Robert Slenes, "Os múltiplos de porcos e diamantes: a economia escravista de Minas Gerais no século XIX," *Cadernos IFCH/UNICAMP* 17 (1985), is another important critique of the Martins. For a recent appraisal that responds to the various historiographical issues see Laird W. Bergad, *Slavery and the Demographic and Economic History of Minas Gerais, Brazil, 1720–1888* (Cambridge: Cambridge University Press, 1999), chapter 2.
46. Wirth, *Minas Gerais in the Brazilian Federation, 1889–1937* (Stanford, Calif.: Stanford University Press, 1977), 2–3.

47. Warren Dean, *With Broadax and Firebrand: The Destruction of the Brazilian Atlantic Forest* (Berkeley: University of California Press, 1995), 187.

48. Francisco Iglésias, *Política econômica do govêrno provincial mineiro (1835–1889)* (Rio de Janeiro: Instituto Nacional do Livro, 1958); Douglas Cole Libby, *Transformação e trabalho em uma economia escravista: Minas Gerais no século XIX* (São Paulo: Editora Brasiliense, 1988); João Heraldo de Lima, *Café e indústria em Minas Gerais, 1870–1920* (Petrópolis: Vozes, 1981); Ana Lúcia Duarte Lanna, *A transformação do trabalho: a passagem para o trabalho livre na Zona da Mata mineira, 1870–1920* (Campinas: Editora da UNICAMP, 1988); John D. Wirth, *Minas Gerais in the Brazilian Federation;* Peter Louis Blasenheim, "A Regional History of the Zona da Mata in Minas Gerais, Brazil, 1870–1906," Ph.D. dissertation, Stanford University, 1982; Maria Efigênia Lage de Resende, "Manifestações oligárquicas na política mineira," *Revista Brasileira de Estudos Políticos* (1979): 7–69.

49. Peter Evans, *Dependent Development: The Alliance of Multinational, State, and Local Capital in Brazil* (Princeton: Princeton University Press, 1979).

50. Marshall C. Eakin, "Creating a Growth Pole: The Industrialization of Belo Horizonte, Brazil, 1897–1987," *The Americas* 47:4 (April 1991): 383–410.

51. The power of political and kinship networks has long been a subject of debate in studies of Minas Gerais. For a recent dissertation that addresses the subject see, Amilcar Vianna Martins, "The White Collar Republic: Patronage and Interest Representation in Minas Gerais, Brazil, 1889–1930," Ph.D. dissertation, University of Illinois, 1987. See also, Cid Rebelo Horta, "Famílias Governamentais de Minas Gerais," in *Segundo Seminário de Estudos Mineiros* (Belo Horizonte: Universidade de Minas Gerais, 1956), 45–91. A new study of patronage, clientelism, and regionalism in the post-1964 era is Frances Hagopian, *Traditional Politics and Regime Change in Brazil* (Cambridge: Cambridge University Press, 1996).

52. "In the early 1960s, private Minas capital was concentrated in the 'traditional' industrial sector, a plethora of small-scale, family-run production units with outmoded managerial practices; low growth rates, low levels of technology, productivity, and efficiency; obsolete equipment; and less than optimal plant locations." Hagopian, *Traditional Politics and Regime Change in Brazil,* 86. Greater Belo Horizonte "received over 80 percent of all new industrial investment from 1970 to 1977, the lion's share of which was targeted to the area's steel industries and the increasingly dense cluster of manufacturing plants in the metropolitan region of the state capital. Metropolitan Belo Horizonte alone acquired one-third of all investment channeled through the Industrial Development Institute from 1969 to 1980." Ibid., 99.

53. Steven Topik, *The Political Economy of the Brazilian State, 1889–1930* (Austin: University of Texas Press, 1987), especially chapter 4, "The Railway Network," 93–128.

54. Martins, 85.

55. See, for example, William Roderick Summerhill, "Railroads and the Brazilian Economy Before 1914," Ph.D. dissertation, Stanford University, 1995.

56. Daniel de Carvalho, "A Formação Histórica de Minas Gerais," in *Primeiro Seminário de Estudos Mineiros* (Belo Horizonte: Universidade Federal de Minas Gerais, 1956), 54.

57. See, for example, Gail D. Triner, *Banking and Economic Delvelopment: Brazil, 1889–1930* (New York: Palgrave, 2000).

58. For a sample of the literature on state planning and the role of technocrats see: Nathaniel H. Leff, *Economic Policy-Making and Development in Brazil, 1947–1964* (New York: John Wiley & Sons, 1968); Robert T. Daland, *Brazilian Planning: Development Politics and Administration* (Chapel Hill: University of North Carolina Press, 1967); Octavio Ianni, *Estado e planejamento econômico no Brasil (1930–1970)* (Rio de Janeiro: Civilização Brasileira, 1971); Luciano Martins, *Estado capitalista e burocracia no Brasil pós–64* (Rio de Janeiro: Paz e Terra, 1985); Ben Ross Schneider, *Politics Within the State: Elite Bureaucrats and Industrial Policy in Authoritarian Brazil* (Pittsburgh, Penn.: University of Pittsburgh Press, 1991). Hagopian's definition of technocrat is "those officeholders who had: an economics degree; an engineering degree; or a record of service" in public sector enterprises such as the state electrical utility (CEMIG), state steel corporation (Usiminas), the state highway division (DER), and the state development bank (BDMG). Hagopian, *Traditional Politics and Regime Change in Brazil,* 115.

59. Peter Louis Blasenheim, "A Regional History of the Zona da Mata in Minas Gerais, Brazil, 1870–1906," Ph.D. dissertation, Stanford University, 1982.

60. Maria Efigênia Lage de Resende, "Uma interpretação sobre a fundação de Belo Horizonte," *Revista Brasileira de Estudos Políticos* 39 (1974): 129–161.

61. See, for example, the classic work of Raimundo Faoro, *Os donos do poder: formação do patronato político brasileiro,* 5a. ed., 2 v. (Porto Alegre: Globo, 1979). See also, Simon Schwartzman, *Bases do autoritarismo brasileiro,* 3a ed. (Rio de Janeiro: Campus, 1988). I should note here that although I agree that corporatism and patrimonialism have long characterized Brazilian society, I reject the ahistorical approach of the "cultural" theorists who place more emphasis on continuity than on change. For the concept of the cartorial state see, Hélio Jaguaribe, *Political Development: A General Theory and a Latin American Case Study* (New York: Harper & Row, 1973), 476.

62. Emília Viotti da Costa, *The Brazilian Empire: Myths and Histories,* esp. chapter 3.

63. Roderick Barman, *Brazil: The Forging of a Nation, 1798–1852* (Stanford: Stanford University Press, 1988).

64. José Murilo de Carvalho, *Teatro de sombras: a política imperial* (São Paulo: Vértice, 1988).

65. Richard Graham, *Patronage and Politics in Nineteenth-Century Brazil* (Stanford: Stanford University Press, 1990).

66. Fernando Uricoechea, *O minotauro imperial* (Rio de Janeiro: Difel, 1978).

67. Victor Nunes Leal, *Coronelismo, enxada e voto: o município e o regime representativo no Brasil* (Rio de Janeiro: Revista Forense, 1948).

68. "The states were given control over federal patronage in exchange for supporting the president's program in congress." John D. Wirth, *Minas Gerais in the Brazilian Federation*, 106.

69. See note 45.

70. See, for example, the classic biography, Afonso Arinos de Melo Franco, *Um estadista da República,* 3 v. (Rio de Janeiro: José Olympio, 1955).

71. Wirth, *Minas Gerais in the Brazilian Federation,* chapter 4; and, Martins, "The White Collar Republic," esp. chapter 4.

72. Nunes Leal, *Coronelismo;* Wirth, *Minas Gerais in the Brazilian Federation;* Joseph Love, *São Paulo in the Brazilian Federation, 1889–1937* (Stanford, Calif.: Stanford University Press, 1980); Robert M. Levine, *Pernambuco in the Brazilian Federation, 1889–1937* (Stanford, Calif.: Stanford University Press, 1978).

73. "By any indicator of political power one chooses to take—the number of high offices in the federal administration held by the state's politicians, the strength and prestige of its delegation in the national congress, or most important of all, the capacity to channel federal resources and sinecures to the state—Minas was second to none. In the period 1902–1930, Minas had three presidents, five vice-presidents, more years in the ministries than any other state, virtual control of certain key commissions in the congress, and the largest single share of other high level positions in the federal administrations." Martins, 1.

74. "[T]he unification of Mineiro politics was primarily achieved through a broad and far-reaching process of political co-optation of all groups and factions in the state . . ." Martins, "White Collar Republic," 8.

75. "The leaders of these factions shared a similar talent for nonideological politics based on pragmatic manipulation. They ran their factions on a patron-client system of reciprocal rights and obligations, in which personal loyalty was the guiding principle and patronage the cement of politics." Wirth, *Minas Gerais in the Brazilian Federation,* 107–108.

76. For an excellent book on recent politics, see Hagopian, *Traditional Politics and Regime Change in Brazil.*

77. "For most coronéis, however, there was but one commandment: never oppose the governor." Wirth, *Minas Gerais in the Brazilian Federation,* 105.

78. Those positions were: director of the Imprensa Oficial, president of the Banco Hipotecário de Minas Gerais, president of the Banco do Estado de Minas Gerais, mayor of Belo Horizonte, state representative, state senator, justice of the state supreme court, secretary of agriculture, secretary of finance, secretary

of the interior, chief of police (after 1927 the secretary of public safety), lieutenant governor, governor, federal representative, federal senator, president of the Banco do Brasil, mayor of the Federal District, minister of the federal supreme court, minister of finance, minister of interior and justice, minister of agriculture, minister of foreign relations, minister of the army, minister of the navy, vice-president, and president of Brazil. Martins, "The White Collar Republic," 113 and 146. Three other important studies of the political elite are Wirth, *Minas Gerais in the Brazilian Federation,* especially chapter 5; David Verge Fleischer, "Political Recruitment in the State of Minas Gerais, Brazil (1890–1970)," Ph.D. dissertation, University of Florida, 1972; and David V. Fleischer, "O Recrutamento Político em Minas 1890/1918," *Revista Brasileira de Estudos Políticos* 30 (1971). Wirth's sample covers the period from 1889 to 1937, and consisted of 214 individuals. He did not include as many positions as Martins.

79. Martins, "White Collar Republic," 277.
80. "Family ties, education, and money were the customary pathways to elite status." Wirth, *Minas Gerais in the Brazilian Federation,* 142.
81. He gives the examples of "the Ottoni family (5 members) from Teófilo Ottoni in the Mucuri region; the Mello Franco family (5 members) from Paracutu; the Pereira Gomes and Santiago families (6 members); the Bueno Brandão, the Silviano Brandão and Bueno de Paiva families (8 members) from the Sul; the Moura family (6 members) from the Mata; the Pena family (5 members) from the Metalúrgica; the Andrada family (6 members) from Barbacena, in the Campos das Vertentes region; and the Ribeiro da Luz, Ferraz, and Coimbra families (10 members) from the Metalúrgica, among others. Many of these families were already in the elite during the Empire, and today they are still actively involved in the Mineiro politics." Martins, 120.
82. Martins, 131.
83. Wirth, *Minas Gerais in the Brazilian Federation,* 141.
84. In the March 1898 election for governor, the newly organized PRM chose Francisco Silviano de Bueno Brandão as its candidate, and he received 112,746 votes out of a total of 112,911 cast! Martins, "White Collar Republic," 160.
85. Martins, "White Collar Republic," 162–163.
86. "In Minas, as (probably) in several other Latin polities of this era, change through clientele politics was authoritarian, from the top down, but garbed in democratic forms. This resulted in technocratic policies, the co-option of interest groups by the state, and the conscious suppression of class politics. Whereas clientelism eroded the development of collective interests, the state government was also beholden to special interest groups and gave them favors to secure their loyalty and prevent tax revolts. Here reciprocity—the key element of clientele politics—hindered basic structural change and was per-

haps a high price to pay for short-term political peace." Wirth, *Minas Gerais in the Brazilian Federation,* 118.

87. As one popular saying went, "Fora do PRM não há salvação." (Outside the PRM there is no salvation.) Martins, "White Collar Republic," 175.

88. As Martins has put it, "The only condition for access to patronage was political loyalty to the center." Martins, "White Collar Republic," 172.

89. Martins, 168–169.

90. Martins, 185.

91. Martins, 185–193.

92. Martins, 188–189.

93. An excellent summary of the various theoretical perspectives can be found in Delgado, "Burguesia e Estado," 8–18.

Chapter 2

1. "It was hoped that the new capital would effectively come to exercise the role of a center for political and economic integration for the 'mineiro mosaic'." Otavio Soares Dulci, *Política e recuperação econômica em Minas Gerais* (Belo Horizonte: Editora UFMG, 1999), 41.

2. Waldemar de Almeida Barbosa, *A verdade sobre a história de Belo Horizonte* (Belo Horizonte: FIMAC, 1985), 74. Vila Rica do Ouro Preto (as it was originally called) had arisen spontaneously as a gold mining camp in the rugged Serra do Espinhaço, and the city sprawled up and down the steep hillsides.

3. "Mensagem do Presidente Augusto de Lima à Assembléia Constituinte Mineira em 17 de abril de 1891," *Annaes do Senado Mineiro* (1891), 15–16.

4. Commissão D'Estudo das Localidades Indicadas para a Nova Capital, *Relatório* (Rio de Janeiro: Imprensa Nacional, 1893); Maria Efigênia Lage de Resende, "Uma interpretação sobre a fundação de Belo Horizonte," *Revista Brasileira de Estudos Políticos* 39 (1974): 7–69; Jeffry Adelman, "Urban Planning and Reality in Republican Brazil: Belo Horizonte, 1890–1930," Ph.D. dissertation, Indiana University, 1974, chapter 1.

5. Commissão Constructora da Nova Capital, *Revista geral dos trabalhos. I. Abril de 1895* and *II. Fevereiro de 1896* (Rio de Janeiro: H. Lombaerts, 1895 and 1896). Good descriptions of the building of the capital are Adelman, "Urban Planning," chapter 2, and eyewitness accounts by Alfredo Camarate reproduced in *Revista do Arquivo Público Mineiro* XXXVI (1985), 23–198.

6. The parish of Curral d'El Rei (founded 1748) became the district of Belo Horizonte in 1890. With the decision to move the capital, the state created the municipio of Belo Horizonte around the city. In 1901, the Cidade de Minas once again became the city of Belo Horizonte in the municipio of the same name. Waldemar de Almeida Barbosa, *Dicionário histórico-geográfico de Minas Gerais* (Belo Horizonte: Promoção-da-Família, 1971), 67–68; Paulo

Kruger Corrêa Mourão, *História de Belo Horizonte de 1897 a 1930* (Belo Horizonte: Imprensa Oficial, 1970), 9–11.

7. Abílio Barreto, *Bello Horizonte: Memória histórica e descriptiva,* 2a ed. (Bello Horizonte: Livraria Rex, 1936), 245.

8. *Memória da economia da cidade de Belo Horizonte* (Belo Horizonte: Iniciativas Culturais Empresas BMG, 1987), 25.

9. *Minas Geraes,* 2–3 January 1898, 1; *Estado de Minas,* 2 July 1988, 14.

10. *Annuario estatístico. anno I—1921,* volume IV, tomo I (Bello Horizonte: Imprensa Official, 1926), 407.

11. The figures are taken from *Sinopse estatístico do município de Belo Horizonte* (Rio de Janeiro: IBGE, 1948), 20. Calculations include only those with known occupations.

12. *Annuário estatístico de Belo Horizonte, anno I—1937* (Belo Horizonte: Serviço de Estatístico Geral, 1937), 75. Prominent exceptions were the Belgo Mineira iron and steel works in Sabará, and the Morro Velho gold mine in Nova Lima.

13. Some examples are found in *Minas Geraes,* 30 January 1907, 5; 19 September 1908, 7; 20 June 1909, 4; 8 July 1909, 5; 26 May 1910, 3; 18 May 1910, 5; 20 May 1910, 4; 9–10 January 1911, 5–6; 1 June 1912, 5; 24–25 June 1912, 3; 16 June 1912, 5; 8 June 1912, 3.

14. For example, "Contratos," 27 May 1910, 63v–64v and 8 July 1910, 64v–65v, Arquivo Público da Cidade de Belo Horizonte. Other examples can be found in the *Relatório da Prefeitura de Bello Horizonte,* v. 1, 57.

15. "50 annos da FIEMG," *Vida Industrial* 30:2 (February 1983): 8–13.

16. *Recenseamento geral do Brasil [1 de setembro de 1940]. série nacional. volume III. censo econômico* (Rio de Janeiro: IBGE, 1950), 185; and Armin K. Ludwig, *Brazil: A Handbook of Historical Statistics* (Boston: G. K. Hall, 1985), 55.

17. Despite an extensive literature on economic history, the history of business, and more specifically, of entrepreneurs, has been barely explored in Latin America. Aside from hagiographic or amateurish studies, scholarly works on entrepreneurs and business are few, and the field of business history has only recently begun to take shape. In the case of Brazil, the list of books on specific firms is very short, and studies of entrepreneurs, equally so. Some recent examples are: Roderick J. Barman, "Business and Government in Imperial Brazil: The Experience of Viscount Mauá," *Journal of Latin American Studies* 13:2 (November 1981): 239–264; Sérgio de Oliveira Birchal, *Entrepreneurship in Nineteenth-Century Brazil: The Formation of a Business Environment* (New York: St. Martin's Press, 1999); Jorge Caldeira, *Mauá: empresário do Império* (São Paulo: Companhia das Letras, 1995); Elizabeth Anne Cobbs, *The Rich Neighbor Policy: Rockefeller and Kaiser in Brazil* (New Haven, Conn.: Yale University Press, 1992); Marshall C. Eakin, *British Enterprise in Brazil: The St. John d'el Rey Mining Company and the Morro Velho Gold Mine, 1830–1960* (Durham, North Carolina: Duke University Press,

1989); Maria Bárbara Levy, *História da Bolsa de Valores do Rio de Janeiro* (Rio de Janeiro: Instituto Brasileiro de Mercado de Capitais, 1977); Duncan Mc-Dowall, *The Light: Brazilian Traction, Light and Power Company Limited, 1899–1945* (Toronto: University of Toronto Press, 1988); Eugene Ridings, *Business Interest Groups in Nineteenth-Century Brazil* (New York: Cambridge University Press, 1994); Elisabeth von de Weid and Anna Marta Rodrigues Bastos, *O fio da meada: estratégia de expansão de uma indústria têxtil: Companhia América Fabril, 1878–1930* (Rio de Janeiro: FCRB-CNI, 1986).

18. "Except for banking, the mineiro entrepreneur just limits himself to making appeals [to the government] and scarcely appears in areas such as the transformation of non-metallic minerals and civil construction." *Diagnóstico da economia mineira* (Belo Horizonte: Banco de Desenvolvimento de Minas Gerais, 1967), v. 1, 18.

19. See, for example, Luis Aureliano Gama de Andrade, "Technocracy and Development: The Case of Minas Gerais," Ph.D. dissertation, University of Michigan, 1980; Clélio Campolina Diniz, *Estado e capital estrangeiro na industrialização mineira* (Belo Horizonte: UFMG/PROED, 1981); Frances Hagopian, *Traditional Politics and Regime Change in Brazil* (New York: Cambridge University Press, 1996); Superintendência de Desenvolvimento da Região Metropolitana (PLAMBEL), Secretaria de Estado do Planejamento e Coordenação Geral, Governor do Estado de Minas Gerais, "O Processo de desenvolvimento de Belo Horizonte: 1897–1970," (Belo Horizonte: PLAMBEL, 1979).

20. See, for example, Ian Roxborough, *Theories of Underdevelopment* (London: Macmillan, 1979); and Robert A. Packenham, *The Dependency Movement: Scholarship and Politics in Development Studies* (Cambridge, Mass.: Harvard University Press, 1992).

21. Some recent dissertations by mineiro scholars have looked at the business community for small periods of time. See, for example, Evantina Pereira Vieira, "Minas Gerais: a dominação burguesa—conflitos políticos e formas de organização (1927–1940)," Ph.D. dissertation, Universidade de São Paulo, 1985; Ignácio José Godinho Delgado, "Burguesia e estado—o caso de Minas Gerais: a estratégia de um revés," M.A. thesis, Departamento de Ciência Política, UFMG, 1989; Maria Auxiliadora Faria, "'A Política da Gleba': as classes conservadoras mineiras: discurso e prática na Primeira República," Ph.D. dissertation, Universidade de São Paulo, 1992. Heloisa Starling, *Os senhores das Gerais: os novos inconfidentes e o golpe militar de 1964,* 5a. ed.(Petrópolis: Vozes, 1986) looks at the business community during the 1960s.

22. The tax was on both firms and individuals, the vast majority of the businesses in operation were run by individuals. As a result, although the table provides a count of firms and individuals, it is very close to a tabulation of individual entrepreneurs. More than three-quarters of those counted are

firmas individuais as opposed to *firmas sociais,* nearly of all of which are small, family firms. *Minas Geraes,* 28 December 1922. The categories in the table are mine and are not used in the census.

23. The tax obviously did not extend to domestic servants, but only the formal service sector.

24. The municipality collected the tax on industries and professions (the basis of data in table 2.3 and appendix A), while the census of mercantile firms in the 1930s comes from the state's registry of businesses, the Junta Comercial do Estado de Minas Gerais. The data on 1950 come from the national census.

25. One thousand mil-reis equalled one *conto* (1,000$). In 1936, 86 mil-reis equalled 1 pound sterling. Annibal Villanova Villela and Wilson Suzigan, *Política do governo e crescimento da economia brasileira, 1889–1945* (Rio de Janeiro: IPEA/INPES, 1973), 425.

26. For accounts of the founding of the ACM, see *Boletim da Associação Comercial de Minas* II, 49 (31 August 1943), 4–6; *Minas Gerais,* 3 January 1951, 8; 6 January 1951, 9–10; 13 January 1951, 13. When the ACM was founded in 1901, the city was known as the Cidade de Minas and had not yet reverted back to its previous name, Belo Horizonte. Hence, the Minas in the association's title did not refer to the state, but to the city. The Cidade de Minas reverted back to Belo Horizonte by Decree 302 of 1 July 1901. *Relatório da Prefeitura de Bello Horizonte* v. 1: 21.

27. *Minas Geraes,* 7–8 January 1901, 3; 9 January 1901, 3; 21–22 January 1901, 2; 24 January 1901, 4; and, Luiz Sayão de Faria and Joaquim Ribeiro Filho, "Resumo histórico da Associação Comercial de Minas," *Revista Social Trabalhista,* December 1947, 360–7.

28. As one article explained it, the ACM "exercised influence and always participated in the development of the state's economy, and, consequently, attracted the respect and recognition of public officials, and tacitly became a collaborator in municipal and state administrations through suggestions that were of interest to the productive forces of the state." Sayão de Faria and Ribeiro Filho, *Revista Social Trabalhista,* 361. For numerous examples of commercial associations in imperial Brazil, see Eugene Ridings, *Business Interest Groups in Nineteenth-Century Brazil* (Cambridge: Cambridge University Press, 1994).

29. Sayão de Faria and Ribeiro Filho, 363; *Minas Geraes,* 7–8 January 1901, 3; 21–22 January 1901, 2. The successful pursuit of the government loan is chronicled in the ACM's *Atas* that are now housed in the "centro de memória" of the ACM on the Avenida Afonso Pena in downtown Belo Horizonte. *Atas da ACM,* 7 February 1915; 26 June and 21 August 1919; 29 September, 11 December, and 18 December 1921; 9 August 1928; 4 July and 29 October 1929.

30. Arquivo da Associação Comercial de Minas, "Livro de Eleições," January 1936 to January 1946.

31. *Minas Geraes,* 1 January 1901, 3; 11 January 1907, 4; 24/25 August 1908, 7.

32. Sayão de Faria and Ribeiro Filho; *Minas Geraes,* 24/25 August 1908, 7. Obituary of Drummond in *Minas Geraes,* 21 November 1923, 11.

33. *Minas Gerais,* 3 September 1970, 4.

34. The Vargas government recognized the FIEMG as the official *entidade sindical* of industrialists in February 1943. Archive of the Federação das Indústrias do Estado de Minas Gerais (hereafter AFIEMG), Pasta 369. See also, *Vida Industrial* 30:2 (February 1983): esp. 10–13.

35. The industries included: ceramics, footwear, construction, sawmills, marble and woodworking, brick and tilemaking, pharmaceuticals, mechanical shops, bottling, soapmaking, papermaking, typographers, chemicals, print shops, food processing, metallurgy, and textiles. AFIEMG, "Livro de transcripção dos socios."

36. The Federação do Comércio was founded in 1938 during the corporatist Estado Novo dictatorship. *Revista Comercial de Minas Gerais* 15 (1938): 85.

37. Associação Comercial de Minas, *Estatutos de fundação* (Cidade de Minas: Imprensa Oficial, 1901).

38. *Minas Gerais,* 8 September 1935. Faria has an excellent and extended analysis of the discourse of the business elite in "A Política da Gleba."

39. *Atas da ACM,* 9 February 1933.

40. *Atas da ACM,* 4 July 1935.

41. The 1935 Congress had committees representing the ACM, the FIEMG, and the Sociedade Mineira de Agricultura. The committees are a who's who of the power elite: ACM—Caetano Vasconcelos, Lauro Jacques, Ismael Libânio, Osorio Diniz, Luiz Haas, Lauro Vidal; FIEMG—Alvimar Carneiro de Rezende, Christiano Guimarães, Américo Giannetti, Janot Pacheco, Arthur Savassi, José da Silva Brandão; SMA—Socrates Alvim, Flávio de Salles Dias, Virgílio Bastos, Antônio Ribeiro de Abreu, José Monteiro Machado, Cândido de Freitas. The secretary general of the commissions was Jair Negrão de Lima. *Atas da ACM,* 21 March 1935.

42. For a detailed analysis of the major figures in the congresses see Maria Auxiliadora Faria, "'A Política da Gleba': as classes conservadoras mineiras: discurso e prática na Primeira República," Ph.D. dissertation, Universidade de São Paulo, 1992, esp. 177, 204–209.

43. Dulci, 160.

44. Quoted in Dulci, *Política e recuperação econômica,* 45.

45. Evantina Pereira Vieira, "Minas Gerais: a dominação burguesa—conflitos políticos e formas de organização (1927–1940)," Ph.D. dissertation, Universidade São Paulo, 1985, 54–55. See also, "A união das classes conservadoras," *Estado de Minas,* 11 May 1928, 1.

46. *Minas Gerais,* 17 September 1935.

47. Quoted in Vieira, 76.

48. *Minas Gerais,* 16 February 1939, 21. Dos Santos was unusual in that he was not a mineiro (he was born in Alagoas). He married into one of the local elite families.

49. *Minas Gerais,* 3 September 1970, 4.

50. Wirth, *Minas Gerais in the Brazilian Federation,* 147.

51. A prominent example was Arthur Haas, an Alsatian Jew who set up retail operations during the initial construction of the city. He became one of the most prominent merchants in Belo Horizonte with one of the first and most important automobile dealerships. His son Luiz also was a major figure in the ACM. Founded in 1894, the Casa Arthur Haas justifiable advertised itself as "the oldest commercial house in Belo Horizonte." *Minas Geraes,* 22 August 1909, 8. A few Lebanese merchants, such as Miguel Abras, also played important roles in local commerce. *Minas Geraes,* 14 January 1938.

52. In Belo Horizonte, despite the decline (that would continue for decades), textiles were still the major industry in the city in 1940 with 32 establishments accounting for nearly 40 percent of capital investment (more than twice the second leading industry, food processing), and 23 percent of the industrial workforce. *Produção industrial do municipio de Belo Horizonte, 1936–1942* (Belo Horizonte: IBGE, 1943).

53. See, for example, Alisson Mascarenhas Vaz, *Cia. Cedro e Cachoeira: história de uma empresa familiar, 1883–1987* (Belo Horizonte: Cia. de Fiação e Tecidos Cedro e Cachoeira S. A., 1990).

54. Ibid.

55. A full obituary of Américo Teixeira Guimarães can be found in *Minas Gerais,* 30 November 1947, 13.

56. Obituary of Benjamim Ferreira Guimarães in *Minas Gerais,* 16 March 1948, 25; *Coronel Benjamim Ferreira Guimarães: tecendo histórias* (Belo Horizonte: Livraria Del Rey Editora, 1997); "Antônio Mourão Guimarães," and "Flávio Pentagna Guimarães," *Dicionário biográfico,* I, 300–1 and 303; "Centenário de Antônio Mourão Guimarães," *Estado de Minas,* 25 June 1988, 4–6.

57. Very little research has been done on banking in Minas Gerais. The most important study is Fernando Nogueira da Costa, "Bancos em Minas Gerais (1889–1964)," Ph.D. dissertation, Universidade Estadual de Campinas, 1978.

58. Two pioneering studies of Brazilian banking and finance are Gail D. Triner, *Banking and Economic Delvelopment: Brazil,* 1889–1930 (New York: Palgrave, 2000); and, Anne Gerard Hanley, "Capital Markets in the Coffee Economy: Financial Institutions and Economic Change in São Paulo, Brazil, 1850–1905," Ph.D. dissertation, Stanford University, 1995.

59. Da Costa, 33–99.

60. Da Costa, 32–43. He argues that the banking "explosion" in Minas after 1920 was partially fostered by the state government. See 144.

61. Naomi R. Lamoreaux, "Banks, Kinship, and Economic Development: The New England Case," *Journal of Economic History* 46:3 (September 1986): 647.
62. See, for example, Noel Maurer, "Banks and Entrepreneurs in Porfirian Mexico: Inside Exploitation or Sound Business Strategy?" *Journal of Latin American Studies* 31:2 (May 1999): 331–61; and Lamoreaux, "Banks, Kinship, and Economic Development," 647–67; Lynne Zucker, "Production of Trust: Institutional Sources of Economic Structure, 1940–1920," in *Research in Organizational Behavior,* v. 8 (1986), Barry M. Staw and L. L. Cummings, editors, 53–111.
63. Faria, 126.
64. The son of a rural colonel in Minas Novas in eastern Minas, Barbosa had degrees from both the law school in São Paulo and Ouro Preto. A prominent journalist, he also founded the Companhia Industrial e Agrícola Riacho Fundo. He was one of the founders of the state's most powerful newspaper in the twentieth century, the *Estado de Minas.* "Juscelino Barbosa," *Dicionário biográfico,* I, 72–3.
65. The information in this paragraph and the next come from Antônio Lopes Sá, *Origens de um banco centenário* (Belo Horizonte: Credireal, 1989); Fernando Nogueira da Costa, "Bancos em Minas Gerais (1889–1964)," Ph.D. dissertation, Universidade Estadual de Campinas, 1978; Cláudio Bastos, *Instituições financeiras de Minas (1819–1995)* (Belo Horizonte: Embalat Editora, 1997); Dulci, *Recuperação e política econômica,* 49–50; Faria, "'A Política da Gleba'," 340–5.
66. Obituary of "Sebastião Augusto de Lima," *Minas Gerais,* 25 November 1953, 8; "Banco Comércio e Indúsria de Minas Gerais, S. A.," in *Belo Horizonte completa 50 anos,* 104–7; "Banco Comércio e Indúsria de Minas Gerais," JUCEMG.
67. "Banco da Lavoura de Minas Gerais," JUCEMG; "Hugo Furquim Werneck," *Dicionário biográfico,* II, 724; Bastos, 111–7.
68. Quoted in Dulci, *Recuperação e política econômica,* 50. See also the analysis of these banks and their role in Faria, "'A Política da Gleba'," 340–5.
69. *Minas Gerais,* 16 February 1939 (for dos Santos); 23 July 1890, 4, and 18 September 1918, 6 (for Vaz de Mellos); and, 14 December 1952, 8 (for Carvalho Brito).
70. Maria Auxiliadora Faria, "'A política da gleba': as classes conservadoras mineiras: discurso e prática na Primeira República," Ph.D. diss., Universidade de São Paulo, 1992; Evantina Pereira Vieira, "Minas Gerais: a dominação burguesa—conflitos políticos e formas de organização (1927–1940)," Ph.D. diss., Universidade de São Paulo, 1985; Ignácio José Godinho Delgado, "Burguesia e estado: o caso de Minas Gerais: a estrategia de um revés," M.A. thesis, Political Science, Universidade Federal de Minas Gerais, 1989; Otavio Soares Dulci, *Política e recuperação econômica em Minas Gerais* (Belo Horizonte: Editora UFMG, 1999); Heloísa Maria Murgel Starling, *Os senhores das*

Gerais: os novos inconfidentes e o golpe militar de 1964, 5a. ed. (Petrópolis: Vozes, 1986).

71. Warren Dean, *The Industrialization of São Paulo, 1880–1945,* chapter 3.
72. *Recenseamento do Brazil . . . 1920,* v. II, 1a parte, 514; v. IV, 5a parte, tomo II, 24–25 and 787–7.
73. The absolute figures in cruzeiros are: Belo Horizonte (2,188,821,000), Rio de Janeiro (29,520,640,000), São Paulo (38, 804,327,000). *Anuário estatístico do Brasil* (Rio de Janeiro: Instituto Brasileiro de Geografia e Estatística, 1953), 330.
74. Dean, *The Industrialization of São Paulo;* and Cano, *Desequilíbrios regionais;* Joseph L. Love, *São Paulo in the Brazilian Federation, 1889–1937* (Stanford, Calif.: Stanford University Press, 1980).
75. Love, *São Paulo in the Brazilian Federation,* 55 and 158- 9.
76. Ako Okochi and Shigeaki Yasuoka, eds., *Family Business in the Era of Industrial Growth* (Tokyo: University of Tokyo Press, n.d.), esp. 1–32 and 171–206. See also, Leslie Hannah, *The Rise of the Corporate Economy,* 2nd ed. (London: Methuen, 1983).
77. Two examples of other studies of business communities in Latin America are: Alex M. Saragoza, *The Monterrey Elite and the Mexican State, 1880–1940* (Austin: University of Texas Press, 1988) and Carlos Dávila L. de Guevara, *El empresariado colombiano: una perspectiva histórica* (Bogotá: Pontificia Universidad Javeriana, 1986).

Chapter 3

1. See, for example, Clélio Campolina Diniz, *Estado e capital estrangeira na industrialização mineira* (Belo Horizonte: UFMG/PROED, 1981); Domingos Antônio Giroletti, "A modernização capitalista em Minas Gerais—a formação do operariado industrial e de uma nova cosmovisão," Ph.D. diss., Universidade Federal do Rio de Janeiro, 1987; João Heraldo Lima, *Café e indústria em Minas Gerais, 1870–1920* (Petrópolis: Vozes, 1981); and, Banco de Desenvolvimento de Minas Gerais, *Diagnóstico da economica mineira,* 6 v. (Belo Horizonte: BDMG, 1968). A recent work that does provide a look at firms and their technological choices for the nineteenth century is Sérgio de Oliveira Birchal, *Entrepreneurship in Nineteenth-Century Brazil: The Formation of a Business Environment* (New York: St. Martin's Press, 1999).
2. Martins, "The White Collar Republic: Patronage and Interest Representation in Minas Gerais, Brazil, 1889–1930," Ph.D. diss., University of Illinois, 1987, chapter 3, "The Non-Export Sector of the Mineiro Economy: The Invisible Giant."
3. Wirth, *Minas Gerais in the Brazilian Federation, 1889–1937* (Stanford: Stanford University Press, 1977), 3.

4. João Heraldo de Lima, "Crescimento Industrial em uma Economia Não-Exportadora: Minas Gerais, 1907–1920," *Estudos Econômicos* 15 (Janeiro-Abril 1985): 138 and Table 12.

5. *Relatório . . . Agricultura,* 1928–1929, 41.

6. Martins, "The White Collar Republic," 259–60.

7. Wilson Suzigan, *Indústria brasileira: origem e desenvolvimento* (São Paulo: Brasiliense, 1986), 122.

8. "Inventário dos teares existentes na Capitania de Minas Gerais 1786," *Revista do Arquivo Público Mineiro* 40 (1995): 1–160; Suzigan, *Indústria brasileira,* 130–133; Alisson Mascarenhas Vaz, "A Indústria Têxtil em Minas Gerais," *Revista de História* 56:111 (1977): 101–118.

9. Mascarenhas Vaz, "A Indústria Têxtil," 108–109; Lima, *Café e indústria,* 82.

10. Stanley J. Stein, *The Brazilian Cotton Manufacture: Textile Enterprise in an Underdeveloped Area, 1850–1950* (Cambridge, Mass.: Harvard University Press, 1957), 104; Lima, *Café e indústria,* 67–70.

11. Lima, *Café e indústria,* 82.

12. Stephen H. Haber, "Business Enterprise and the Great Depression in Brazil: A Study of Profits and Losses in Textile Manufacturing," *Business History Review* 66 (summer 1992): 335–363; Campolina Diniz, *Estado e capital estrangeiro,* 29.

13. *Produção industrial do municipio de Belo Horizonte, 1936- 1942* (Belo Horizonte: IBGE, 1943).

14. *Plano de recuperação econômica e fomento da produção,* 8 and 26.

15. Campolina Diniz, *Estado e capital estrangeiro,* chapter 1.

16. Lima, *Café e indústria,* 82–83.

17. Rodolfo Jacob, *Minas Geraes no XX século* (Rio de Janeiro: 1911), 271; *Indústria de fiação e tecelagem 1944* (Belo Horizonte: Oficinas Gráficas da Estatística, 1946), 4–9

18. *Indústria de fiação,* 4–6.

19. See, for example, Alisson Mascarenhas Vaz, *Cia. Cedro e Cachoeira: história de uma empresa familiar, 1883–1987* (Belo Horizonte: Gráfica Editora Formato Ltda., 1990).

20. Ibid.

21. Substantial obituaries of Américo Teixeira Guimarães and Christiano Teixeira França Guimarães can be found in *Minas Gerais,* 30 November 1947, 13, and 3 September 1970, 4.

22. *Minas Gerais,* 3 September 1970, 4.

23. The Lowell Machine Shop, for example, sold less than $50,000 of equipment in all South America prior to 1900—only $20,000 to one mill in Brazil. George Sweet Gibb, *The Saco-Lowell Shops: Textile Machinery Building in New England, 1813–1949* (Cambridge, Mass.: Harvard University Press, 1950), 272. This should not be surprising considering that every area of the world, except the United States, was dependent on English textile

machinery at least until the 1930s. Platt Brothers of Oldham had a productive capacity in 1914 "that was probably greater than the entire American textile machinery industry combined." Thomas R. Navin, *The Whitin Machine Works Since 1831: A Textile Machinery Company in an Industrial Village* (Cambridge, Mass.: Harvard University Press, 1950), 324–325.

24. "Mania de proteção," *Veja* (26 julho 1995): 99–100.

25. See, for example, Frédéric Mauro, "Political and Economic Structures of Empire, 1580–1750," in *Colonial Brazil,* Leslie Bethell, ed.(Cambridge: Cambridge University Press, 1987), 39–66; and, James Lang, *Portuguese Brazil: The King's Plantation* (New York: Academic Press, 1979).

26. Quoted in Stanley J. Stein, *The Brazilian Cotton Manufacture: Textile Enterprise in an Underdeveloped Area, 1850–1950* (Cambridge, Mass.: Harvard University Press, 1957), 2.

27. See, for example, Alan K. Manchester, *British Preeminence in Brazil: Its Rise and Decline: A Study in European Expansion* (Chapel Hill: University of North Carolina Press, 1933); Richard Graham, *Britain and the Onset of Modernization in Brazil, 1850- 1914* (Cambridge: Cambridge University Press, 1968).

28. Warren Dean, "Economy," in *Brazil: Empire and Republic, 1822–1930,* Leslie Bethell, ed.(Cambridge: Cambridge University Press, 1989), 246.

29. Douglas Cole Libby, *Transformação e trabalho em uma economia escravista: Minas Gerais no século XIX* (São Paulo: Brasiliense, 1988), 212.

30. Dean, "Economy," 246.

31. L. S. Garry, *Textile Markets of Brazil,* Department of Commerce, Bureau of Foreign and Domestic Commerce, Special Agents Series, No. 203, (Washington, DC: Government Printing Office, 1920), 22.

32. Stein, *The Brazilian Cotton Manufacture,* 20–21.

33. Libby, *Transformação,* 214–226; Birchal, *Entrepreneurship in Nineteenth-Century Brazil,* esp. chapters 2 and 4.

34. Vaz, *Cia. Cedro e Cachoeira: história de uma empresa familiar, 1883–1987* (Belo Horizonte: Gráfica Editora Formato Ltda., 1990), 48–51; Birchal, *Entrepreneurship in Nineteenth-Century Brazil* 164–69. For a fine description of the seemingly endless problems with foreign technicians sent out to the factories in Brazil, see Giroletti, *Fábrica convento disciplina* (Belo Horizonte: Imprensa Oficial, 1991), chapter 2.

35. Platt Brothers supplied machinery to more than 30 textile firms in Minas Gerais in the half-century prior to the Second World War. Platt-Saco-Lowell Archive, Lancashire Record Office, Preston, England, DDPS1 5/2/5. See, also, DDPSL/2 4/3, Dobson & Barlow Ltd of Bolton, Customers' Contract Summary Books, 'M' Book no. 1, 1897–1914.

36. Vaz, *Cia. Cedro e Cachoeira,* 73–75.

37. Nelson Lage Mascarenhas, *Bernardo Mascarenhas—o surto industrial de Minas Gerais* (Rio de Janeiro: Editora Aurora, 1954).

38. Suzigan, *Indústria brasileira,* 145; and, W. A. Graham Clark, *Cotton Goods in Latin America, Part II. Brazil, Colombia, and Venezuela,* Department of Commerce and Labor, Bureau of Manufactures, Special Agents Series, no. 1 36 (Washington, DC: Government Printing Office, 1910), 48. A survey of 32 plants in the Zona Metalurgica in the 1960s showed that 14 plants were entirely equipped with English equipment and another 12 had some English technology. The other dominant suppliers were Germany (10 plants), United States, Japan, Sweden, France, Czechoslovakia, Switzerland (14 plants total). John Philip Dickenson, "Zona Metalúrgica: A Study of the Geography of Industrial Development in Minas Gerais, Brazil," Ph.D. diss., University of Liverpool, 1970, 284.

39. See, for example, Elisabeth von der Weid and Ana Marta Rodrigues Bastos, *O fio da meada: estrategia de expansão de uma indústria têxtil, Companhia América Fabril, 1878–1930* (Rio de Janeiro: FCRB-CNI, 1986), 268–269. The most important of the foreign electrical utilities has been analyzed by Duncan McDowall, *The Light: Brazilian Traction, Light and Power Company Limited, 1899–1945* (Toronto: University of Toronto Press, 1988). The company was Canadian.

40. Suzigan, *Indústria brasileira,* 147.

41. Ibid., 148–149.

42. Stephen H. Haber, "Industrial Concentration and the Capital Markets: A Comparative Study of Brazil, Mexico, and the United States, 1830–1930," *Journal of Economic History* 51:3 (September 1991): 573.

43. Suzigan, *Indústria brasileira,* 149. One analyst at the beginning of the century observed that nearly all machinery came from England (Platt Brothers, Brooks & Doxey, and Howard & Bullough dominating the market). Even Northrop batteries (an American invention) were imported from English manufacturers using the American patent. Some dyeing and finishing machinery came from Germany and France, and a few knitting and winding machines came from the United States. Clark, *Cotton Goods in Latin America,* 48.

44. Suzigan, *Indústria brasileira,* 155.

45. Flávio Rabelo Versiani, "Technical Change, Equipment Replacement and Labor Absorption: The Case of the Brazilian Textile Industry," Ph.D. diss., Vanderbilt University, 1971, especially chapter IV, "Brazilian Cotton Manufacture Before 1940," 52–65.

46. Stein, *The Brazilian Cotton Manufacture,* 144.

47. Stein, 144.

48. "The failure of this quite substantial textile industry to stimulate the growth of ancillary industries such as chemicals and machinery should be noted." Dickenson, "A Study of the Geography," 285. For an analysis of similar efforts to control internal markets through oligopolistic practices see Stephen Haber's *Industry and Underdevelopment in Mexico, 1870–1940* (Stanford: Stanford University Press, 1989).

49. The literature on Brazilian iron and steel is voluminous. Some key works are: Humberto Bastos, *A conquista siderúrgica no Brasil* (São Paulo: Martins, 1959); Dermeval José Pimenta, *Implantação da grande siderurgia em Minas Gerais* (Belo Horizonte: UFMG, 1967); William Stuart Callaghan, "Obstacles to Industrialization"; Werner Baer, *The Development of the Brazilian Steel Industry* (Nashville, Tenn.: Vanderbilt University Press, 1969); and, John D. Wirth, *The Politics of Brazilian Development, 1930–1954* (Stanford: Stanford University Press, 1970), part II.

50. Cláudio Scliar, *Geopolítica das minas do Brasil* (Rio de Janeiro: Revan, 1996), 65–66; William Stuart Callaghan, "Obstacles to Industrialization: The Iron and Steel Industry in Brazil During the Old Republic," Ph.D. Diss., University of Texas, 1981.

51. Wilhelm Ludwig von Eschwege, *Pluto brasiliensis,* trans. Domício de Figueiredo, 2 v. (Belo Horizonte: Editorial Itatiaia, 1979).

52. Diniz, *Estado e capital estrangeiro,* 28.

53. Quoted in Maria Olivia A. B. P. Couto, *Ventos do sul nas montanhas de Minas* (Belo Horizonte: SENAI-MG,1992), 64.

54. See, for example, *Atas da ACM,* 9 September 1920 and 20 November 1934; and Giannetti speech in Couto, *Ventos do sul,* 64- 68.

55. The Portuguese original is: "A mineria não da duas safras." Charles A. Gauld, *The Last Titan: Percival Farquhar, An American Entrepreneur in Latin America* (Stanford: Institute of Hispanic American and Luso-Brazilian Studies, 1964), esp. 281–336; and, Callaghan, "Obstacles to Industrialization," chapters 5–6.

56. "Amaro Lanari" in Norma de Góis Monteiro, coord., *Dicionário biográfico de Minas Gerais—período republicano—1889–1991,* 2 v. (Belo Horizonte: Assembléia Legislativa do Estado de Minas Gerais, 1994), I, 332–333; Gil Guatimosim Júnior, "No Cinqüentenário da Belgo-Mineira," *Usiminas-Revista* 2:4 (1971), 13–15. For a list of the initial investors and the founding statutes of the company, see *Minas Geraes,* 22–23 January 1917, 7.

57. Júnior, "No Cinqüentenário da Belgo-Mineira," 15. The state government of Minas also loaned the new company 1,800 contos at 5 percent to be paid back in 10 annual installments. *Minas Geraes,* 11 August 1923, 3.

58. The Companhia Brasileira de Usinas Metalúrgicas was founded by the Hime family from São Paulo in 1925. In Minas its plant was located in Barão de Cocais around the old Gongo Soco gold mine. It produced pig iron. Baer, *The Development of the Brazilian Steel Industry,* 170.

59. Giannetti deserves a full-fledged biography. For the moment, the closest approximation is Couto's celebratory volume, *Ventos do sul nas montanhas de Minas.*

60. "Giannetti, Américo Renné (*sic*)," *Dicionário biográfico de Minas Gerais—período republicano—1889–1991,* coord. Norma de Góis Monteiro (Belo Horizonte: Assembléia Legislativa do Estado de Minas Gerais, 1994), I, 284;

Campolina Diniz, *Estado e capital estrangeiro,* 30; and Renato Falci, inter-viewed by Lígia Pereira and Otávio Dulci, Belo Horizonte, 18 December 1999, 9 February 1990, and 12 March 1990.

61. Campolina Diniz, *Estado e capital estrangeiro,* 34.

62. Ibid., 31.

63. *Revista Comercial de Minas Gerais* 35 (1940), 60–61.

64. Wirth, *Politics of Brazilian Development,* chapters 5–6 and, Baer, *Brazilian Steel Industry,* 68–76.

65. Paulo Macedo Gontijo, interviewed by Lígia Pereira and Adriana Simões, Belo Horizonte, 13 December 1990, 18 December 1990, and 6 March 1991.

66. José Murilo de Carvalho, *A Escola de Minas de Ouro Preto: o peso da glória* (São Paulo: Companhia Editora Nacional, 1978); Campolina Diniz, *Estado e capital estrangeiro,* 40–41. The principal business of the Pinheiro family for decades was a ceramics factory begun by João Pinheiro in Caeté. Among other things, the factory produced the paving stones ("paralelepípedos") for the Avenida da Liberdade that terminated at the front entrance of the gov-ernor's palace. The street was later renamed the Avenida João Pinheiro. *Re-latório da Prefeitura de Belo Horizonte,*(hereinafter *RPBH*) v. 1, unpublished (1902), 51–52.

67. See, for example, Dermeval José Pimenta, *A Vale do Rio Doce e sua história* (Belo Horizonte: Vega, 1981); and, Silvia Raw, "The Making of a State-Owned Conglomerate: A Brazilian Case Study," Working Paper #97, August 1987, The Helen Kellogg Institute for International Studies, University of Notre Dame.

68. Pimenta, *A Vale do Rio Doce e sua história,* 107–26; and Campolina Diniz, *Estado e capital estrangeiro,* 55–57.

69. Bernhard Fischer, Juan-Carlos Herken-Frauer, Matthias Lüke, and Peter Nunnenkamp, *Capital-Intensive Industries in Newly Industrializing Coun-tries: The Case of the Brazilian Automobile and Steel Industries* (Tübingen: Mohr, 1988), 198–202.

70. Baer, *Development of the Brazilian Steel Industry,* 9–10, 63; Edward Jonathan Rogers, "A Study of the Brazilian Iron and Steel Industry and its Associated Resources," Ph.D. diss., Stanford University, 1957, 323–64.

71. For a good description of the technology employed at Belgo Mineira in its early years, see Francisco Magalhães Gomes, *História da siderurgia no Brasil* (Belo Horizonte: Itatiaia, 1983), 189–94.

72. Born in Luxembourg, Ensch married into the prominent Azeredo Coutinho family from Caratinga. One of the most powerful figures in the mineiro business community, he was decorated by Getúlio Vargas with the Order of the Southern Cross in 1940 for his work in the iron and steel in-dustry. He eventually led not only Belgo Mineira (as well as other enter-prises), but he also became a member of the board of ARBED. "Louis

Jacques Ensch," *Dicionário biográfico,* I, 233–4; "Luto: Sra. Maria Campos Coutinho Ensch," *Minas Gerais,* 27 January 1966, 34.

73. Donald Edmund Rady, *Volta Redonda: A Steel Mill Comes to a Brazilian Coffee Plantation: Industrial Entrepreneurship in a Developing Economy* (privately printed, 1973), 145 and 152–4.

74. Ibid., 365–427; Baer, *Development of the Brazilian Steel Industry,* 68–79.

75. The use of waterwheels in gold mining began in the eighteenth century in Minas. See, for example, A. J. R. Russell-Wood, "The Gold Cycle, c. 1690–1750," in *Colonial Brazil,* Leslie Bethell, ed. (Cambridge: Cambridge University Press, 1987), 223; and Eschwege, *Pluto brasiliensis,* esp. v. I, 167–80.

76. Nelson Lage Mascarenhas, *Bernardo Mascarenhas—o surto industrial de Minas Gerais* (Rio de Janeiro: Editora Aurora, 1954).

77. Campolina Diniz, *Estado e capital estrangeiro,* 38.

78. Minas Gerais, Secretaria de Viação e Obras Públicas, *Plano de eletrificação de Minas Gerais,* 5 v. (Rio de Janeiro: Companhia Brasileira de Engenharia, 1950), IV, 85.

79. Marshall C. Eakin, *British Enterprise in Brazil: The St. John d'el Rey Mining Company and the Morro Velho Gold Mine, 1830–1960* (Durham, North Carolina: Duke University Press, 1989), 45–46, 60, and 129; *Plano de eletrificação,* IV, 85–92.

80. An early concession to construct and run the city's bonde service (6 December 1900) is described in *RPBH,* v. 1 (1902), 130- 2. The concession went to Julio Viveiros Brandão e Cia. After laying the rails the company had problems getting enough power to run the electric trolleys.

81. *RPBH,* v. 7 (1908/9), 39. For detailed descriptions of the construction of Rio das Pedras see *Minas Geraes,* 24 July 1906, 5; 25 July 1906, 3; 26 July 1906, 6; 28 July 1906, 4; 29 July 1906, 2–3; 1 August 1906, 4–5; 3 August 1906, 3; 4 August 1906, 4–5; 20 February 1907, 6–7.

82. *Minas Geraes,* 31 January 1912, 1–5 and 29 March 1912, 4.

83. The founder of the company was Dr. Manuel Tomás de Carvalho Brito, the president and treasurer were his brothers, Dr. Elysio de Carvalho Brito and Dr. Eusebio de Brito. Afonso Pena Júnior, the son of the former governor and president was on the *conselho fiscal.* Carvalho Brito died at the age of 80 in Rio de Janeiro in 1952. *Minas Geraes em 1925,* 1145–60. "Luto: Dr. Manuel Tomaz de Carvalho Brito," *Minas Gerais,* 14 December 1952, 8; "Brito, Manuel Tomás de Carvalho," *Dicionário biográfico,* I, 117- 118; Wirth, *Minas Gerais in the Brazilian Federation,* 97, 111, 133; Afonso Arinos de Melo Franco, *Um estadista da República (Afrânio de Melo Franco e seu tempo),* 2a ed. (Rio de Janeiro: Editora Nova Aguilar, 1976), v. 3, 505, 991–92.

84. According to some sources, Governor Antônio Carlos sold the concession to raise money for the uprising against the government of Washington Luís in 1930. Campolina Diniz, *Estado e capital estrangeiro,* 38, citing Paul Singer

and Hélio Silva. The contract was negotiated and signed without any public bidding process in late September and early October 1929 for 34.000:000$000. Joubert C. Diniz, "Estudo do mercado energético da Cia Força e Luz de Minas Gerais," vol. I, Faculdade de Ciências Econômicas, UFMG, 1964. The signing of the contract is described in *Minas Gerais,* 6 October 1929, 1.

85. Diniz, "Estudo do mercado energético da Cia Força e Luz de Minas Gerais," 6 and 30.
86. *RPBH,* v. 5 (1906/7), 51; v. 10, 27–8; v. 13, 28; v. 14, 12.
87. *RPBH,* v. 16 (1922/23), 13.
88. *Estado de Minas,* 21 June 1928, 1.
89. *RPBH,* v. 36 (1959/60), 6–7.
90. Thomas F. O'Brien, *The Revolutionary Mission: American Enterprise in Latin America, 1900–1945* (Cambridge: Cambridge University Press, 1996), 35–36.
91. The ACM formally asked Governor Antônio Carlos to consult with its leaders about the government plans to sell to a new concessionary in 1929. *Atas da ACM,* 26 September 1929.
92. Campolina Diniz, *Estado e capital estrangeiro,* 53–54.
93. *Atas da ACM,* 31 December 1911; 16 February 1933; 20 April 1933; 9 August 1934.
94. *Atas da ACM,* 10 October 1935 and 21 January 1937. The industrial park contained a number of small firms producing shoes, coffee, processed foods, lard, cigarettes, and soap, as well as the Companhia Industrial Belo Horizonte and a small branch of Belgo Mineira. *RPBH,* v. 24 (1935/36), 40–42.
95. *Atas da ACM,* 15 September 1932.

Chapter 4

1. Peter Evans, *Dependent Development: The Alliance of Multinational, State, and Local Capital in Brazil* (Princeton, New Jersey: Princeton University Press, 1979).
2. Werner Baer, *The Brazilian Economy: Growth and Development,* 4th ed. (Westport, Conn.: Praeger, 1995), 47.
3. Kathryn Sikkink, *Ideas and Institutions: Developmentalism in Brazil and Argentina* (Ithaca, New York: Cornell University Press, 1991), esp. 32–33.
4. Thomas E. Skidmore, *Politics in Brazil, 1930–1964: An Experiment in Democracy* (New York: Oxford University Press, 1967), 164.
5. Flávio Rabelo Versiani, "Technical Change, Equipment Replacement and Labor Absorption: The Case of the Brazilian Textile Industry," Ph.D. diss., Vanderbilt University, 1971, esp. chapter V.
6. Banco de Desenvolvimento de Minas Gerais, *A indústria têxtil em Minas Gerais: condições e reequipamento* (Belo Horizonte: BDMG, 1965), 10–11.

7. *A indústria têxtil em Minas Gerais* (Belo Horizonte: INDI, 1972), 11.

8. JUCEMG, "Cia Siderúrgica Belgo Mineira"; *Raízes do successo empresarial: a experiência de três empresas bem-sucedidas: Belgo Mineira, Metal Leve e Weg S.A.* (São Paulo: Atlas, 1995), 74–77, 87–90, 101–4, 117–25; "Eng. Albert Scharlé," *Mensagem Econômica* (July 1956): 18–19.

9. *Usiminas, 25 anos. depoimento: Lucas Lopes* (Belo Horizonte: Fundação João Pinheiro, 1987), 10–11.

10. Ibid., and Werner Baer, *The Development of the Brazilian Steel Industry* (Nashville, Tenn.: Vanderbilt University Press), 80.

11. *Diagnóstico da economia mineira* (Belo Horizonte: Banco de Desenvolvimento de Minas Gerais, 1968), II, 109. The largest were the CSN, Belgo Mineira, Usiminas, and Acesita.

12. Edward Jonathan Rogers, "A Study of the Brazilian Iron and Steel Industry and its Associated Resources," Ph.D. diss., Stanford University, 1957, 281–4.

13. Usiminas has produced an excellent series of oral histories by the key Brazilian technocrats and entrepreneurs who brought the company into existence: Gabriel A. Janot Pacheco, Luiz Verano, Paulo Pinto, Jayme de Andrade Peconick, and Lucas Lopes.

14. Baer, *The Development of the Brazilian Steel Industry,* 81- 82.

15. *Diagnóstico da economia mineira,* II, 109 and 112.

16. Baer, *The Development of the Brazilian Steel Industry,* 83 and Appendix II.

17. For the dependence on foreign technology see, for example, Baer, *The Development of the Brazilian Steel Industry;* and, Maria Amélia M. Dantes and Joseleide Souza Santos, "Siderurgia e tecnologia (1918–1964)," in *Tecnologia e industrialização no Brasil: uma perspectiva histórica,* Shozo Motoyama, org. (São Paulo: Editora da Universidade de São Paulo, Centro Estadual da Educação Tecnológica Paula Souza, 1994), 209–32. For specific examples see the oral histories of some of the founders of Usiminas cited in note 13 above.

18. *Memórias do desenvolvimento: Lucas Lopes—depoimento* (Rio de Janeiro: Centro de Memória da Eletricidade no Brasil, 1991), 127–31.

19. John Philip Dickenson, "Zona Metalúrgica: A Study of the Geography of Industrial Development in Minas Gerais Brazil," Ph.D. diss., University of Liverpool, 1970, 90.

20. In the late twenties, a subsidiary of General Electric (Electric Bond & Share Corporation) formed its own subsidiary (the American and Foreign Power Company or Amforp) to expand its interests outside the United States. Bond & Share, in turn, created a Brazilian subsidiary (Companhia Auxiliar de Empresas Elétricas Brasileiras or CAEEB), which obtained concessions to operate in various parts of Brazil, including Rio Grande do Sul, the interior of São Paulo, and the mineiro capital. *Panorama do setor de energia elétrica no Brasil* (Rio de Janeiro: Centro de Memória da Eletricidade, 1988), 62–3.

21. Paul Israel Singer, *Desenvolvimento econômico e evolução urbana: análise da evolução econômica de São Paulo, Blumenau, Pôrto Alegre, Belo Horizonte e Recife* (São Paulo: Editôra Nacional e Editôra da USP, 1968), 259–60. The CFLMG attempted to keep up with demand by purchasing excess power from other producers, primarily the St. John d'el Rey Mining Company, Limited in Nova Lima.

22. *Plano de eletrificação de Minas Gerais,* 5 v. (Rio de Janeiro: Companhia Brasileira de Engenharia, 1950).

23. *Plano de eletrificação,* v. 5, 20.

24. *Diagnóstico da economia mineira,* I, 161. "Offering to the consumer energy at a low price will be, in short, the keystone of the industrial expansion of the state which, with this, will attain a more elevated level of civilization." *Plano,* 2.

25. Born in Niterói in 1896, Seabra was trained as an engineer in Rio and at Westinghouse (Pittsburgh) in the United States. After the Revolution of 1930 he became the *prefeito* of Itajubá in southern Minas. He served as president of the State Assembly (1936–37) and then as secretary of Viação e Obras Públicas (1935–37). He was elected to the Federal Assembly (1946–59) and served as the secretary again under Milton Campos (1947–50). He moved easily between political and technocratic roles. *Dicionário biográfico de Minas Gerais—período republicano—1889–1991,* coord. Norma de Góis Monteiro (Belo Horizonte: Assembléia Legislativa do Estado de Minas Gerais, 1994), II, 625.

26. *John Reginald Cotrim: depoimento de história oral* (Belo Horizonte: CEMIG, 1994), 39; *Memórias do desenvolvimento,* 128–9. Seabra's son, Licínio, would later be on the board of directors of CEMIG, president of Furnas and Nuclebrás. *Lucas Lopes: depoimento de história oral* (Belo Horizonte: CEMIG, 1986), 18. "José Rodrigues Seabra," *Dicionário biográfico,* 625.

27. Marshall C. Eakin, *British Enterprise in Brazil: The St. John d'el Rey Mining Company and the Morro Velho Gold Mine, 1830–1960* (Durham, North Carolina: Duke University Press), 45–46 and 303.

28. *Panorama,* 110.

29. The SALTE Plan was an effort by the administration of President Eurico Dutra (1946–51) to coordinate public expenditures in health (*Saúde*), food (*Alimentação*), transportation (*Transportação*), and energy (*Energia*). Skidmore, *Politics in Brazil,* 71.

30. *Diagnóstico da economia mineira,* III, 175.

31. CEMIG was created by Decree No. 3.710 in February 1952 as one of the pet projects of Kubitschek. Giannetti described the plans for CEMIG in a speech at the FIEMG on 22 November 1950 as he was making the transition from secretary of agriculture to prefeito of Belo Horizonte. *Atas da FIEMG,* 22 November 1950, Federação das Indústrias do Estado de Minas Gerais, Centro de Memória, Belo Horizonte.

32. *Panorama,* 156–9. According to Tendler, "In Brazilian power circles there was one point on which opposing sides always agreed. The Light and the anti-foreign company nationalists, the *privatistas* and *estatistas* (those against and in favor of state-sponsored power), the World Bank and the Brazilian Development Bank—all said that Minas Gerais' state power company, CEMIG, was one of the best enterprises in Brazil." Judith Tendler, *Electric Power in Brazil: Entrepreneurship in the Public Sector* (Cambridge, Mass.: Harvard University Press, 1968), 175.
33. *Panorama,* 171; and *Diagnóstico,* I, 161.
34. In 1965, industry consumed 70 percent of the power generated by CEMIG, and other utilities another 20 percent. Ivana Santos Mayer, "A CEMIG e a industrialização de Minas Gerais," Bachelor's thesis, Faculdade de Ciências Econômicas, UFMG, 1988, 27, 30 and 35.
35. Mayer, "A CEMIG," 26.
36. Tendler, *Electric Power in Brazil,* 36–7; *John Reginald Cotrim.*
37. By 1988, São Paulo had reached an installed capacity of 12,443,000, Minas was at 10,277,000, and Rio was a distant third at 2,791,000 kW. *A CERJ e a história da energia elétrica no Rio de Janeiro* (Rio de Janeiro: Centro da Memória da Eletricidade no Brasil, 1993), 211.
38. Júlio César Assis Kühl, "Energia Elétrica," in Motoyama, *Tecnologia e industrialização no Brasil: uma perspectiva histórica* (São Paulo: Editora da Universidade Estadual de São Paulo), 250–91, esp. 280–81.
39. *A CEMIG e o desenvolvimento econômico de Minas Gerais, 1952–1975* (Belo Horizonte: CEMIG, 1971), 78–80.
40. See, for example, John D. Wirth, *The Politics of Brazilian Development, 1930–1954* (Stanford, Calif.: Stanford University Press, 1970).
41. Dermeval José Pimenta, *A vale do Rio Doce e sua história* (Belo Horizonte: Vega, 1981), 69–127.
42. Donald Edmund Rady, *Volta Redonda: A Steel Mill Comes to a Brazilian Coffee Plantation: Industrial Entrepreneurship in a Developing Economy* (Albuquerque, New Mexico: Rio Grande Publishing Company, 1973); Silvia Raw, *The Making of a State-Owned Conglomerate: A Brazilian Case Study* (South Bend, Indiana: Kellogg Institute, University of Notre Dame, Working Paper #97, August 1987); Iran F. Machado, *Recursos minerais: política e sociedade* (São Paulo: Editora Edgard Blucher Ltda., 1989), 363–9.
43. Rogers, "A Study of the Brazilian Iron," 141–2.
44. Ibid., 144–5.
45. H. W. D. Mayers, "The Story of Iron and Steel in Brazil," *Bulletin of the Pan American Union* 72:10 (October 1938): 598.
46. Machado, *Recursos minerais,* 370.
47. JUCEMG, "Companhia de Cimento Portland Itaú"; *Minas Gerais,* 21 Feb 1946, 9–12; 15 Feb 1951, 15–16; 4 Mar 1956, 8–9; 23 Mar 1961, 21–22; 12 Apr 1966, 25–26.

48. Dickenson, "A Study of the Geography," 160.

49. Dias was the father-in-law of Newton Pereira, a president of the FIEMG (1946–52). Pereira ran a shoe factory that Dias had purchased in the 1940s. *Diário de Minas,* 28 July 1957; "Newton Antônio da Silva Pereira," *Dicionário biográfico,* II, 531.

50. Ibid., 161.

51. JUCEMG, "Companhia Cimento Portland Cauê"; *Minas Gerais,* 13 Apr 1956, 17; 30 Mar 1961, 13; 20 Apr 1966, 22; *Dicionário biográfico,* I, 219.

52. Paulo Luiz Esteves, "O moderno entre a iniciativa e a fabricação," *O Tempo,* 6 July 1997, 5.

53. In 1961, COMINCI produced 220,000 tons of cement. Dickenson, "A Study of the Geography," 161.

54. *Diagnóstico,* V, 97.

55. Ibid., V, 74.

56. Ibid., V, 80.

57. JUCEMG, "Magnesita S/A."

58. Dickenson, "A Study of the Geography," 155–6.

59. Eakin, *British Enterprise in Brazil.*

60. Alisson Mascarenhas Vaz, *Israel: uma vida para história* (Rio de Janeiro: CVRD, 1996), esp. 170–73.

61. Esteves, "O moderno," 5.

62. Clélio Campolina Diniz, *Estado e capital estrangeiro na industrializaçao mineira* (Belo Horizonte: PROED/UFMG, 1981) and Luis Gama de Andrade, "Technocracy and Development: The Case of Minas Gerais," Ph.D. diss., University of Michigan, 1980.

63. See, for example, Luciano Martins, *Estado capitalista e burocracia no Brasil pós–64* (Rio de Janeiro: Paz e Terra, 1985); Ben Ross Schneider, *Politics Within the State: Elite Bureaucrats and Industrial Policy in Authoritarian Brazil* (Pittsburgh, Penn.: University of Pittsburgh Press, 1991); Angela de Castro Gomes, coord., *Engenheiros e economistas: novas elites burocráticas* (Rio de Janeiro: Editora da Fundação Getúlio Vargas, 1994); Gilda Portugal Gouvêa, *Burocracia e elites burocráticas no Brasil* (São Paulo: Editora Paulicéia, 1994).

64. Frances Hagopian, *Technocrats and Regime Change in Brazil* (Cambridge: Cambridge University Press, 1995).

65. Two excellent studies that also make this same argument are the previously cited volume by Castro Gomes and Otavio Soares Dulci, *Política e recuperação econômica em Minas Gerais* (Belo Horizonte: Editora UFMG, 1999).

66. An excellent volume that also argues against these restrictive categories is Angela de Castro Gomes (coord.), José Luciano de Mattos Dias, and Marly Silva da Motta, *Engenheiros e economistas,* esp. 2 and 6. "The dichotomy, so clear in the discourse, that opposes 'technocrat' to 'politician' is not sustained theoretically nor empirically." This notion, they argue, is an "invented tradition" in Brazil.

67. Campolina Diniz, *Estado e capital estrangeiro*, 41.
68. This is similar to the technocratic movement in the United States in the 1920s and 1930s. See, for example, Edwin T. Layton, Jr., *The Revolt of the Engineers: Social Responsibility and the American Engineering Profession* (Cleveland, Ohio: Press of Case Western Reserve University, 1971); Thorstein Veblen, *The Engineers and the Price System* (New York: B. W. Huebsch, Inc., 1921).
69. José Murilo de Carvalho, *A Escola de Minas de Ouro Preto: o peso da glória* (São Paulo: FINEP/Companhia Editora Nacional, 1978); Andrade, "Technocracy and Development."
70. "Israel Pinheiro da Silva," *Dicionário biográfico*, II, 641- 42; Martins and Martins, *Engenheiro da utopia* is the only biography of Israel Pinheiro and it is a work obviously commissioned by the family. Done largely through research in the personal papers of Pinheiro and interviews, it has no scholarly documentation.
71. *Folha de Minas*, 21 March 1947.
72. *Estado de Minas*, 24 March 1945 (in FIEMG archives, book of recortes, volume 1, hereafter, Recortes). Dulci argues that there are four phases in the planning and promotion of industrialization. Up until 1940, the focus of the government was on agricultural modernization. From 1941–46 industrial expansion received greater attention with a third phase of comprehensive planning from 1947–50. Finally, From 1951–55 the so-called "mineiro model" of industrial specialization within the larger national economy took shape. Dulci, *Política e recuperação econômica*, 61.
73. "In reality, moving into the industrialization phase profoundly modifies all the economic panorama of our State. Agricultural products or primary extractive activity offer low prices and the capacity for limited commercial transactions. Their market problems are very different than those which manufactured goods present." *Mensagem Econômica*, November 1958, 9; Campolina Diniz, *Estado e capital estrangeiro*, 42.
74. Quoted in Vaz, *Israel*, 135.
75. For decades, mineiros by the thousands had migrated to other states in search of work. For a look at the mentality of industrialists on this issue, see "A Indústria Acabará com a Exportação (de Gente)," *Vida Industrial* (August-October 1962): 16–20.
76. *O Diário*, 13 May 1945 (FIEMG, Recortes, v. 1).
77. Campolina Diniz, *Estado e capital estrangeiro*, 42–61.
78. William Stuart Callaghan, "Obstacles to Industrialization: The Iron and Steel Industry in Brazil During the Old Republic," Ph.D. diss., University of Texas, 1981, 342–452.
79. Pimenta, *A Vale do Rio Doce e sua história*, 107–26.
80. *Memórias do desenvolvimento*, 65–70. The most complete study of the topic is Celina Albano, "The Making of a Brazilian Industrial City: The Experience of Contagem," Ph.D. diss., University of Manchester, 1980.

81. Oral tradition has it that Pinheiro simply picked the Canberra design right out of a book and purely for aesthetic reasons.

82. Celina Albano, "The Making of a Brazilian Industrial City," 119–66; John P. Dickenson, "Industrial Estates in Brazil," *Geography* 55 (1970), 326–29; Andrade, "Technocracy and Development: The Case of Minas Gerais," Ph.D. dissertation, University of Michigan, 1980, 51. The size and location of the Cidade Industrial had their drawbacks. Giannetti remarked in 1950 that it "was poorly located, because it was not possible to establish large-scale industry there." FIEMG, *Relatório—1950*, Federação das Indústria do Estado de Minas Gerais, Centro de Memória, Belo Horizonte.

83. Albano, "The Making of a Brazilian Industrial Ciry,"177, 198, 254.

84. *Plano de recuperação econômica e fomento da produção* (Belo Horizonte: Imprensa Oficial, 1947).

85. Obituary, *Minas Gerais,* 7 September 1954, 7.

86. *Plano de recuperação,* 1–26; Andrade, "Technocracy and Development," 298.

87. "The cornerstone of state industrial expansion will be the supply to the consumer of low cost energy, and with this the highest level of civilization will be attained." *Plano de recuperação,* 2.

88. According to an old popular saying before the 1960s, "Where the road ends, Minas begins." Quoted in Albano, "The Making of a Brazilian Industrial City," 170.

89. Campolina Diniz, *Estado e capital estrangeiro,* 62–68.

90. For an excellent analysis of these developments see Sikkink, *Ideas and Institutions,* especially chapter 2.

91. Evantina Pereira Vieira, "Minas Gerais: a dominação burguesa—conflitos políticos e formas de organização (1927–1940)," Ph.D. dissertation, Universidade de São Paulo, 1985, 50–54. In the late 1950s, the business elite was still referring to itself as the *"classes produtoras"* and *"classes conservadoras."* *O Jornal* (Rio de Janeiro), 7 January 1958.

92. The Secretaria da Agricultura, Indústria, Comércio e Trabalho had been created in 1935 out of the old Secretaria de Viação e Obras Públicas and served as something of a secretariat of economics. Dulci, *Política e recuperação econômica,* 65.

93. Pereira Vieira, "Minas Gerais," 123.

94. "Benedito Valadares Ribeiro," *Dicionário biográfico,* II, 584–85. Dulci, *Política e recuperação econômica,* 66.

95. "Juscelino Kubitschek de Oliveira," *Dicionário biográfico,* II, 476–77; Juscelino Kubitschek, *Meu caminho para Brasília. 1o volume. a experiência da humildade* (Rio de Janeiro: Bloch Editores, 1974).

96. Kubitschek was also related by marriage to other prominent elite families. His marriage to Sara Gomes de Lima in 1931 connected him to the Negrão de Lima family, her cousins. *Dicionário biográfico,* II, 477.

97. Quotes in Dulci, *Política e recuperação econômica,* 103–4.

98. Juscelino Kubitschek, *Meu caminho para Brasília, v. II. a escalada política* (Rio de Janeiro: Bloch, 1976), esp. 185–89.

99. Judith Tendler, *Electric Power in Brazil,* 36–37, 120–22, and 175–76; John P. Dickenson, "Electric Power Development in Minas Gerais, Brazil," *Revista Geográfica* 70 (June 1969): 213–21.

100. Campolina Diniz, *Estado e capital estrangeiro,* 79–80; "As 200 maiores empresas do Brasil," *Visão,* 2 September 1987, 59–67. JUCEMG.

101. Andrade, "Technocracy and Development," 298–300.

102. Dulci refers to this group as "tecno-empresários." *Política e recuperação econômica,* 160.

103. Campolina Diniz, *Estado e capital estrangeiro,* 72–75; Ivana Santos Mayer, "A CEMIG e a industrialização de Minas Gerais," Bachelor's thesis, Faculdade de Ciências Econômicas, Universidade Federal de Minas Gerais, 1988; *Lucas Lopes: depoimento de história oral* (Belo Horizonte: CEMIG, 1986); *John Reginald Cotrim: depoimento de história oral* (Belo Horizonte: CEMIG, 1994).

104. The CEMIG has published some important oral histories of the company directors. In addition to those cited in the previous note, see, for example, *João Camilo Pena: depoimento de história oral* (Belo Horizonte: CEMIG, 1986).

105. For an excellent study of the rise of the ideology of developmentalism in both Brazil and Argentina see, Kathryn Sikkink, *Ideas and Institutions: Developmentalism in Brazil and Argentina* (Ithaca, New York: Cornell University Press, 1991).

106. For an excellent study of the rise of the auto industry see, Helen Shapiro, *Engines of Growth: The State and Transnational Auto Companies in Brazil* (Cambridge: Cambridge University Press, 1994). See also, Caren Addis, *Taking the Wheel: Auto Parts Firms and the Political Economy of Industrialization in Brazil* (University Park, Penn.: The Pennsylvania State University Press, 1999) and Glauco Arbix e Mauro Zilbovicius, org., *De JK a FHC: a reinvenção dos carros* (São Paulo: Scritta, 1997).

107. "Américo Renné Giannetti," *Dicionário biográfico,* I, 284.

108. For an excellent account of the creation of SESI and SENAI (focusing on São Paulo), see Barbara Weinstein, *For Social Peace in Brazil: Industrialists and the Remaking of the Working Class in São Paulo, 1920–1964* (Chapel Hill: University of North Carolina Press, 1996).

109. *Minas Gerais,* 7 September 1954, 7; "Giannetti foi a grande vítima," *Diário da Tarde,* 4–5 August 1990, E6; Dickenson, "A Study of the Geography," 200–1; Campolina Diniz, *Estado e capital estrangeiro,* 58–60.

110. Many observers blamed Giannetti's death by a massive heart attack on his enormous business and political burdens. According to Paulo Macedo Gontijo, one of his contemporaries, Giannetti did not just die, he exploded (*estorou*). Gontijo Interview.

111. Obituary, *Minas Gerais*, 3 September 1970, 4; and "Cristiano França Teixeira Guimarães," *Dicionário biográfico*, I, 302.

112. *Minas Geraes*, 22–23 September 1917, 7; 11 August 1923, 3.

113. JUCEMG, "Banco Comércio e Indústria de Minas Gerais" *Minas Gerais*, 11–12 May 1925, 13; 20 March 1926, 10; "Banco Comércio e Indústria de Minas Gerais, S.A.," in *BH completa 50 anos*, 104–7.

114. *Diário de Minas*, 11 December 1957.

115. "José de Magalhães Pinto," *Dicionário biográfico*, II, 546- 7. JUCEMG.

116. FIEMG, *Atos de reuniões plenárias—1949*, 10 June 1949, Federação das Indústrias do Estado de Minas Gerais, Centro de Memória, Bela Horizonte. The speaker was Newton Pereira.

117. *Ignacio Ballesteros, História Oral, no. 3* (Belo Horizonte: Fundação João Pinheiro, 1996).

118. *Gil Nogueira, História oral, no. 6* (Belo Horizonte: Fundação João Pinheiro, 1996); *Minas Gerais: maiores e melhores, Gazeta Mercantil*, no. 3 (1995): 26.

119. "Lucas Lopes," *Dicionário biográfico*, I, 365–6; *Memórias do desenvolvimento*.

120. Antônio Augusto Pereira da Rocha, engineer and key figure in the textile firm, Companhia Renascença Industrial, quoted in "Dia da Indústria," *Vida Industrial* (Belo Horizonte), May 1980: 17.

121. According to one ally of Magalhães Pinto, Valadares "always tried to create problems for the Association." *Atas da ACM*, 30 January 1944. Paulo Gontijo discusses the crisis in the ACM created by Valadares's efforts to block the election of Pinto and his allies. Gontijo Interview.

122. "A visita do Presidente Getúlio Vargas à Associação Comercial," *Minas Gerais*, 19 July 1938, 5. Magalhães Pinto lost his job and caused an upheaval in the ACM in 1944 when he signed the famous *Manifesto dos Mineiros* calling for Vargas to step down from power.

123. FIEMG, *Relatório, 1945*, Federação das Indústria do Estado de Minas Gerais, Centro de Memória, Bela Horizonte.

124. See, for example, FIEMG, *Relatório—1944; Estado de Minas*, 24 November 1943, 7 April 1944, 12 July 1944, 15 November 1944; *Vida Industrial*, December 1961, 30–36; *Mensagem Econômica*, February 1953, 6–10; April 1954, 44–65; January 1956, 11–18; August 1957, 3–6.

125. *Mensagem Econômica*, October 1955, 19–21; November 1958, 11- 13.

126. Ibid., August-September 1960, 3–27.

127. For a typical statement on the need for foreign capital, but to work in conjunction with mineiro "interests," see *Boletim da ACM* (Belo Horizonte), IV, 93 (30 September 1946): 2–4.

128. Dulci has a chart that presents a nice sample of the overlapping elites. It shows 13 major figures who headed state secretariats between 1945–70, alongside their principal roles in the FIEMG, ACM, and other corporate interest groups. Among these figures are Antônio Mourão Guimarães, Jair

Negrão de Lima, Américo Giannetti, José de Magalhães Pinto, Miguel Augusto Gonçalves de Souza, and Celso Melo de Azevedo. Lima, Giannetti, and Azevedo all served as *prefeito* for Belo Horizonte in this period as well. Dulci, *Política e recuperação econômica,* 170.

Chapter 5

1. Wayne A. Selcher, ed., *Brazil in the International System: The Rise of a Middle Power* (Boulder, Colorado: Westview Press, 1981); Thomas E. Skidmore, *Politics in Brazil, 1930–1964: An Experiment in Democracy* (New York: Oxford University Press, 1967).

2. Peter Evans, *Dependent Development: The Alliance of Multinational, State, and Local Capital in Brazil* (Princeton, New Jersey: Princeton University Press, 1979), esp. 3–13 and 274–326.

3. From 1970 to 1977 Greater Belo Horizonte received 80 percent of all new industrial investment, mainly directed to the steel and manufacturing sectors. "One-third of all new employment was generated in the metropolitan region" of Belo Horizonte. Frances Hagopian, *Traditional Politics and Regime Change in Brazil* (Cambridge: Cambridge University Press, 1996), 99–100.

4. Clélio Campolina Diniz, *Estado e capital estrangeiro na industrializaçã mineira* (Belo Horizonte: UFMG/PROED, 1981), p. 225; Luis Aureliano Gama de Andrade, "Technocracy and Development: The Case of Minas Gerais," Ph.D. dissertation, University of Michigan, 1980, 292; James Brooke, "Inland Region of Brazil Grows Like Few Others," *New York Times,* 11 August 1994, C1; *Veja,* 26 Abril 1995, 104; "O Desempenho da Economia Brasileira e de Minas," *Vida Industrial* (January 1991): 13.

5. Hagopian, *Traditional Politics,* 83–4; *Brasil em números,* v. 4, 1995/96 (Rio de Janeiro: IBGE, 1996), 47.

6. Hagopian, *Traditional Politics,* 30.

7. The state government contracted with the Fundação João Pinheiro in 1971 to elaborate a *Plano da Area Metropolitana de Belo Horizonte,* a process that led to the creation of PLAMBEL, a planning agency that lasted into the 1990s to help shape the rapid growth of the city and surrounding region. *Relatório da Prefeitura de Belo Horizonte,* v. 45.

8. *Anuário estatístico do Brasil* (Rio de Janeiro: IBGE, 1995), 2–14.

9. Campolina Diniz, *Estado e capital estrangeiro,* 183–204.

10. Banco de Desenvolvimento de Minas Gerais, *Diagnóstico da economia mineira,* 6 v. (Belo Horizonte: BDMG, 1968).

11. Nansen Araujo of the FIEMG agreed with the document's analysis, but emphasized that the report was not a cause for pessimism but for hope—to begin to address the serious problems in the state's economy. Nansen Araujo, "Palavras . . . Palavras . . . Palavras . . . ," *Vida Industrial* (April 1969).

12. *Diagnóstico,* v. 1; Luis Aureliano Gama de Andrade, "Technocracy and Development: The Case of Minas Gerais," Ph.D. diss., University of Michigan, 1980, 111.

13. Campolina Diniz, *Estado e capital estrangeiro,* 206–8; "Região Metropolitana de Belo Horizonte, Projetos Decididos para Minas Gerais com Assistência do INDI," Archives of the Instituto de Desenvolvimento Industrial, Belo Horizonte.

14. *Comportamento da economia mineira: periodo 1960–77. Indústria de transformação* (Belo Horizonte: SEPLAN, 1978), 70.

15. Hagopian, *Traditional Politics,* 99–100.

16. "Contagem tem 18.700 operários," *Vida Industrial* (February and March 1969); "Contagem," *Vida Industrial* (May 1969); "Contagem, concentração operária," *Vida Industrial* (June 1969).

17. Interview, José Eduardo de Lima Pereira, Diretor de Assuntos Corporativos, Fiat do Brasil S.A., Nova Lima, Minas Gerais, 16 June 2000.

18. Campolina Diniz, *Estado e capital estrangeiro,* 213–4; *Vida Industrial* (Belo Horizonte), special issue (1984): 49–50.

19. "Estado sai da Fiat com um terço do que investiu," *Estado de Minas,* 26 February 1988; "Fiat converte a dívida brasileira," *Veja,* 24 February 1988.

20. SEPLAN, *As principais sociedades anónimas de Minas Gerais—1976* (Belo Horizonte: Superintendência de Estatísticas e Informacões, 1978).

21. Andrade, "Technocracy and Development," 165.

22. Prefeitura Municipal de Belo Horizonte, Secretaria Municipal de Planejamento, Coordenadoria de Informações Técnicas, *Perfil de Belo Horizonte* (Belo Horizonte: Prefeitura Municipal de Belo Horizonte, 1985), "As Maiores Sociedades Anónimas de Belo Horizonte," 44–48.

23. *Balanço anual—Minas Gerais,* v. 5, no. 5 (October 1998): 66–67. The leading companies (and their rankings) were Cedro e Cachoeira (1), Santanense (3), São José Tecelagem (4), Itaunense (5), Renascença (7), Estamparia (9), Divinópolis (12), and Itabirito (14).

24. Patrícia Duarte, *Diogo Bethonico: a trajetória de um empreendedor* (Belo Horizonte: Dossiê Agência de Investigação Histórica, 1993), 48–49; Edmundo de Macedo Soares e Silva, *As instituições de indústria e comércio do Brasil* (Rio de Janeiro: Crown, 1972), 375.

25. Ibid., 70–71.

26. Ibid., 79; *A economia mineira: perfil das empresas do Estado 1991/1992* (Belo Horizonte: Fundação João Pinheiro, 1994), 70–71.

27. *Anuário Estatístico de Minas Gerais 1987* (Belo Horizonte: SEPLAN, 1987), 474. Furnas was created in 1957 with capital from the federal government, the states of Minas Gerais and São Paulo, and two foreign-owned companies, Light (Canadian) serving Rio and São Paulo, and the Companhia Paulista de Força e Luz (U.S. owned). The state of Minas Gerais controlled

half of all electricity produced at Furnas. Francisco de Assis Magalhães Gomes, *A electrificação no Brasil* (São Paulo: Eletropaulo, 1986), 44. See also Judith Tendler, *Electric Power in Brazil: Entrepreneurship in the Public Sector* (Cambridge, Mass.: Harvard University Press, 1968), 37–38.

28. "Minas Amplia Parque Gerador," *Vida Industrial* (October 1994), 39.

29. "Cemig Chega a 5 Milhões de Ligações," *CEMIG Notícias* 26:4 (May 2000). In the 1980s CEMIG also changed its name to Centrais *Energéticas* de Minas Gerais.

30. *Anuário estatístico . . . 1987,* 474.

31. Tendler, *Electric Power in Brazil,* 179–80.

32. Ibid., 121–22.

33. *Anuário Estatístico . . . 1987,* 475, and Centro da Memória da Eletricidade no Brasil, *Panorama do setor de energia elétrica no Brasil* (Rio de Janeiro: CEMB, 1988), 263.

34. Ibid., 478, and Mayer, "A CEMIG e a industrialização em Minas Gerais," 37. In the early 1970s, 6 large consumers (CVRD, Aluminas, Alcominas, Usiminas, Mannesmann, and the Companhia Brasileira de Carbureto de Cálcio) consumed 2 million kWh or one-quarter of all the energy CEMIG produced. Less than 10 percent of power generated went to residential and commercial consumers. Of the energy consumed by industries, nearly 12,000 industrial firms used 15 percent of the power generated, and 11 companies consumed the rest! *A CEMIG e o desenvolvimento econômico de Minas Gerais, 1952–1975* (Belo Horizonte: CEMIG, 1971).

35. Thibau, although born and educated in Rio, spent the rest of his career in Minas. He was on the board of CEMIG until 1967, was vice president of the FIEMG (1962–64), and later president of the Banco do Estado de Minas Gerais S.A. (1972–74). *Dicionário biográfico de Minas Gerais—período republicano—1889–1991,* coord. Noma de Góis Monteiro (Belo Horizonte: Assembléia Legislativa do Estado de Minas Gerais, 1994), II, 685. Cotrim was born in Manchester, raised in Rio, but came to Minas as an engineer with experience working for Amforp. He effectively became part of Lucas Lopes and Seabra's group and spent the rest of his career in technocratic positions in the electric power industry. *John Reginald Cotrim: depoimento de história oral* (Belo Horizonte: CEMIG, 1994).

36. Tendler, *Electric Power in Brazil,* 175.

37. Bernhard Fischer, Juan-Carlos Herken-Krauer, Matthias Lücke, and Peter Nunnenkamp, *Capital-Intensive Industries in Newly Industrializing Countries: The Case of the Brazilian Automobile and Steel Industries* (Tübingen: J. C. B. Mohr, 1988), 170–1.

38. "Estudo: ferro-gusa, produção não-integrada," *Vida Industrial* (January 1991): 42–44.

39. "Estudo: panorama da fundição no Brasil e em Minas," *Vida Industrial* (November 1990): 36–38.

40. According to Amaro Lanari Júnior, Usiminas had to constantly beg for more financing from the BNDE and the federal treasury. *Amaro Lanari Júnior: a realização* (Belo Horizonte: Fundação João Pinheiro, 1987), 11.

41. The North American firm Booz-Allen, according to Lanari, taught Usiminas how to administer (*gerenciar*) the operation. Ibid., 13. Taeko Taniura, "Economic Development Effects of an Integrated Iron and Steel Works: A Case Study of Minas Gerais Steel in Brazil," *The Developing Economies* XXIV-2 (June 1986): 169–77.

42. Taniura, "Economic Development," 169–88; Fischer, *Capital-Intensice Industries,* et al., 170–1; Macedo Soares, *Dicionário histórico-biográfico brasileiro: 1930–1983,* 411; *Informador Comercial* (7 December 1957), in FIEMG, *Recortes,* v. 4.

43. Gil Guatimosim Júnior, "No Cinqüentenário da Belgo-Mineira," *Usiminas—Revista* 2:4 (1971): 13–15; Paulo Gontijo interview.

44. *Usiminas conta sua história* (Belo Horizonte: Editora Anchieta, 1990), 33; and FIEMG documents.

45. *Usiminas conta sua história,* 141; *Amaro Lanari Júnior: a realização,* 7–9.

46. "Usiminas: uma empresa que deu certo," *Vida Industrial* (July 1991): 8–9.

47. Ibid., 9, 10, 15, 30. Antônia Cristina De Filippo, "A Usiminas Investe Pesado," *Vida Industrial* (August 1994): 6–9. Dahlman and Fonseca argue that by the late 1970s Usiminas had "passed from the know-how to the know-why stage" and was ready to move "beyond importing and adapting technology to creating new techniques, new processes and new products." Despite this optimism the company remains dependent on technology developed elsewhere and then adapted to local conditions. Carl J. Dahlman and Fernando Valadares Fonseca, "From Technological Dependence to Technological Development: The Case of the USIMINAS Steel Plant in Brazil," in *Technology Generation in Latin American Manufacturing Industries,* Jorge M. Katz, ed. (New York: St. Martin's Press, 1987), 154–82, quotes from 171–2.

48. The initial board of directors consisted of three Japanese from Nippon Steel and four Brazilians: Lídio Lunardi (president of the FIEMG and the Conselho Nacional de Indústria), Amaro Lanari Júnior, Sebastião Dayrell de Lima (son of one of the original founders of the precursor to Belgo Mineira), and Osvaldo Fontini (former mayor of Barbacena). *Informador Comercial* (7 December 1957), located in FIEMG Archive, *Recortes,* v. 4.

49. "Açominas na rota da privatização," *Vida Industrial* (February 1993): 47.

50. *Dicionário biográfico de Minas Gerais,* 675–6; Miguel Augusto Gonçalves de Souza, *Açominas: aspiração de várias gerações de mineiros* (Belo Horizonte: Aço Minas Gerais S.A., 1985); Interview, Miguel Augusto Gonçalves de Souza, Belo Horizonte, 5 March 1997.

51. *Acesita, uma história de aço* (Belo Horizonte: Editora Anchieta, 1989); Edmundo de Macedo Soares e Silva, *As instituições de indústria e comércio do Brasil* (Rio de Janeiro: Crown, 1972), 382–3.

52. "Edmundo de Macedo Soares," *Dicionário histórico-biográfico brasileiro: 1930–1983* (Rio de Janeiro: Editora Forense-Universitária, 1984), 3221–5.

53. Silva, *As instituições*, 41, 49, 55, 57, 61, 67, 99–103.

54. "Minas, uma visão geral da economia em 1975," *Vida Industrial* (November 1975): 12.

55. "Força do Aço de Minas Gerais Ultrapassa Barreiras da Crise," *Vida Industrial* (November 1992): 10–13.

56. Edson Vaz Musa, "A competitividade da indústra têxtil brasileira," *Vida Industrial* (December 1992): 20.

57. Instituto de Desenvolvimento Industrial Minas Gerais, *Panorama do setor têxtil de Minas Gerais 1995/1996*. All the information in this section comes from this unpublished report graciously given to me by Marcus Vinicius M. de Oliveira Lima of the INDI.

58. "O Setor Têxtil no Brasil," FIEMG Archives. For the perspective of an industry leader, the president of Rhodia S. A., see Edson Vaz Musa, "A competitividade da indústria têxtil brasileira," 20–23.

59. Sérgio de Oliveira Birchal, "O empresariado mineiro: cinco casos de sucesso," M.A. thesis, Faculdade de Ciências Econômicas, Universidade Federal de Minas Gerais, 1989, 110–28.

60. My thanks to Marcus Vinicius M. de Oliveira for giving me the benefit of his knowledge of the industry. "Os desafios da modernização e da sucessão entre parentes," *Vida Industrial* (April 1993): 5–9.

61. About half of this ore went to Asia (Japan, South Korea, China) and the rest to Europe (primarily Germany, Belgium, France, England, and Italy). Just 3 percent went to the U.S. *Vida Industrial* (May 1994): 18.

62. *Balanço anual—Minas Gerais* 5:5 (October 1998): 70–71; *Balanço anual—Nacional* 22:22 (June 1998): 212.

63. JUCEMG, "Companhia de Cimento Portland Itaú," and Macedo Soares, 523.

64. Geraldo Corrêa, *Pequena história de um grande industrial* (Belo Horizonte: n.p., 1968); Interview, Vitória Dias, Belo Horizonte, 5 August 1999; *Balanço anual—Minas Gerais* 5:5 (October 1998): 82.

65. "CIMINAS: mais um milhão de toneladas de cimento," *Vida Industrial* (April 1975): 10–11.

66. *Anuário estatístico do Brasil—1995*, 4–26.

67. Ibid., 70–71.

68. "Benjamim Ferreira Guimarães," *Dicionário biográfico de Minas Gerais*, 301; *Coronel Benjamim Ferreira Guimarães: tecendo histórias* (Belo Horizonte: Livraria Del Rey Editora, 1997).

69. "Antônio Mourão Guimarães," and "Flávio Pentagna Guimarães," *Dicionário biográfico de Minas Gerais*, 300–2; "Centenário de Antônio Mourão Guimarães," *Estado de Minas* 25 June 1988, 4. Antônio Chagas Diniz was another founder of Magnesita. He was a physician who married into the

Guimarães family. He was also a founder of the Centro das Indústrias da Cidade Industrial. *Vida Industrial* (June 1969): n.p.

70. Fiat was largest both in terms of total current assets (roughly US$2.5 billion) and operating income (roughly US$11.5 billion). *Balanço anual—nacional* 22:22 (June 1998): 116–7.

71. *A economia mineira,* 127 and 136.

72. The municipios of Betim, Contagem, and Belo Horizonte alone accounted for one-third of the value of all industrial production in the state in 1985. *Anuário estatístico de Minas Gerais 1990- 1993* (Belo Horizonte: Fundação João Pinheiro, 1994), 331–43. *Expresso Fiat—Edição de Ouro, Especial 100 anos,* 11 July 1999, 90–102.

73. *O grupo Fiat no Brasil, edição 2000,* March 2000, 21–29.

74. "Implantação da Fiat consolida a economia mineira," *Estado de Minas,* 9 July 1986, 3; *Dicionário biográfico,* v. 1, 193–4.

75. "Miguel Augusto Gonçalves de Sousa," *Dicionário biográfico de Minas Gerais,* 675–6; Interview, Miguel Augusto Gonçalves de Souza.

76. *Dicionário biográfico,* v. 1, 265–6.

77. Brian Loveman and Thomas M. Davies, Jr., eds., *The Politics of Antipolitics: The Military in Latin America* (Wilmington, Delaware: Scholarly Resources, 1997).

78. The classic statement on bureaucratic-authoritarianism is Guillermo O'-Donnell, *Modernization and Bureaucratic- Authoritarianism: Studies in South American Politics* (Berkeley, Calif.: Institute of International Studies, University of California, 1973). See also, David Collier, ed., *The New Authoritarianism in Latin America* (Princeton, New Jersey: Princeton University Press, 1979); Luciano Martins, *Estado capitalista e burocracia no Brasil pós–64* (Rio de Janeiro: Paz e Terra, 1985).

79. Clélio Campolina Diniz, *Estado e capital estrangeiro na industrialização mineira* (Belo Horizonte: UFMG/PROED, 1981).

80. Luís Aureliano Gama de Andrade, "Technocracy and Development: The Case of Minas Gerais," Ph.D. diss., University of Michigan, 1980, 300.

81. Hagopian, *Traditional Politics,* 33 and 106.

82. For an interesting study of this phenomenon at the national level, see Angela de Castro Gomes, coord., *Engenheiros e economistas: novas elites burocráticas* (Rio de Janeiro: Editora Fundação Getúlio Vargas, 1994).

83. The FACE's home in downtown Belo Horizonte was built with funds from the state government through the efforts of then federal deputy José de Magalhães Pinto. Maria Arminda do Nascimento Arruda, "A Modernidade Possível: Cientistas e Ciências Sociais em Minas Gerais," in *História das ciências sociais no Brasil,* vol. 1, Sergio Miceli, org. (São Paulo: Vértice, 1989), 234–315, esp. 252 and 257.

84. Andrade, "Technocracy and Development," 74.

85. Ibid., 75–80.

232   *Tropical Capitalism*

86. BDMG, *Relatório 1963/1964* (Belo Horizonte, 1965), 3, as cited in Andrade, 83.
87. Andrade, "Technocracy and Development," 83–84.
88. *Dicionário biográfico*, I, 221.
89. CEMIG and the BDMG each provided half of the financing for INDI, although the former later took over a larger share and political control of the INDI. The original board consisted of three directors, one appointed by the BDMG, one by CEMIG, and one by the Secretaria de Indústria e Comércio. Andrade, "Technocracy and Development," 236. Between 1972 and 1993 the INDI assisted in the creation of more than a thousand industrial projects with a combined investment of more than US$7 billion. "Novas Perspectivas para Minas Gerais," *Vida Industrial* (November 1993): 32.
90. *Dicionário biográfico*, I, 221; Andrade, "Technocracy and Development," 92–101.
91. Andrade, "Technocracy and Development," 306.
92. Ibid., 113–30.
93. "O Comércio Exterior e o Desenvolvimento de Minas Gerais," *Vida Industrial* (July 1970): quadro 4.
94. *Dicionário biográfico*, II, 569.
95. Andrade, "Technocracy and Development," 304.
96. Ibid., 307.
97. Hagopian, *Traditional Politics*, 125.
98. Ibid., 241.
99. Hagopian, 242.
100. *Dicionário biográfico*, II, 537.
101. *Dicionário biográfico*, II, 710–11.
102. *Dicionário biográfico*, I, 329.
103. Nansen Araujo, "Política e Políticos," *Vida Industrial* (September 1970).
104. For details see the very fine work of Heloísa Maria Murgel Starling, *Os senhores das Gerais: os novos inconfidentes e o golpe militar de 1964* (Petrópolis: Vozes, 1986).
105. "Classes Produtoras Firmam Posição," *Mensagem Econômica* (March 1964): 9; Nansen Araujo, "O Brasil Prossegue," *Vida Industrial* (September 1969).
106. This group was divided into various sectors, each with its leadership: clothing, food, shelter, medicine, transportation, means of combat. *Vida Industrial* (October-December 1964).
107. *Mensagem Econômica* (October 1960): 6.
108. Ibid., July 1964, 4.
109. "Minas à Margem do Processo Desenvolvimentista do País," *Mensagem Econômica* (July 1966): 14–16.
110. Nansen Araujo, "Imperialismo Interno," *Vida Industrial* (July 1975).
111. "Sugestões e Reivindicações Junto aos Govêrnos Estadual e Federal," *Mensagem Econômica* (June 1964): 3–8; "Problemas de Crédito e de Infra-Estru-

tura da Economia Mineira," *Mensagem Econômica,* (May 1965): 3–17; "Documento da Indústria ao Govêrno Estadual é Síntese das Aspirações dos Mineiros," *Vida Industrial* (October 1971).

112. Nansen Araujo, "O Flagelo da Estatização," *Vida Industrial* (May 1968).

113. Warren Dean, *The Industrialization of São Paulo, 1889–1940* (Austin, Texas: University of Texas Press, 1969); Wilson Cano, *Raízes da concentração industrial em São Paulo* (São Paulo: Difel, 1977).

114. João Heraldo Lima, *Café e indústria em Minas Gerais, 1870- 1920* (Petrópolis: Vozes, 1981).

115. Unless otherwise noted, the information in the following section comes from Claudio Bastos, *Instituições financeiras de Minas (1819–1995)* (Belo Horizonte: Embalart Editora, 1997), 20–42.

116. "Banco da Lavoura de Minas Gerais," JUCEMG.

117. Roberto Pompeu de Toledo, ed., *História do Unibanco* (São Paulo: Instituto Moreira Salles, 1994).

118. "Estado em disparada," *Veja,* 26 April 1995, 104.

119. Founded by Nansen Araujo in 1930, the company "took off" in 1930 when the *prefeito,* Otacílio Negrão de Lima, gave Araujo an exclusive contract to supply water meters to the *prefeitura*—a guaranteed order for 100,000 units, 15 years without taxes, and a large advance on the purchase. Araujo then persuaded powerful business figures (Sebastião Augusto de Lima, in particular, and Antônio Mourão Guimarães, Juventino Dias) to capitalize the new corporation. S. A. de Lima was a relative of Araujo. It has long manufactured water and electric meters using licensed foreign technology, primarily German, North American, Swiss, and Canadian. "Nansen, 40 Anos," *Vida Industrial* (October 1971); "Meio Século da Nansen," *Vida Industrial* (August 1980): 26–28; Sérgio de Oliveira Birchal, "O empresariado mineiro: cinco casos de successo," M.A. thesis, Faculdade de Ciências Econômicas, Universidade Federal de Minas Gerais, 1989, 163–206.

120. Motta was born in Diamantina and entered into the business world in 1934. He founded the Companhia Mineira de Cerveja in 1961 and he ran two chemical companies. He also served as vice president of the National Confederation of Industries (CNI). *Minas Gerais,* 10 July 1969, 2; *Dicionário biográfico,* II, 440.

Conclusion

1. See, for example, Philip D. Oxhorn and Graciela Ducatenzeiler, eds., *What Kind of Democracy? What Kind of Market?: Latin America in the Age of Neoliberalism* (University Park, Penn.: Pennsylvania State University Press, 1998); and Menno Vellinga, ed., *The Changing Role of the State in Latin America* (Boulder, Colorado: Westview Press, 1998).

2. Jacob Knifl, "The Most Important Government Ploys," *Global Finance* (February 1998): 52–3. On some of the difficulties of privatizing the telephone companies see *Folha de São Paulo,* 29 July 1999, 6 brasil.

3. Werner Baer and Claudio Paiva, "Brazil's Drifting Economy: Stagnation and Inflation During 1987–1996," in Oxhorn and Ducatenzeiler, 89–126.

4. *Folha de São Paulo,* 18 January 2000, 1; *Conjuntura Econômica* 54:10 (October 2000), xvii.

5. See, for example, Will Hutton and Anthony Giddens, eds., *On the Edge: Living with Global Capitalism* (London: Jonathan Cape, 2000).

6. Aymoré, for example, traditionally the largest food processing firm in Minas, joined forces with Danone in order to remain competitive in an increasingly open market for retailers. Marta Vieira, "Brasil Terá Nova Onda e Fusões," *Estado de Minas,* 25 July 1999, Economia, 4.

7. Heberth Xavier, "Indústria Têxtil Agora na Ofensiva," *Estado de Minas,* 12 June 2000, Economia, 14.

8. Marta Vieira, "Belgo Entra no Mercado Canadense," *Estado de Minas,* 13 June 2000, Economia, 15; *Jornal do Brasil,* 31 May 2000, 1; Wilson Peres, coord., *Grandes empresas y grupos industriales latinoamericanos: expansión y desafíos en la era de la apertura y la globalización* (México, D. F.: Siglo Veintiuno Editores, 1998), 261–6.

9. Cardoso's comment came after the announcement of the impending merger of Brazil's two largest beverage firms, Brahma and Antarctica, to confront competition from Coca-Cola. "FH Apóia Fusão de Empresas para Enfrentar Multinacionais," *Jornal do Brasil,* 4 July 1999, 1.

10. Leonardo Attuch, "STJ Abre Caminho para Acerto entre Mendes e BB," *Estado de Minas,* 17 June 2000, Economia, 11.

11. *O Grupo Fiat do Brasil* (Belo Horizonte: Fiat do Brasil, 1999).

12. The best recent analysis of what many mineiro analysts have called the "revolution from above" is Otavio Soares Dulci's excellent *Política e recuperação econômica em Minas Gerais* (Belo Horizonte: Editora UFMG, 1999).

13. For a recent volume that emphasizes the survival of clientelism in contemporary Brazilian politics, see Peter R. Kingstone and Timothy J. Power, eds., *Democratic Brazil: Actors, Institutions, and Processes* (Pittsburgh, Penn.: University of Pittsburgh Press, 2000), esp. 7.

14. For efforts to block the privatization of Furnas, see "Fiemg quer Furnas em Minas," *Folha de São Paulo,* 1 August 1999, 4.

15. Hélio Garcia, "Queremos Criar Novo Modelo de Estado," *Vida Industrial* (November 1991): 8–9.

16. For examples of the mentality of mineiro industrialists in the 1990s see, for example, Silvio Diniz Ferreira, "Reduzir o Tamanho do Estado na Economia," *Vida Industrial* (June 1991): 7–8; "A Verdade Sobre as Emergências do Desenvolvimento Econômico Mineiro," *Vida Industrial* (February 1994): entire issue.

17. The population of Mexico City today is more than 20 percent of Mexico's total population. Buenos Aires is home to one of every three Argentines, Montevideo accounts for 40 percent of all Uruguayans. Greater Santiago is home to one in three Chileans. Even São Paulo, considered by some the third- or fourth-largest city in the world, accounts for just 10 percent of Brazil's total population. A dozen Brazilian cities have more than one million inhabitants. Robert N. Gwynne, *New Horizons? Third World Industrialization in an International Framework* (New York: Longman, 1990), 166.

18. A pioneering study of secondary cities is James R. Scobie, *Secondary Cities of Argentina: The Social History of Corrientes, Salta, and Mendoza, 1850–1910* (Stanford, Calif.: Stanford University Press, 1988) completed and edited by Samuel L. Baily.

19. For Monterrey, see Alex M. Saragoza, *The Monterrey Elite and the Mexican State, 1880–1940* (Austin: University of Texas Press, 1988); Menno Vellinga, *Economic Development and the Dynamics of Class: Industrialization, Power and Control in Monterrey, Mexico* (Assen, The Netherlands: Van Gorcum, 1979); Mario Cerutti, *Burguesía y capitalismo en Monterrey (1850–1910)* (México: Claves Latinoamericanas, 1983). The literature on Medellín is sparse. See Jorge Restrepo Uribe, *Medellín, su origen, progreso y desarrollo* (Medellín: Servigráficas, 1981).

20. For a carefully argued definition and discussion of patronage and clientelism see Luis Roniger, *Hierarchy and Trust in Modern Mexico and Brazil* (Westport, Conn.: Praeger, 1990), 3–4.

21. For a recent reconsideration of populism, see Michael Conniff, ed., *Populism in Latin America* (Tuscaloosa: University of Alabama Press, 1999), especially chapter 10, by Kurt Weyland, "Populism in the Age of Neoliberalism."

22. For a look at family networks and economic growth in a somewhat similar case, see Sudipt Dutta, *Family Business in India* (New Delhi: Response Books, 1997). For some other examples of the importance of family enterprise in Latin America, see Carlos Dávila and Rory Miller, eds., *Business History in Latin America: The Experience of Seven Countries* (Liverpool: Liverpool University Press, 1999).

23. *Vida Industrial* (April 1993): 9; Wilson Peres, coord. *Grandes empresas y grupos industriales latinoamericanos: expansión y desafíos en la era de la apertura y la globalización,* (Mexico, D. F.: Siglo Veintiuno Editores, 1998), 230.

24. The classic account of the rise of the modern business enterprise is Alfred D. Chandler, Jr., *The Visible Hand: The Managerial Revolution in American Business* (Cambridge, Mass.: Belknap Press, 1977). See also, Mansel G. Blackford, *The Rise of Modern Business in Great Britain, the United States, and Japan* (Chapel Hill: University of North Carolina Press, 1988).

25. Every year, for example, the FIEMG awards medals to leading entrepreneurs in more than a dozen industries. Throughout the nineties, occasionally, a

woman can be found among the recipients. See, for example, *Vida Industrial* (December 1992): 25.

26. Peter Evans, *Embedded Autonomy: States and Industrial Transformation* (Princeton, New Jersey: Princeton University Press, 1995).

27. Mauricio Mesquita Moreira persuasively argues that the key to understanding economic growth in Brazil and South Korea is not state intervention in itself, but selective state intervention. *Industrialization, Trade and Market Failures: The Role of Government Intervention in Brazil and South Korea* (New York: St. Martin's Press, 1995).

28. In a number of widely read recent publications Michael Porter has argued that the "old distinctions between *laissez-faire* and intervention are obsolete. Government, first and foremost, must strive to create an environment that supports rising productivity. This implies a minimalist government role in some areas (e.g., trade barriers, pricing) and an activist role in others (e.g., ensuring vigorous competition, providing high-quality education and training)." Michael E. Porter, *The Competitive Advantage of Nations* (New York: The Free Press, 1990), xiii.

29. Barbara Geddes, *The Politician's Dilemma* (Berkeley: University of California Press, 1994).

30. Some important recent studies of policy choice and the role of what I have called public entrepreneurs, see Miguel Ángel Centeno, *Democracy Within Reason: Technocratic Revolution in Mexico,* 2nd ed. (University Park, Penn.: The Pennsylvania State University Press, 1997); Merilee S. Grindle and John W. Thomas, *Public Choices and Policy Change: The Political Economy of Reform in Developing Countries* (Baltimore, Maryland: The Johns Hopkins University Press, 1991); Ben Ross Schneider, *Politics Within the State: Elite Bureaucrats and Industrial Policy in Authoritarian Brazil* (Pittsburgh, Penn.: University of Pittsburgh Press, 1991).

31. See, Thomas K. McCraw, ed., *Creating Modern Capitalism: How Entrepreneurs, Companies, and Countries Triumphed in Three Industrial Revolutions* (Cambridge, Mass.: Harvard University Press, 1997); Tetsuji Okazaki and Masahiro Okuno-Fujiwara, eds., *The Japanese Economic System and Its Historical Origins* (Oxford: Oxford University Press, 1999).

32. Some good examples of these studies are Ernest Bartell, C. S. C. and Leigh A. Payne, eds., *Business and Democracy in Latin America* (Pittsburgh, Penn.: University of Pittsburgh Press, 1995); Leigh A. Payne, *Brazilian Industrialists and Democratic Change* (Baltimore, Maryland: Johns Hopkins University Press, 1994); Ben Ross Schneider, *Politics Within the State;* Gilda Portugal Gouvea, *Burocracia e elites burocráticas no Brasil* (São Paulo: Editora Paulicéia, 1994).

33. Following the example of some other late industrializers, Belo Horizonte is also trying to develop an informatics industry. See, for example, "BH Vira Incubadora," *Vida Industrial* (August 1994): 10–12.

34. *Jornal do Brasil,* 10 July 2001, 1.
35. In a speech to the Center for Technology in the Chemical and Textile Industries, H. Joseph Sperber, president of Gerber Scientific, told gathered industrialists that, "If you gentlemen do not put technology at your disposal, it will be used against you." "Tudo Sob Medida: A Chave da Sobrevivência," *Vida Industrial* (March 1992): 15.
36. Schumpeter, *Capitalism, Socialism, and Democracy* (New York: Harper & Brothers, 1947), 110.
37. Sandra Kiefer, "BH Empurra a Miséria para a Periferia," *Estado de Minas,* 2 June 2000, 25, Gerais/Urbanismo; and, 4 June 2000, 43, Gerais/Comunidade.
38. "Situação de BH se Repete pelo País," *Vida Industrial* (July 1993): 13.
39. Evelyne Huber, "Assessments of State Strengths," in *Latin American in Comparative Perspective: New Approaches to Methods and Analysis,* Peter H. Smith, ed. (Boulder, Colorado: Westview, 1995), 163–93.
40. The infant mortality rate in Rio Grande do Sul (the lowest in all Brazil) equals the rate in Canada in the late 1960s. *Veja,* 14 June 2000, 32. A recent survey showed that half of the population of the city of São Paulo (or 5.5 million people) live in "irregular" housing. "Metade de SP Mora em habitação irregular," *Folha de São Paulo,* 4 June 2000, C1. Another recent survey placed the salary of Brazilian executives (directors and presidents of firms) in a range from $20,000 to $70,000 per month! Only U.S. executives received higher salaries. Consuelo Dieguez, "Poucos Com Muito," *Veja,* 7 June 2000, 144–5.
41. Schumpeter, *Capitalism, Socialism, and Democracy,* 82–3.
42. Peter F. Drucker, *Post-Capitalist Society* (New York: HarperCollins, 1993).

Bibliography

Archives

Arquivo Público da Cidade de Belo Horizonte
Arquivo Público Mineiro
Assembléia Legislativa de Minas Gerais
Associação Comercial de Minas, Centro de Memória
Câmara Municipal de Belo Horizonte
Federação das Indústria do Estado de Minas Gerais, Centro de Memória
Instituto de Desenvolvimento Industrial
Junta Comercial do Estado de Minas Gerais
Museu Abílio Barreto
Platt-Saco-Lowell Archive, Lancashire Record Office, Preston, England
Prefeitura Muncipal de Belo Horizonte

Interviews and Oral Histories

Ignacio Ballesteros, História Oral, no. 3. Belo Horizonte: Fundação João Pinheiro, 1996.
Mauricio Chagas Bicalho: depoimento de história oral. Rio de Janeiro: CEMIG, 1986.
John Reginald Cotrim: depoimento de história oral. Belo Horizonte: CEMIG, 1994.
Vitória Dias. Interviewed by author. Belo Horizonte, 5 August 1999.
Renato Falci. Interviewed by Ligia Leite and Otávio Dulci. Belo Horizonte, 18 December 1989, 9 February 1990, 12 March 1990.
Paulo Macedo Gontijo. Interviewed by Lígia Pereira and Adriana Simões. Belo Horizonte, 13 December 1990, 18 December 1990, 6 March 1991.
Amaro Lanari Júnior: a realização. Belo Horizonte: Fundação João Pinheiro, 1987.
Lucas Lopes: a criação de Usiminas. Belo Horizonte: Fundação João Pinheiro, 1987.
Lucas Lopes: depoimento de história oral. Belo Horizonte: CEMIG, 1986.
Memórias do desenvolvimento: Lucas Lopes–depoimento. Rio de Janeiro: Centro de Memória da Eletricidade no Brasil, 1991.
Usiminas, 25 anos. depoimento: Lucas Lopes. Belo Horizonte: Fundação João Pinheiro, 1987.
Gil Nogueira, História oral, no. 6. Belo Horizonte: Fundação João Pinheiro, 1996.

Gabriel A. Janot Pacheco: a criação de Usiminas. Belo Horizonte: Fundação João Pinheiro, 1987.

Jayme de Andrade Peconick: idealização. Belo Horizonte: Fundação João Pinheiro, 1987.

Paulo Pinto: o aspecto social. Belo Horizonte: Fundação João Pinheiro, 1987.

João Camilo Pena: depoimento de história oral. Belo Horizonte: CEMIG, 1986.

José Eduardo de Lima Pereira, Diretor de Assuntos Corporativos, Fiat do Brasil S. A. Interviewed by the author. Nova Lima, Minas Gerais, 16 June 2000.

Edmundo de Macedo Soares e Silva: um construtor do nosso tempo: depoimento ao CPDOC, Lucia Hippolito and Ignez Cordeiro de Farias, orgs. Rio de Janeiro: Iarte Impressos de Arte, 1998.

Miguel Augusto Gonçalves de Souza. Interviewed by the author. Belo Horizonte, 5 March 1997.

Luiz Verano: a implantação. Belo Horizonte: Fundação João Pinheiro, 1987.

Dissertations and Theses

Adelman, Jeffry. Urban Planning and Reality in Republican Brazil: Belo Horizonte, 1890–1930. Ph.D. dissertation, Indiana University, 1974.

Albano, Celina. The Making of a Brazilian Industrial City: The Experience of Contagem. Ph.D. dissertation, University of Manchester, 1980.

Andrade, Luis Aureliano Gama de. Technocracy and Development: The Case of Minas Gerais. Ph.D. dissertation, University of Michigan, 1980.

Barbosa, Maria Lígia de Oliveira. Reconstruindo as Minas e planejando os Gerais: os engenheiros e a constituição dos grupos sociais. Ph.D. dissertation, UNICAMP, 1993.

Birchal, Sérgio de Oliveira. O empresariado mineiro: cinco casos de sucesso. M.A. thesis, Faculdade de Ciências Econômicas, Universidade Federal de Minas Gerais, 1989.

Blasenheim, Peter Louis. A Regional History of the Zona da Mata in Minas Gerais, Brazil, 1870–1906. Ph.D. dissertation, Stanford University, 1982.

Callaghan, William Stuart. Obstacles to Industrialization: The Iron and Steel Industry in Brazil during the Old Republic. Ph.D. dissertation, University of Texas, 1981.

Cammack, Paul. State and Federal Politics in Minas Gerais, Brazil. Ph.D. dissertation, Oxford University, 1980.

Costa, Fernando Nogueira da. Bancos em Minas Gerais (1889–1964). Ph.D. dissertation, Universidade Estadual de Campinas, 1978.

Delgado, Ignácio José Godinho. Burguesia e estado–o caso de Minas Gerais: a estratégia de um revés. M.A. thesis, Departamento de Ciência Política, Universidade Federal de Minas Gerais, 1989.

Dickenson, John Philip. "Zona Metalúrgica: A Study of the Geography of Industrial Development in Minas Gerais, Brazil." Ph.D. dissertation, University of Liverpool, 1970.

Diniz, Joubert C. Estudo do mercado energético da Cia Força e Luz de Minas Gerais. M.A. thesis, Faculdade de Ciências Econômicas, Universidade Federal de Minas Gerais, 1964.

Faria, Maria Auxiliadora. "A Política da Gleba": as classes conservadoras mineiras: discurso e prática na Primeira República. Ph.D. dissertation, Universidade de São Paulo, 1992.

David Verge Fleischer, Political Recruitment in the State of Minas Gerais, Brazil (1890–1970). Ph.D. dissertation, University of Florida, 1972.

Giroletti, Domingos Antônio. A industrialização de Juiz de Fora, 1850 a 1930. M.A. thesis, Universidade Federal de Minas Gerais, 1976.

———. A modernização capitalista em Minas Gerais—a formação do operariado industrial e de uma nova cosmovisão. Ph.D. dissertation, Universidade Federal do Rio de Janeiro, 1987.

Hanley, Anne Gerard. Capital Markets in the Coffee Economy: Financial Institutions and Economic Change in São Paulo, Brazil, 1850–1905. Ph.D. dissertation, Stanford University, 1995.

Le Ven, Michel Marie. Classes sociais e poder política na formação espacial de Belo Horizonte (1893–1914). M.A. thesis, Universidade Federal de Minas Gerais, 1977.

Machado, Barry. Farquhar and Ford in Brazil: Studies in Business Expansion and Foreign Policy. Ph.D. dissertation, Northwestern University, 1975.

Martins Filho, Amilcar Vianna. The White Collar Republic: Patronage and Interest Representation in Minas Gerais, Brazil, 1889–1930. Ph.D. dissertation, University of Illinois, 1987.

Mayer, Ivana Santos. A CEMIG e a industrialização de Minas Gerais. Bachelor's thesis, Faculdade de Ciências Econômicas, Universidade Federal de Minas Gerais, 1988.

Paula, João Antônio de. O Prometeu no sertão: economia e sociedade da Capitania das Minas dos Matos Gerais. 2 V., Ph.D. dissertation, Universidade de São Paulo, 1988.

Paula, Maria Carlota de Souza. As vicissitudes da industrialização periférica: o caso de Juiz de Fora (1930–70). M.A. thesis, Universidade Federal de Minas Gerais, 1976.

Pereira, Paulo Afonso Carvalho. Padrões de concentração e crescimento industrial na região polarizada por Belo Horizonte. M. A. thesis, CEDEPLAR, Universidade Federal de Minas Gerais, 1980.

Rogers, Edward Jonathan. A Study of the Brazilian Iron and Steel Industry and its Associated Resources. Ph.D. dissertation, Stanford University, 1957.

Silva, Celson José da. Marchas e contramarchas do mandonismo local. (Caeté–um estudo de caso). M.A. thesis, Universidade Federal de Minas Gerais, 1972.

Silva, Vera Alice Cardoso. A política regionalista e o atraso da industrialização em Minas Gerais. M.A. thesis, Universidade Federal de Minas Gerais, 1977.

Summerhill, William Roderick. Railroads and the Brazilian Economy Before 1914. Ph.D. dissertation, Stanford University, 1995.

Versiani, Flávio Rabelo. Technical Change, Equipment Replacement and Labor Absorption: The Case of the Brazilian Textile Industry. Ph.D. dissertation, Vanderbilt University, 1971.

Vieira, Evantina Pereira. Minas Gerais: a dominação burguesa—conflitos políticos e formas de organização (1927–1940). Ph.D. dissertation, Universidade de São Paulo, 1985.

Journals and Periodicals Consulted

Annaes do Senado Mineiro
Boletim da Associação Comercial de Minas
CEMIG Notícias
Conjuntura Econômica
Diário da Tarde (Belo Horizonte)
Diário de Minas (Belo Horizonte)
Estado de Minas (Belo Horizonte)
Folha de Minas (Belo Horizonte)
Folha de São Paulo
Jornal do Brasil (Rio de Janeiro)
Minas Gerais
Mensagem Econômica (ACM)
Revista Comercial de Minas Gerais
Revista do Arquivo Público Mineiro
O Tempo (Belo Horizonte)
Veja
Vida Industrial (FIEMG)

Statistical Sources

Andrade, Afranio Alves de, Maria Auxiliadora Faria, and João Heraldo Lima. *Estatísticas históricas: a República em Minas Gerais*, 4 V. Belo Horizonte: FINEP/CEM/CEDEPLAR, 1982. [unpublished manuscript]

Annuario estatístico. anno I—1921. Volume IV, Tomo I. Bello Horizonte: Imprensa Official, 1926.

Annuário estatístico de Belo Horizonte, anno I—1937. Belo Horizonte: Serviço de Estatístico Geral, 1937.

Anuário estatístico de Minas Gerais 1987. Belo Horizonte: SEPLAN, 1987.

Anuário estatístico de Minas Gerais 1990–1993. Belo Horizonte: Fundação João Pinheiro, 1994.

Anuário estatístico do Brasil. Rio de Janeiro: Instituto Brasileiro de Geografia e Estatística, 1953.

Anuário estatístico do Brasil. Rio de Janeiro: IBGE, 1995.

Balanço anual–Minas Gerais. V. 5, No. 5 (October 1998).

Balanço anual–Nacional. V. 22, No. 22 (June 1998).

Brasil em números. V. 4, 1995/96. Rio de Janeiro: IBGE, 1996.

Brazil. Ministério da Agricultura. *Atlas econômico de Minas Gerais.* Rio de Janeiro, 1938.

Centro das Indústrias das Cidades Industriais de Minas Gerais. *A Cidade Industrial de Contagem em números–1966/1967.* Belo Horizonte: CICI, 1968.

Federação das Indústrias do Estado de Minas Gerais. *Anuário industrial de Minas Gerais.* Belo Horizonte: FIEMG, various years.

Indústria de fiação e tecelagem 1944. Belo Horizonte: Oficinas Gráficas da Estatística, 1946.

Ludwig, Armin K. *Brazil: A Handbook of Historical Statistics.* Boston: G. K. Hall, 1985.

Meirelles, Olyntho. *Recenseamento de Bello Horizonte em 1912.* Bello Horizonte: Imprensa Official, 1913.

Minas Gerais. Secretaria da Agricultura. *Synopse estatística do município de Bello Horizonte, 1928–1934.* Belo Horizonte, 1935.

———. Secretaria de Planejamento. *As principais sociedades anónimas de Minas Gerais–1976.* Belo Horizonte: Superintendência de Estatísticas e Informacões, 1978.

———. *Minas Gerais: indicadores socio-econômicos, 1950–1980.* Belo Horizonte: SEPLAN, 1983.

Pinto, Alfredo Moreira. *Monographia de Bello Horizonte em 1901.* Bello Horizonte: Imprensa Official, 1913.

Produção industrial do municipio de Belo Horizonte, 1936–1942. Belo Horizonte: Instituto Brasileiro de Geografia e Estatística, 1943.

Sinopse estatístico do município de Belo Horizonte. Rio de Janeiro: Instituto Brasileiro de Geografia e Estatística, 1948.

Usinas siderúrgicas em Minas Gerais. Belo Horizonte: Instituto Brasileiro de Geografia e Estatística, 1944.

Brazilian national censuses, 1872, 1890, 1920, 1940, 1950, 1960, 1970, 1980, 1991.

Reports and Plans

Banco de Desenvolvimento de Minas Gerais. *Economia mineira–1989: diagnóstico e perspectivas.* 5V in 7. Belo Horizonte: BDMG, 1989.

———. *A indústria têxtil em Minas Gerais: condições e reequipamento.* Belo Horizonte: BDMG, 1965.

Belo Horizonte. Prefeitura. *Plano de ação municipal: diagnóstico e diretrizes.* Belo Horizonte: Minas Gráfica Editora, 1984.

———. *Quarto plano de ação municipal: diagnóstico e diretrizes.* Belo Horizonte: Prefeitura Municipal de Belo Horizonte, 1985.

Clark, W. A. Graham. *Cotton Goods in Latin America, Part II. Brazil, Colombia, and Venezuela.* Department of Commerce and Labor, Bureau of Manufactures, Special Agents Series, No. 1. Washington, DC: Government Printing Office, 1910.

Diagnóstico da economia mineira. 6 V. Belo Horizonte: Banco de Desenvolvimento de Minas Gerais, 1968.

A economia mineira: perfil das empresas do Estado 1991/1992. Belo Horizonte: Fundação João Pinheiro, 1994.

Giannetti, Américo Renê. *Plano-programa de administração para Belo Horizonte, 1951.* Belo Horizonte: Estabelecimentos Gráficos Santa Maria, 1951.

Instituto de Desenvolvimento Industrial Minas Gerais. "Panorama do setor têxtil de Minas Gerais 1995/1996." [unpublished report]

Kehdy, Mitiko Okazaki, coord. "Relatório de pesquisa. Projeto IV: arquivos mineiros da Repùblica Velha." 5V. Belo Horizonte: Faculdade de Ciências Econômicas, 1982. [unpublished report]

Minas Gerais, Brazil. Companhia de Distritos Industriais. *Distritos industriais: Montes Claros, Pirapora, Uberaba, Juiz de Fora, Santa Luzia, Sete Lagoas, Uberlândia.* Belo Horizonte: Imprensa Oficial, 1971.

———. Secretaria da Agricultura. *Plano de recuperação econômica e fomento da produção.* Belo Horizonte: Imprensa Oficial, 1947.

———. Secretaria das Finanças. *O Estado de Minas Gerais: sua evolução econômica.* Bello Horizonte: Imprensa Oficial, 1922.

———. Secretaria de Planejamento. *Análises setoriais da economia urbana: setor industrial.* Belo Horizonte: Plambel, 1978.

———. *Áreas industriais na região metropolitana de Belo Horizonte.* Belo Horizonte: Plambel, 1973.

———. *Comportamento da economia mineira: periodo 1960–77. Indústria de transformação.* Belo Horizonte: SEPLAN, 1978.

———. *Diagnóstico das áreas industriais existentes na região metropolitana de Belo Horizonte.* Belo Horizonte: Plambel, 1978.

Garry, L. S. *Textile Markets of Brazil.* Department of Commerce, Bureau of Foreign and Domestic Commerce, Special Agents Series, No. 203. Washington, DC: Government Printing Office, 1920.

A indústria têxtil em Minas Gerais. Belo Horizonte: INDI, 1972.

Minas Gerais, Secretaria de Viação e Obras Públicas. *Plano de eletrificação de Minas Gerais.* 5 V. Rio de Janeiro: Companhia Brasileira de Engenharia, 1950.

Relatórios da Prefeitura de Bello Horizonte. various years.

Superintendência de Desenvolvimento da Região Metropolitana (PLAMBEL), Secretaria de Estado do Planejamento e Coordenação Geral, Governor do Estado de Minas Gerais. *Plano metropolitano de Belo Horizonte. a estrutura econômica da região metropolitana. diagnóstico e proposições. relatório intermediário.* Belo Horizonte: Plambel, 1971.

———. "O Processo de desenvolvimento de Belo Horizonte: 1897–1970. Belo Horizonte: PLAMBEL, 1979. [unpublished manuscript]

Books and Articles

Abreu, Marcelo de Paiva, org. *A ordem do progresso: cem anos de política econômica republicana, 1889–1989.* Rio de Janeiro: Campus, 1990.

Acesita, uma história de aço. Belo Horizonte: Editora Anchieta, 1989.

Adas, Michael. *Machines as the Measure of Men: Science, Technology, and Ideologies of Western Dominance.* Ithaca, New York: Cornell University Press, 1989.

Addis, Caren. *Taking the Wheel: Auto Parts Firms and the Political Economy of Industrialization in Brazil.* University Park, Penn.: The Pennsylvania State University Press, 1999.

Araujo, Laís Corrêa, org. *Sedução do Horizonte.* Belo Horizonte: Fundação João Pinheiro, 1996.

Arbix, Glauco and Mauro Zilbovicius, org. *De JK a FHC: A reinvenção dos carros.* São Paulo: Scritta, 1997.

Arruda, Maria Arminda do Nascimento. "A Modernidade Possível: Cientistas e Ciências Sociais em Minas Gerais." In *História das ciências sociais no Brasil, vol. 1,* edited by Sergio Miceli. São Paulo: Vértice, 1989, 234–315.

Ashton, T. S. *The Industrial Revolution.* Oxford: Oxford University Press, 1948.

Baer, Werner. *The Brazilian Economy: Growth and Development,* 4th ed. Westport, Conn.: Praeger, 1995.

———. *The Development of the Brazilian Steel Industry.* Nashville, Tenn.: Vanderbilt University Press, 1969.

Baeta, Nilton. *A indústria siderúrgica em Minas Gerais.* Belo Horizonte: Imprensa Oficial, 1973.

Bairoch, Paul. "International Industrialization Levels from 1750 to 1980." *Journal of European Economic History* 11:2 (fall 1982): 269–333.

Barbosa, Waldemar de Almeida. *Dicionário histórico-geográfico de Minas Gerais.* Belo Horizonte: Promoção-da-Família, 1971.

———. *A verdade sobre a história de Belo Horizonte.* Belo Horizonte: FIMAC, 1985.

Barman, Roderick. *Brazil: The Forging of a Nation, 1798–1852.* Stanford: Stanford University Press, 1988.

———. "Business and Government in Imperial Brazil: The Experience of Viscount Mauá." *Journal of Latin American Studies* 13:2 (November 1981): 239–264.

Barreto, Abílio. *Bello Horizonte: Memória histórica e descriptiva.* 2a ed. Bello Horizonte: Livraria Rex, 1936.

Bartell, Ernest, C. S. C. and Leigh A. Payne, eds. *Business and Democracy in Latin America.* Pittsburgh, Penn.: University of Pittsburgh Press, 1995.

Bastos, Cláudio. *Instituições financeiras de Minas (1819–1995).* Belo Horizonte: Embalat Editora, 1997.

Bastos, Humberto. *A conquista siderúrgica no Brasil.* São Paulo: Martins, 1959.

Beloch, Israel and Alzira Alves de Abreu, coord. *Dicionário histórico-biográfico brasileiro: 1930–1983.* Rio de Janeiro: Editora Forense-Universitária, 1984.

Belo Horizonte & o comércio: 100 anos de história. Belo Horizonte: Fundação João Pinheiro, 1997.

Bergad, Laird W. *Slavery and the Demographic and Economic History of Minas Gerais, Brazil, 1720–1888.* Cambridge: Cambridge University Press, 1999.

Bethell, Leslie, ed. *Colonial Brazil.* Cambridge: Cambridge University Press, 1987.

Birchal, Sérgio de Oliveira. *Entrepreneurship in Nineteenth-Century Brazil: The Formation of a Business Environment.* New York: St. Martin's Press, 1999.

Blackford, Mansel G. *The Rise of Modern Business in Great Britain, the United States, and Japan.* Chapel Hill: University of North Carolina Press, 1988.

Boxer, C. R. *The Golden Age of Brazil, 1695–1750: Growing Pains of a Colonial Society.* Berkeley, Calif.: University of California Press, 1969.

Brooke, James. "Inland Region of Brazil Grows Like Few Others." *New York Times,* 11 August 1994, C1.

Bulmer-Thomas, Victor. *The Economic History of Latin America Since Independence.* Cambridge: Cambridge University Press, 1994.

Caldeira, Jorge. *Mauá: empresário do Império.* São Paulo: Companhia das Letras, 1995.

———. *A nação mercantilista.* São Paulo: Editora 34, 1999.

Cameron, Rondo. *A Concise Economic History of the World from Paleolithic Times to the Present.* 2nd ed. New York: Oxford University Press, 1993.

Cano, Wilson. *Desequilíbrios regionais e concentração industrial no Brasil: 1930–1970.* São Paulo: Global, 1985.

Cardoso, Fernando Henrique. *Empresário industrial e desenvolvimento econômico no Brasil.* São Paulo: Difusão Européia do Livro, 1964.

———. *Política e desenvolvimento em sociedades dependentes: ideologias do empresariado industrial argentino e brasileiro.* Rio de Janeiro: Zahar, 1971.

Cardoso, Fernando Henrique and Enzo Faletto. *Dependencia y desarrollo en América Latina.* México: Siglo XXI, 1971.

Carvalho, Daniel de. *Notícia histórica sobre o algodão em Minas.* Rio de Janeiro: Typ. do Jornal do Commercio, 1916.

Carvalho, José Murilo de. *A Escola de Minas de Ouro Preto: o peso da glória.* São Paulo: Companhia Editora Nacional, 1978.

———. *Teatro de sombras: a política imperial.* São Paulo: Vértice, 1988.

Castañeda, Jorge G. *Utopia Unarmed: The Latin American Left After the Cold War.* New York: Vintage Books, 1993.

A CEMIG e o desenvolvimento econômico de Minas Gerais, 1952–1975. Belo Horizonte: CEMIG, 1971.

Centeno, Miguel Ángel. *Democracy within Reason: Technocratic Revolution in Mexico.* 2nd ed. University Park, Penn.: The Pennsylvania State University Press, 1997.

Centro da Memória da Eletricidade no Brasil. *A CERJ e a história da energia elétrica no Rio de Janeiro.* Rio de Janeiro: CMEB, 1993.

————. *História do Centro de Pesquisas de Energia Elétrica: CEPEL.* Rio de Janeiro: Eletrobrás, 1991.

————. *Panorama do setor de energia elétrica no Brasil.* Rio de Janeiro: CMEB, 1988.

Cerutti, Mario. *Burguesía y capitalismo en Monterrey (1850–1910).* México: Claves Latinoamericanas, 1983.

Chandler, Alfred C., Jr. *The Visible Hand: The Managerial Revolution in American Business.* Cambridge, Mass.: Belknap Press of Harvard University Press, 1977.

Cintra, Antônio Octávio and Luis Aureliano Gama de Andrade. "Planejamento: Reflexões sobre uma Experiência Estadual." In *Dilemas do planejamento urbano e regional no Brasil,* edited by Antônio Octávio Cintra and Paulo Roberto Haddad. Rio de Janeiro: Zahar, 1978, 25–33.

Cipolla, Carlo, ed. *The Fontana Economic History of Europe.* V. 3, *The Industrial Revolution,* and V. 4, *The Emergence of Industrial Societies.* Glasgow: Fontana/Collins, 1973 and 1976.

Coatsworth, John H. and Alan M. Taylor, eds. *Latin America and the World Economy Since 1800.* Cambridge, Mass.: Harvard University, David Rockefeller Center for Latin American Studies, 1998.

Cobbs, Elizabeth Anne. *The Rich Neighbor Policy: Rockefeller and Kaiser in Brazil.* New Haven, Conn.: Yale University Press, 1992.

Collier, David, ed. *The New Authoritarianism in Latin America.* Princeton, New Jersey: Princeton University Press, 1979.

Commissão Constructora da Nova Capital. *Revista geral dos trabalhos. I. Abril de 1895* and *II. Fevereiro de 1896.* Rio de Janeiro: H. Lombaerts, 1895 and 1896.

Commissão D'Estudo das Localidades Indicadas para a Nova Capital. *Relatório.* Rio de Janeiro: Imprensa Nacional, 1893.

Conniff, Michael, ed. *Populism in Latin America.* Tuscaloosa: University of Alabama Press, 1999.

Conrad, Robert. *The Destruction of Brazilian Slavery, 1850–1888.* Berkeley, Calif.: University of California Press, 1972.

Coronel Benjamim Ferreira Guimarães: tecendo histórias. Belo Horizonte: Livraria Del Rey Editora, 1997.

Corrêa, Geraldo. *Pequena história de um grande industrial.* Belo Horizonte: n.p., 1968.

Costa, Emilia Viotti da. *The Brazilian Empire: Myths and Histories.* rev. ed. Chapel Hill: University of North Carolina Press, 2000.

Couto, Maria Olivia A. B. P. *Ventos do sul nas montanhas de Minas.* Belo Horizonte: SENAI-MG, 1992.

Dahlman, Carl J. and Fernando Valadares Fonseca. "From Technological Dependence to Technological Development: The Case of the USIMINAS Steel Plant in Brazil." In *Technology Generation in Latin American Manufacturing Industries.* edited by Jorge M. Katz. New York: St. Martin's Press, 1987, 154–82.

Daland, Robert T. *Brazilian Planning: Development Politics and Administration.* Chapel Hill: University of North Carolina Press, 1967.

248   *Tropical Capitalism*

Dantes, Maria Amélia M. and Joseleide Souza Santos. "Siderurgia e tecnologia (1918–1964)." In *Tecnologia e industrialização no Brasil: uma perspectiva histórica.* organized by Shozo Motoyama. São Paulo: Editora da Universidade de São Paulo, Centro Estadual da Educação Tecnológica Paula Souza, 1994, 209–32.

Dávila L. de Guevara, Carlos. *El empresariado colombiano: una perspectiva histórica.* Bogotá: Pontificia Universidad Javeriana, 1986.

Dávila, Carlos and Rory Miller, eds. *Business History in Latin America: The Experience of Seven Countries,* trans. Garry Mills and Rory Miller. Liverpool, England: Liverpool University Press, 1999.

Dean, Warren. Economy. In *Brazil: Empire and Republic, 1822–1930.* edited by Leslie Bethell. Cambridge: Cambridge University Press, 1989, 217–56.

———. *The Industrialization of São Paulo, 1880–1945.* Austin: University of Texas Press, 1969.

———. "The Planter as Entrepreneur: The Case of São Paulo." *Hispanic American Historical Review* 46:2 (February 1966): 138–52.

———. *With Broadax and Firebrand: The Destruction of the Brazilian Atlantic Forest.* Berkeley: University of California Press, 1995.

Deane, Phyllis. *The First Industrial Revolution.* Cambridge: Cambridge University Press, 1967.

Dickenson, John P. "Electric Power Development in Minas Gerais, Brazil." *Revista Geográfica* 70 (June 1969): 213–21.

———. "Industrial Estates in Brazil." *Geography* 55 (1970): 326–29.

Diniz, Clélio Campolina. "Economia e planejamento em Minas Gerais." *Revista Brasileira de Estudos Políticos* 58 (January 1984): 259-95.

———. *Estado e capital estrangeiro na industrialização mineira.* Belo Horizonte: UFMG/PROED, 1981.

Diniz, Eli. *Empresariado, Estado e capitalismo no Brasil, 1930-1945.* Rio de Janeiro: Paz e Terra, 1978.

Diniz, Eli and Renato Boschi. *Empresariado nacional e Estado no Brasil.* Rio de Janeiro: Editora Forense Universitária, 1978.

Dreifuss, René Armand. *A Internacional capitalista: estrategia e táticas do empresariado transnacional (1918–1986).* Rio de Janeiro: Espaço e Tempo, 1986.

Drucker, Peter F. *Post-Capitalist Society.* New York: HarperCollins, 1993.

Duarte, Patrícia. *Diogo Bethônico: a trajetória de um empreendedor.* Belo Horizonte: Dossiê Agência de Investigação Histórica, 1993.

Dulci, Octavio Soares. *Política e recuperação econômica em Minas Gerais.* Belo Horizonte: Editora UFMG, 1999.

Dutta, Sudipt. *Family Business in India.* New Delhi: Response Books, 1997.

Eakin, Marshall C. *British Enterprise in Brazil: The St. John d'el Rey Mining Company and the Morro Velho Gold Mine, 1830–1960.* Durham, North Carolina: Duke University Press, 1989.

———. "Creating a Growth Pole: The Industrialization of Belo Horizonte, Brazil, 1897–1987." *The Americas* 47:4 (April 1991): 383–410.

Eschwege, Wilhelm Ludwig von. *Pluto brasiliensis,* trad. Domício de Figueiredo. 2 V. Belo Horizonte: Editorial Itatiaia, 1979.

Evans, Eric J. *The Forging of the Modern State: Early Industrial Britain, 1783–1870.* 2nd ed. London: Longman, 1996.

Evans, Peter. *Dependent Development: The Alliance of Multinational, State, and Local Capital in Brazil.* Princeton, New Jersey: Princeton University Press, 1979.

———. *Embedded Autonomy: States and Industrial Transformation.* Princeton, New Jersey: Princeton University Press, 1995.

Expresso Fiat–Edição de Ouro, Especial 100 anos, 11 July 1999.

Falkus, M. E. *The Industrialization of Russia, 1700–1914.* London: Macmillan, 1972.

Faoro, Raimundo. *Os donos do poder: formação do patronato político brasileiro.* 5a. ed., 2 v. Porto Alegre: Globo, 1979.

Faria, Luiz Sayão de and Joaquim Ribeiro Filho. "Resumo histórico da Associação Comercial de Minas." *Revista Social Trabalhista* (December 1947): 360–7.

Fischer, Bernhard, Juan-Carlos Herken-Frauer, Matthias Lüke, and Peter Nunnenkamp. *Capital-Intensive Industries in Newly Industrializing Countries: The Case of the Brazilian Automobile and Steel Industries.* Tübingen: Mohr, 1988.

Fishlow, Albert. "Brazilian Development in Long-Term Perspective." *American Economic Review* 70:2 (1980): 102–12.

Fleischer, David V. "O Recrutamento Político em Minas 1890/1918." *Revista Brasileira de Estudos Políticos* 30 (1971).

Franco, Afonso Arinos de Melo. *Um estadista da República.* 3 V. Rio de Janeiro: José Olympio, 1955.

Friedman, Milton. *Capitalism and Freedom.* Chicago: University of Chicago Press, 1962.

Fukuyama, Francis. "The End of History?" *The National Interest* 16 (summer 1989).

———. *The End of History and the Last Man.* New York: The Free Press, 1992.

Furtado, Celso. *Economic Development of Latin America: A Survey from Colonial Times to the Cuban Revolution.* 2nd ed. Cambridge: Cambridge University Press, 1976.

———. *Formação econômica do Brasil.* Rio de Janeiro: Editôra Fundo de Cultura, 1959.

Gauld, Charles A. *The Last Titan: Percival Farquhar, An American Entrepreneur in Latin America.* Stanford: Institute of Hispanic American and Luso-Brazilian Studies, 1964.

Geddes, Barbara. *The Politician's Dilemma.* Berkeley: University of California Press, 1994.

Gerschenkron, Alexander. *Economic Backwardness in Historical Perspectives: A Book of Essays.* Cambridge, Mass.: Belknap Press, 1962.

Gibb, George Sweet. *The Saco-Lowell Shops: Textile Machinery Building in New England, 1813–1949.* Cambridge, Mass.: Harvard University Press, 1950.

Giroletti, Domingos. *Fábrica convento disciplina.* Belo Horizonte: Imprensa Oficial, 1991.

Gomes, Angela de Castro, coord. *Engenheiros e economistas: novas elites burocráticas.* Rio de Janeiro: Editora da Fundação Getúlio Vargas, 1994.

Gomes, Francisco de Assis Magalhães. *A electrificação no Brasil.* São Paulo: Eletropaulo, 1986.

———. *História da siderurgia no Brasil.* Belo Horizonte: Itatiaia, 1983.

Gouvêa, Gilda Portugal. *Burocracia e elites burocráticas no Brasil.* São Paulo: Editora Paulicéia, 1994.

Graham, Richard. *Britain and the Onset of Modernization in Brazil, 1850–1914.* Cambridge: Cambridge University Press, 1968.

———. *Patronage and Politics in Nineteenth-Century Brazil.* Stanford: Stanford University Press, 1990.

———. "Sepoys and imperialists: Techniques of British Power in Nineteenth-Century Brazil." *Inter-American Economic Affairs* 23:2 (Autumn 1969): 23–37.

Gravatá, Hélio. Contribuição bibliográfica sobre Belo Horizonte. *Revista do Arquivo Público Mineiro* 33 (1982): 9–176.

Grindle, Merilee S. and John W. Thomas. *Public Choices and Policy Change: The Political Ecoomy of Reform in Developing Countries.* Baltimore, Maryland: The Johns Hopkins University Press, 1991.

O Grupo Fiat do Brasil. Belo Horizonte: Fiat do Brasil, 1999.

O Grupo Fiat no Brasil, edição 2000, March 2000.

Guatimosim Júnior, Gil. No cinqüentenário da Belgo-Mineira," *Usiminas-Revista.* 2:4 (1971): 13–15.

Guimarães, Berenice Martins and Sérgio de Azevedo, orgs. *Belo Horizonte em tese.* Belo Horizonte: Centro de Estudos Urbanos, Universidade Federal de Minas Gerais, 1995.

Gwynne, Robert N. *New Horizons? Third World Industrialization in an International Framework.* New York: Longman, 1990.

Haber, Stephen H. "Business Enterprise and the Great Depression in Brazil: A Study of Profits and Losses in Textile Manufacturing." *Business History Review* 66 (summer 1992): 335–63.

———. "Industrial Concentration and the Capital Markets: A Comparative Study of Brazil, Mexico, and the United States, 1830–1930." *Journal of Economic History* 51:3 (September 1991): 559–80.

———. *Industry and Underdevelopment in Mexico, 1870–1940.* Stanford: Stanford University Press, 1989.

———. "The Worst of Both Worlds: The New Cultural History of Mexico." *Mexican Studies* 13:2 (summer 1997): 363–83.

———, ed. *How Latin America Fell Behind: Essays on the Economic Histories of Brazil and Mexico, 1800–1914.* Stanford: Stanford University Press, 1997.

Hagopian, Frances. *Traditional Politics and Regime Change in Brazil.* Cambridge: Cambridge University Press, 1996.

Hannah, Leslie. *The Rise of the Corporate Economy.* 2nd ed. London: Methuen, 1983.

Haring, Clarence H. *Empire in Brazil: A New World Experiment with Monarchy.* Cambridge, Mass.: Harvard University Press, 1958.

Herrero, Daniel. Le développement industriel de Medellin (1925–1965). In *Ville et commerce: deux essais d'histoire hispano-américaine.* Paris: Editions Klincksieck, 1974, 95–207.

Holloway, Thomas H. *Immigrants on the Land: Coffee and Society in São Paulo, 1886–1934.* Chapel Hill: University of North Carolina Press, 1980.

Horowitz, Irving Louis. *Three Worlds of Development: The Theory and Practice of International Stratification.* New York: Oxford University Press, 1966.

Horta, Cid Rebelo. "Famílias governamentais de Minas Gerais," *Segundo Seminário de Estudos Mineiros.* Belo Horizonte: Universidade de Minas Gerais, 1956, 45–91.

Huber, Evelyne. "Assessments of State Strengths." In *Latin American in Comparative Perspective: New Approaches to Methods and Analysis.* edited by Peter H. Smith. Boulder, Colorado: Westview, 1995, 163–93.

Hudson, Pat. *The Industrial Revolution.* London: Edward Arnold, 1992.

Hutton, Will and Anthony Giddens, eds. *On the Edge: Living with Global Capitalism.* London: Jonathan Cape, 2000.

Ianni, Octavio. *Estado e planejamento econômico no Brasil (1930–1970).* Rio de Janeiro: Civilização Brasileira, 1971.

Iglésias, Francisco. *A industrialização brasileira.* São Paulo: Editora Brasiliense, 1985.

————. *Política econômica do govêrno provincial mineiro (1835–1889).* Rio de Janeiro: Instituto Nacional do Livro, 1958.

"Inventário dos teares existentes na Capitania de Minas Gerais 1786." *Revista do Arquivo Público Mineiro* 40 (1995): 1–160.

Jacob, Rodolfo. *Minas Geraes no XX século.* Rio de Janeiro: Gomes Irmaos, 1911.

Jaguaribe, Hélio. *Political Development: A General Theory and a Latin American Case Study.* New York: Harper & Row, 1973.

James, Preston. "Bello Horizonte and Ouro Prêto. A Comparative Study of Two Brazilian Cities." In *Papers of the Michigan Academy of Science and Letters,* V. 18, edited by Eugene S. McCartney and Peter Okkelberg. Ann Arbor: University of Michigan Press, 1933, 239–58.

Jeremy, David J. *Transatlantic Industrial Revolution: The Diffusion of Textile Technologies Between Britain and America, 1790–1830s.* Cambridge, Mass.: The MIT Press, 1981.

Jones, E. L. *The European Miracle: Environments, Economies, and Geopolitics in the History of Europe and Asia.* 2nd ed. Cambridge: Cambridge University Press, 1987.

Kemp, Tom. *Industrialization in Nineteenth-Century Europe.* London: Longman, 1969.

Industrialization in the Non-Western World. 2nd ed. New York: Longman, 1989.

Kennedy, Paul. *The Rise and Fall of the Great Powers: Economic Change and Military Conflict from 1500 to 2000.* New York: Random House, 1987.

252   *Tropical Capitalism*

Kingstone, Peter R. and Timothy J. Power, eds. *Democratic Brazil: Actors, Institutions, and Processes.* Pittsburgh: University of Pittsburgh Press, 2000.

Knifl, Jacob. "The Most Important Government Ploys." *Global Finance* (February 1998): 52–3.

Kranzberg, Melvin and Carroll W. Pursell, Jr., eds. *Technology in Western Civilization: v. 1. The Emergence of Modern Industrial Society: Earliest Times to 1900.* New York: Oxford University Press, 1967.

Kubitschek, Juscelino. *Meu caminho para Brasília. 1o volume. a experiência da humildade.* Rio de Janeiro: Bloch Editores, 1974.

———. *Meu caminho para Brasília, v. II. a escalada política.* Rio de Janeiro: Bloch, 1976.

Lamoreaux, Naomi R. "Banks, Kinship, and Economic Development: The New England Case." *Journal of Economic History* 46:3 (September 1986): 647–67.

Landes, David S. *The Unbound Prometheus: Technological Change and Industrial Development in Western Europe from 1750 to the Present.* Cambridge: Cambridge University Press, 1969.

———. *The Wealth and Poverty of Nations: Why Some are So Rich and Some So Poor.* New York: W. W. Norton, 1998.

Lanna, Ana Lúcia Duarte. *A transformação do trabalho: a passagem para o trabalho livre na Zona da Mata mineira, 1870–1920.* Campinas: Editora da UNICAMP, 1988.

Laue, Theodore von. *Sergei Witte and the Industrialization of Russia.* New York: Columbia University Press, 1963.

Layton, Edwin T., Jr. *The Revolt of the Engineers: Social Responsibility and the American Engineering Profession.* Cleveland, Ohio: Press of Case Western Reserve University, 1971.

Leal, Victor Nunes. *Coronelismo, enxada e voto: O município e o regime representativo no Brasil.* Rio de Janeiro: Revista Forense, 1948.

Leff, Nathaniel H. *The Brazilian Capital Goods Industry, 1929–1964.* Cambridge, Mass.: Harvard University Press, 1968.

———. *Economic Policy-Making and Development in Brazil, 1947–1964.* New York: John Wiley & Sons, 1968.

Leloup, Yves. *Les paysages urbains: Belo Horizonte: capitale champignon.* Paris: Institut des Hautes Études de l'Amérique Latine, 1970.

Levine, Robert M. *Pernambuco in the Brazilian Federation, 1889–1937.* Stanford, Calif.: Stanford University Press, 1978.

Levy, Maria Bárbara. *História da Bolsa de Valores do Rio de Janeiro.* Rio de Janeiro: Instituto Brasileiro de Mercado de Capitais, 1977.

Libby, Douglas Cole. *Transformação e trabalho em uma economia escravista: Minas Gerais no século XIX.* São Paulo: Editora Brasiliense, 1988.

Lima, João Heraldo de. *Café e indústria em Minas Gerais, 1870–1920.* Petrópolis: Vozes, 1981.

———. "Crescimento Industrial em uma Economia Não-Exportadora: Minas Gerais, 1907–1920." *Estudos Econômicos* 15 (January-April 1985).

Lima, José Luiz. *Estado e energia no Brasil: o setor elétrico no Brasil: das origens à criação da Eletrobrás (1890–1962)*. São Paulo: Instituto de Pesquisas Econômicas da USP, 1984.

Love, Joseph. *São Paulo in the Brazilian Federation, 1889–1937*. Stanford, Calif.: Stanford University Press, 1980.

Loveman, Brian and Thomas M. Davies, Jr., eds. *The Politics of Antipolitics: The Military in Latin America*. Wilmington, Delaware: Scholarly Resources, 1997.

Luz, Nícia Villela. *A luta pela industrialização no Brasil: 1808–1930*. São Paulo: Difusão Européia do Livro, 1961.

Machado, Iran F. *Recursos minerais: política e sociedade*. São Paulo: Editora Edgard Blucher Ltda., 1989.

Maddison, Angus. *Monitoring the World Economy, 1820–1992*. Paris: Organization for Economic Cooperation and Development, 1995.

Manchester, Alan K. *British Preeminence in Brazil*. Chapel Hill: University of North Carolina Press, 1933.

Martins, Luciano. *Estado capitalista e burocracia no Brasil pós- 64*. Rio de Janeiro: Paz e Terra, 1985.

Martins Filho, Amilcar and Roberto B. Martins. "Slavery in a Nonexport Economy: Nineteenth-Century Minas Gerais Revisited." *Hispanic American Historical Review* 63:3 (August 1983): 537–68.

Martins, Kao and Sebastião Martins. *O engenheiro da utopia: Israel Pinheiro e seu tempo*. Belo Horizonte: Armazém de Idéias, 1992.

Marx, Karl. *Capital: A Critique of Political Economy*. V. 1, trans. Ben Fowkes. New York: Vintage Books, 1977 [1867].

Mascarenhas, Geraldo Magalhães. *Centenário da Fábrica do Cedro: histórico, 1872–1972*. Belo Horizonte: Companhia de Fiação e Tecidos Cedro e Cachoeira, 1972.

Mascarenhas, Nelson Lage. *Bernardo Mascarenhas—o surto industrial de Minas Gerais*. Rio de Janeiro: Editora Aurora, 1954.

Maurer, Noel. "Banks and Entrepreneurs in Porfirian Mexico: Inside Exploitation or Sound Business Strategy?" *Journal of Latin American Studies* 31:2 (May 1999): 331–61.

Mauro, Frédéric. "Le développement économique de Monterrey, 1890–1960." *Caravelle* 2 (1964): 35–126.

Mayers, H. W. D. "The Story of Iron and Steel in Brazil." *Bulletin of the Pan American Union* 72:10 (October 1938).

McCraw, Thomas K. "The Creative Destroyer: Schumpeter's *Capitalism, Socialism, and Democracy.*" EH.NET Project 2000, ehreview@eh.net.

McCraw, Thomas K., ed. *Creating Modern Capitalism: How Entrepreneurs, Companies, and Countries Triumphed in Three Industrial Revoltuions*. Cambridge, Mass.: Harvard University Press, 1997.

McDowall, Duncan. *The Light: Brazilian Traction, Light and Power Company Limited, 1899–1945*. Toronto: University of Toronto Press, 1988.

McNeill, William H. *The Rise of the West: A History of the Human Community.* Chicago: University of Chicago Press, 1963.

Medeiros, Jarbas. *Govêrno e planejamento em Minas Gerais.* Belo Horizonte: n.p., 1968.

Mello, José Waldemar Teixeira de. *Santanense: revolução filosófica e industrial em Sanct'Anna do São João Acima.* Belo Horizonte: Rumos Editorial, 1991.

Memória da economia da cidade de Belo Horizonte. Belo Horizonte: Iniciativas Culturais Empresas BMG, 1987.

Minas Gerais: maiores e melhores, Gazeta Mercantil. no. 3 (1995).

Mokyr, Joel, ed. *The Economics of the Industrial Revolution.* Totowa, New Jersey: Rowman & Allanheld, 1985.

―――, ed. *The British Industrial Revolution: An Economic Perspective.* Boulder, Colorado: Westview, 1993.

Mommsen, W. J. *Britain and Germany, 1800–1914: Two Development Paths Toward Industrial Society.* London: German Historical Institute, 1986.

Monteiro, Norma de Góis, coord. *Dicionário biográfico de Minas Gerais–período republicano–1889–1991,* 2 V. Belo Horizonte: Assembléia Legislativa do Estado de Minas Gerais, 1994.

Moore, Barrington, Jr. *Social Origins of Dictatorship and Democracy: Lord and Peasant in the Making of the Modern World.* Boston: Beacon Press, 1966.

Moreira, Mauricio Mesquita. *Industrialization, Trade and Market Failures: The Role of Government Intervention in Brazil and South Korea.* New York: St. Martin's Press, 1995.

Motoyama, Shozo, org. *Tecnologia e industrialização no Brasil: uma perspectiva histórica.* São Paulo: Editora da Universidade Estadual de São Paulo, 1994.

Mourão, Paulo Kruger Corrêa. *História de Belo Horizonte de 1897 a 1930.* Belo Horizonte: Imprensa Oficial, 1970.

Musson, A. E. and Eric Robinson. *Science and Technology in the Industrial Revolution.* Toronto: University of Toronto Press, 1969.

Navin, Thomas R. *The Whitin Machine Works Since 1831: A Textile Machinery Company in an Industrial Village.* Cambridge, Mass.: Harvard University Press, 1950.

O'Brien, Thomas F. *The Revolutionary Mission: American Enterprise in Latin America, 1900–1945.* Cambridge: Cambridge University Press, 1996.

O'Donnell, Guillermo. *Modernization and Bureaucratic- Authoritarianism: Studies in South American Politics.* Berkeley, Calif.: Institute of International Studies, University of California, 1973.

Okazaki, Tetsuji and Masahiro Okuno-Fujiwara, eds. *The Japanese Economic System and Its Historical Origins.* Oxford: Oxford University Press, 1999.

Okochi, Ako and Shigeaki Yasuoka, eds. *Family Business in the Era of Industrial Growth.* Tokyo, n.d.

Omnibus: uma história dos transportes coletivos em Belo Horizonte. Belo Horizonte: Fundação João Pinheiro, 1996.

Oxhorn, Philip D. and Graciela Ducatenzeiler, eds. *What Kind of Democracy? What Kind of Market?: Latin America in the Age of Neoliberalism.* University Park, Penn.: The Pennsylvania State University Press, 1998.

Packenham, Robert A. *The Dependency Movement: Scholarship and Politics in Development Studies.* Cambridge, Mass.: Harvard University Press, 1992.

Panorama do setor de energia elétrica no Brasil. Rio de Janeiro: Centro de Memória da Eletricidade, 1988.

Payne, Leigh A. *Brazilian Industrialists and Democratic Change.* Baltimore: Johns Hopkins University Press, 1994.

Peres, Wilson, coord. *Grandes empresas y grupos industriales latinoamericanos: expansión y desafíos en la era de la apertura y la globalización.* México, D. F.: Siglo Veintiuno Editores, 1998.

Pereira, Lígia Maria Leite and Maria Auxiliadora de Faria. *Presidente Antônio Carlos: um Andrada da República.* Rio de Janeiro: Nova Fronteira, 1998.

Pereira, Luís Carlos Bresser. *Development and Crisis in Brazil, 1930–1983.* Boulder, Colorado: Westview, 1984.

Pimenta, Dermeval José. *Implantação da grande siderurgia em Minas Gerais.* Belo Horizonte: UFMG, 1967.

———. *A Vale do Rio Doce e sua história.* Belo Horizonte: Vega, 1981.

Platt, D. C. M. *Business Imperialism, 1840–1930: An Inquiry Based on British Experience in Latin America.* Oxford: Oxford University Press, 1977.

Pollard, Sidney. *Peaceful Conquest: The Industrialization of Europe 1760–1970.* Oxford: Oxford University Press, 1981.

Porter, Michael E. *The Competitive Advantage of Nations.* New York: The Free Press, 1990.

Prefeitura Municipal de Belo Horizonte, Secretaria Municipal de Planejamento, Coordenadoria de Informações Técnicas. *Perfil de Belo Horizonte.* Belo Horizonte: Prefeitura Municipal de Belo Horizonte, 1985.

Rady, Donald Edmund. *Volta Redonda: A Steel Mill Comes to a Brazilian Coffee Plantation: Industrial Entrepreneurship in a Developing Economy.* Albuquerque: University of New Mexico Press, 1973.

Raízes do sucesso empresarial: a experiência de três empresas bem-sucedidas: Belgo Mineira, Metal Leve e Weg S.A. São Paulo: Atlas, 1995.

Raw, Silvia. "The Making of a State-Owned Conglomerate: A Brazilian Case Study." Working Paper #97, August 1987, The Helen Kellogg Institute for International Studies, University of Notre Dame.

"Representantes de Minas Geraes (eleitos de 1821 a 1896)." *Revista do Arquivo Público Mineiro* I (1896).

Resende, Maria Efigênia Lage de. "Uma interpretação sobre a fundação de Belo Horizonte." *Revista Brasileira de Estudos Políticos* 39 (1974): 129–161.

———. "Manifestações oligárquicas na política mineira." *Revista Brasileira de Estudos Políticos* (1979): 7–69.

Restrepo Uribe, Jorge. *Medellín, su origen, progreso y desarrollo.* Medellín: Servigráficas, 1981.

Ridings, Eugene. *Business Interest Groups in Nineteenth-Century Brazil.* Cambridge: Cambridge University Press, 1994.

Roett, Riordan. "Brazilian Politics at Century's End." In *Brazil under Cardoso,* edited by Susan Kaufman Purcell and Riordan Roett. Boulder, Colorado: Lynne Rienner, 1997, 19–41.

Roniger, Luis. *Hierarchy and Trust in Modern Mexico and Brazil.* Westport, Conn.: Praeger, 1990.

Rosenberg, Nathan and L. E. Birdell, Jr. *How the West Grew Rich: The Economic Transformation of the Industrial World.* New York: Basic Books, 1986.

Roxborough, Ian. *Theories of Underdevelopment.* London: Macmillan, 1979.

Russell-Wood, A. J. R. "The Gold Cycle, c. 1690–1750." In *Colonial Brazil,* edited by Leslie Bethell. Cambridge: Cambridge University Press, 1987, 190–243.

Sá, Antônio Lopes. *Origens de um banco centenário.* Belo Horizonte: Credireal, 1989.

Sánchez Flores, Ramón. *Historia de la tecnología y la invención en México: Introducción a su estudio y documentos para los anales de la técnica.* México: Fomento Cultural Banamex, 1980.

Saragoza, Alex M. *The Monterrey Elite and the Mexican State, 1880–1940.* Austin: University of Texas Press, 1988.

Schneider, Ben Ross. *Politics Within the State: Elite Bureaucrats and Industrial Policy in Authoritarian Brazil.* Pittsburgh, Penn.: University of Pittsburgh Press, 1991.

Schumpeter, Joseph A. *Capitalism, Socialism, and Democracy.* New York: Harper & Brothers, 1947.

Schwartzman, Simon. *Bases do autoritarismo brasileiro,* 3a ed. Rio de Janeiro: Campus, 1988.

Scliar, Cláudio. *Geopolítica das minas do Brasil.* Rio de Janeiro: Revan, 1996.

Scobie, James R. *Secondary Cities of Argentina: The Social History of Corrientes, Salta, and Mendoza, 1850–1910,* completed and edited by Samuel L. Baily. Stanford, Calif.: Stanford University Press, 1988.

Selcher, Wayne A., ed. *Brazil in the International System: The Rise of a Middle Power.* Boulder, Colorado: Westview Press, 1981.

Shapiro, Helen. *Engines of Growth: The State and Transnational Auto Companies in Brazil.* Cambridge: Cambridge University Press, 1994.

Sikkink, Kathryn. *Ideas and Institutions: Developmentalism in Brazil and Argentina.* Ithaca, New York: Cornell University Press, 1991.

Silva, Edmundo de Macedo Soares e. *As instituições de indústria e comércio do Brasil.* Rio de Janeiro: Crown, 1972.

Silveira, Victor, org. and ed. *Minas Geraes em 1925.* Bello Horizonte: Imprensa Oficial, 1926.

Singer, Paul Israel. *Desenvolvimento econômico e evolução urbana: análise da evolução econômica de São Paulo, Blumenau, Pôrto Alegre, Belo Horizonte e Recife.* São Paulo: Editôra Nacional e Editôra da USP, 1968.

Skidmore, Thomas E. *Politics in Brazil, 1930–1964: An Experiment in Democracy.* New York: Oxford University Press, 1967.

———. *The Politics of Military Rule in Brazil, 1964–1985.* New York: Oxford University Press, 1988.

Slenes, Robert. "Os múltiplos de porcos e diamantes: a economia escravista de Minas Gerais no século XIX." *Cadernos IFCH/UNICAMP,* 17 (1985).

Smith, Adam. *An Inquiry into the Nature and Causes of the Wealth of Nations,* edited by R. H. Campbell and A. S. Skinner, 2 v. Oxford: Clarendon Press, 1976 [1776].

Smith, Peter H. "The State and Development in Historical Perspective." In *Americas: New Interpretive Essays,* edited by Alfred Stepan. New York: Oxford University Press, 1992, 30–56.

Somarriba, Maria das Mercês Gomes, Maria Gezica Valadares, and Mariza Rezende Afonso. *Lutas urbanas em Belo Horizonte.* Petrópolis: Vozes, 1984.

Souza, Miguel Augusto Gonçalves de. *Açominas: aspiração de várias gerações de mineiros.* Belo Horizonte: Aço Minas Gerais S.A., 1985.

———. *História de Itaúna,* 2 V. Belo Horizonte: Ed. Littera Maciel Ltda., 1986.

Starling, Heloisa. *Os senhores das Gerais: os novos inconfidentes e o golpe militar de 1964,* 5a. ed. Petrópolis: Vozes, 1986.

Stearns, Peter N. *The Industrial Revolution in World History.* 2nd ed. Boulder, Colorado: Westview Press, 1998.

Stein, Stanley J. *The Brazilian Cotton Manufacture: Textile Enterprise in an Underdeveloped Area, 1850–1950.* Cambridge, Mass.: Harvard University Press, 1957.

Stone, Irving. "British Direct and Portfolio Investment in Latin America before 1914." *The Journal of Economic History* 37:3 (September 1977): 690–722.

Strauch, Ney. *Zona metalúrgica de Minas Gerais e Vale do Rio Doce.* Rio de Janeiro: Conselho Nacional de Geografia, 1958.

Suzigan, Wilson. *Indústria brasileira: origem e desenvolvimento.* São Paulo: Editôra Brasiliense, 1986.

———. *Política do governo e crescimento da economia brasileira, 1889–1945.* Rio de Janeiro: IPEA/INPES, 1973.

Tamm, Paulo. *A família Mascarenhas e a indústria têxtil em Minas.* Belo Horizonte: Velloso & Cia Ltda, 1939.

Taniura, Taeko. "Economic Development Effects of an Integrated Iron and Steel Works: A Case Study of Minas Gerais Steel in Brazil." *The Developing Economies* XXIV-2 (June 1986): 169–77.

Tendler, Judith. *Electric Power in Brazil: Entrepreneurship in the Public Sector.* Cambridge, Mass.: Harvard University Press, 1968.

Teulières, Roger. *Belo-Horizonte: Étude de géographie urbaine.* Saigon: Huong-Van, 1961.

———. "Favelas de Belo Horizonte." *Boletim Mineiro de Geografia* 1 (July 1957): 7–37.

Toledo, Roberto Pompeu de, ed. *História do Unibanco.* São Paulo: Instituto Moreira Salles, 1994.

Topik, Steven. *The Political Economy of the Brazilian State, 1889–1930.* Austin: University of Texas Press, 1987.

Toplin, Robert Brent. *The Abolition of Slavery in Brazil.* New York: Atheneum, 1971.

Trebat, Thomas J. *Brazil's State-Owned Enterprises: A Case Study of the State as Entrepreneur.* Cambridge: Cambridge University Press, 1983.

Trebilcock, Clive. *The Industrialization of the Continental Powers 1780–1914.* London: Longman, 1981.

Triner, Gail D. *Banking and Economic Development: Brazil, 1889–1930.* New York: Palgrave, 2000.

Tucker, Barbara M. *Samuel Slater and the Origins of the American Textile Industry, 1790–1860.* Ithaca, New York: Cornell University Press, 1984.

Uricoechea, Fernando. *O minotauro imperial.* Rio de Janeiro: Difel, 1978.

Vargas, Milton, org. *História da técnica e da tecnologia no Brasil.* São Paulo: Editora da Universidade Estadual de São Paulo, 1994.

Vaz, Alisson Mascarenhas. *Cia. Cedro e Cachoeira: história de uma empresa familiar, 1883–1987.* Belo Horizonte: Cia. de Fiação e Tecidos Cedro e Cachoeira S. A., 1990.

———. "A Indústria têxtil em Minas Gerais." *Revista de História* 56:111 (1977): 101–118.

———. *Israel: uma vida para história.* Rio de Janeiro: CVRD, 1996.

Veblen, Thorstein. *The Engineers and the Price System.* New York: B. W. Huebsch, Inc., 1921.

Vellinga, Menno, ed. *The Changing Role of the State in Latin America.* Boulder, Colorado: Westview Press, 1998.

———. *Economic Development and the Dynamics of Class: Industrialization, Power and Control in Monterrey, Mexico.* Assen, The Netherlands: Van Gorcum, 1979.

Villela, Annibal Villanova and Wilson Suzigan. *Política do governo e crescimento da economia brasileira, 1889–1945.* Rio de Janeiro: IPEA/INPES, 1973.

Weid, Elisabeth von de and Anna Marta Rodrigues Bastos. *O fio da meada: estratégia de expansão de uma indústria têxtil: Companhia América Fabril, 1878–1930.* Rio de Janeiro: FCRB-CNI, 1986.

Weinstein, Barbara. *For Social Peace in Brazil: Industrialists and the Remaking of the Working Class in São Paulo, 1920–1964.* Chapel Hill: University of North Carolina Press, 1996.

Wirth, John D. *Minas Gerais in the Brazilian Federation, 1889–1937.* Stanford: Stanford University Press, 1977.

———. *The Politics of Brazilian Development, 1930–1954.* Stanford: Stanford University Press, 1970.

Wrigley, E. A. *Continuity, Chance and Change: The Character of the Industrial Revolution in England.* Cambridge: Cambridge University Press, 1988.

Zucker, Lynne. "Production of Trust: Institutional Sources of Economic Structure, 1940–1920." In *Research in Organizational Behavior,* V. 8 (1986), edited by Barry M. Staw and L. L. Cummings, 53–111.

Index